THE MONSTER
IN EMMA

TACKLING THE TUMOUR WITH HUMOUR

EMMA SHEILS

FOREWORD BY MATT LUCAS

DEDICATION

This book is dedicated to my good friends Cheryl Langridge (1969-1993) who died from liver cancer while at Teaching College and David Reed (1969-2017) who died while walking in his beloved Munros.

TABLE OF CONTENTS

FOREWORD

Through anecdotes, quotes, funny stories and tales from her past, Emma describes her breast cancer story in a unique, personal and absorbing way. She faces the Monster with humour, and it was through laughter and smiling that she was able to face surgery, chemotherapy and radiotherapy all in the space of a year.

In her own words, a' cross between Miranda Hart and Bridget Jones', Emma is a likeable and endearing woman who has emerged smiling through both mental and physical health problems and life-changing events.

Cleverly entwined with stories from her childhood, this bittersweet autobiography becomes a record of her fight with cancer from diagnosis to end of treatment and a source of inspiration for the millions of women around the world suffering with breast cancer.

ABOUT THE AUTHOR

Approaching fifty and recently divorced, Emma Sheils is a school teacher and a mother of two girls and a pug. Having spent her childhood in Kent and secondary school years in Edinburgh, she attended the University of St Andrews and completed a PGCE in Canterbury.

Emma met her Moroccan husband of 22 years in her own words "in the street" in Sicily 1990 and married in 1994.

Having suffered from eczema as a child, it became severe and regularly infected and began to take over her life. Fighting this debilitating skin condition illness, in 1996 she was eventually admitted as an outpatient at St Thomas' Hospital.

In 2015 she was diagnosed with Pernicious Anaemia, Vitamin B12 Deficiency and Vitamin D Deficiency. The previous misdiagnosis of these conditions had led to bipolar outbursts, manic depression, psychotic behaviour and many neurological disorders.

Now on B12 injections and medication for life, Emma has made a full recovery from a year battling a mental illness. Although it cost her marriage and almost her life, she has been able to gain a deeper understanding of what it is like to live with both a physical and mental illness and the effect it has on others around her.

The sting in the tail came in October 2017, two months into a new job, when she was then diagnosed with an aggressive form of breast cancer.

A month later her mother too was diagnosed with cancer.

PROLOGUE

The late Ronnie Corbett used to regularly deliver after-dinner speeches at his and my former secondary school -The Royal High, Edinburgh. I envied the way he could tell anecdotes from his life, and although they were simple tales, he had me reeling with laughter. He had a way with words and impeccable delivery. He used to sit in his chair too during The Two Ronnie's Show and do the same, recounting funny stories and making his audience giggle and laugh. I suppose he was one of my inspirations for this book.

My friends and colleagues used to tell me I should write my tales down and create them a holiday book to read. I began retelling odd occurrences that had happened to me to friends both on and off Facebook. The stories were met with both laughter and squeals of "OMG!" They clamoured for me to write a book.

When I was diagnosed with cancer, I was determined to stay positive and document "my journey". With my friends' pleas in mind, I have put together an amalgamation of tales from my past and a diary of my battle with cancer, tenuously linked together and almost in chronological order.

If I were reading this collection of tales, I would honestly think 'how could all of this have happened to one person?' but it has, the tales are true. I also want it to be a positive read for anyone going on their own cancer journey or know of someone who is going through anything similar. This book is also a positive one for anyone battling a mental illness too.

Where friends and family have wished to remain anonymous, I have respected their wishes. They have shared in my embarrassments, my triumphs, my despair, but most of all you the reader can either emphasise or sympathise. What would like you have done in the same situation? I would you to enjoy reading my tales. After all, fortunately, they didn't happen to you. I honestly feel like Kent's very own Bridget Jones, but unlike Bridget, my life is real.

1
A SPANNER IN THE WORKS

"If you hadn't have rolled around in the grass with your loved one, then you wouldn't be in this predicament."

AN ODD FEELING

I loved being a pug owner. I was greeted by a waggy, curly tail and lots of licks on my return from work and we both enjoyed nothing more than a bundle and a roll in the garden.

We would play "hide the toy in the socks" and "yank the sheep toy" and similar such made up games.

On one such occasion in October 2017, I was lying on the garden grass playing with my dog, and it felt like my bra underwire was digging into me. The advantages of having a garden that was not overlooked meant that I could fling my bra off and resume the playing. So I did. The pain didn't go away, and I could feel hardness. Not quite a lump, but more of a thickening of the skin and it bothered me all evening. I had never felt this before, and it worried me.

I visited the doctor a couple of days later, and he wasn't happy with what he felt, although he did reassure me that eight out of every ten lumps or bumps turn out to be nothing more than cysts. I didn't have a lump, or a bead or a "moveable marble" as mentioned in all the breast self-checking awareness adverts. It hurt to press and felt like a long strip of hardness. The doctor said he would refer me to the breast clinic.

"Did you not notice the discolouration?" said the nurse in mid-blue at the Breast Care Unit.

The appointment had come through within a couple of days. Not really, I thought. I'd been in the sun a lot over the summer, and there were various tan lines visible.

"What about the dimpling here?" she said prodding underneath. "Surely you noticed this in the mirror?" Mirror? There was no time spent looking at myself in any mirror, let alone looking for discolouration or dimpling! I did check my breasts regularly in the shower, but only for lumps.

Usually, the routine at home was to shower and dash back into the bedroom stark naked to save taking the wet towel back to the bathroom. "The landing streak," I call it in our house. More often than not, the heating wasn't on, so it was pretty chilly. There was no time spent peering at breasts in a mirror.

The nurse in mid-blue looked straight at me and said they were going to do both a mammogram and an ultrasound that afternoon and that in her professional opinion, she was, or rather I was, looking at breast cancer.

THE MAMMOGRAM

It was an odd feeling sitting there in the Breast Care Clinic. I had gone on my own. The nurses and receptionists were all friendly; there were posters and thank you cards pinned to the walls and business cards you could take. There were adverts for support groups and leaflets about where to get the best wigs too. It was all a bit overwhelming.

Had I got cancer?

I fiddled with my fingers. Oh my goodness, my nails were yellow! How come I hadn't noticed? Was this a sign of cancer? The worry of my nails passed the short time spent waiting and thankfully as my name was called, I realised I had peeled a large orange earlier.

Contrary to popular belief a mammogram isn't a form of sexting; it wasn't sending topless pictures via social media! At 48 I was too young to have been summoned for my well-woman check, so this was my first experience of this machine. I had heard a lot about it, and I was intrigued as to how it all worked. In Europe, women over 40 are offered a mammogram. In England, it is the age of 50.

I am very sure, however, that the inventor of the mammogram was male. You are supposed to put your breast on a platform which then turns into a vice – trapping your breast between two heavy metal plates and then you are supposed to hold very still.

Well, I put one of my breasts on the platform. There was a very unladylike slap sound as if a piece of meat had been thrown onto the counter. I did wonder then how those women less well endowed coped. How could they lay their wares on the slab?

All was well until the cold vice-like machine closed its jaws onto me. I honestly thought I would pop or burst or end up with a pancake. "Stay very still," said the radiographer in white.

I wasn't going anywhere.

I tried to gauge the look of the lady in white. Did she look worried? Had she seen something on the screen? I was given my clothes and told not to redress but to nip to the room across the corridor. She was not allowed to reveal any information.

You will read from now on that I recount tales from the past whenever I mention a keyword or subject. At times the tales may seem a bit random, but they make sense to me in this order and have occurred to me as I've reached certain points on my journey. I promise I will not leave anyone lingering about what has happened to me – and this journey will have a beginning, middle and an end that will give this book a structure. So please bear with me as I venture back into my childhood and teenage years and then through my university years into adulthood.

The reason for this is that my cancer diagnosis has put everything into perspective. I'm beginning to know now what is important and what isn't. My real friends are starting to rally round and time spent with my family is precious.

It's also all about living for the future and not dwelling on the past.

When you think that there may not be a future, you learn to value it more. You want it so badly, and the only thing you can do is live every day as though it was your last. It does sound like one big cliché, but it's true. It makes so much sense.

I'm a historian. I love the past, but I know that I can never go back (of course, I'm not Dr Who!) but it's nice to think back on stories and tales as they have made me who I am today. I have perhaps learnt from my mistakes or not as the case may be.

Remembering the past has helped me realise what I value the most. Sometimes I look too hard for the story to be funny and it's hard to recreate the time place and atmosphere for someone who wasn't there, but I've tried my best, and I hope you can imagine me talking or playing the role that I do.

I wanted to share these memories as a record of my life for my children and my friends- my legacy, perhaps a primary source for the future, except I am careful not to mention politics or name names in this book where possible.

THE CORRIDOR

As a teenager, many a secondary school trip involved dodging the teachers on patrol of the corridors at night-time and running across the corridors into each other's rooms. Each year group had a different bedtime, and the challenge was to defy it as much as possible. On one music trip, we smuggled one of the older boys into our girls' room because he was a good singer and we wanted him to sing to us. He was quite a willing 'kidnappee', but every time there were room inspections we had to find a different place to hide him! It seemed unfair that the year above could stay up half an hour longer, (similarly the older sibling has a later bedtime).

The 'Corridor' also seemed to be an excellent analogy for this book of my cancer journey. There is an obvious direction and way forward, but lots of doors or tangents on the way to open and to find out what went on in that room or on that occasion. Some doors remain firmly shut, bolted and locked, never to be opened and for only me to know what is in that room.

Some doors are just pushed shut and can be opened with a key or a link, and some are left ajar to step in and briefly have a look. The last few doors have the sign 'Do not disturb' on but can always be opened later when the time is right.

THE ULTRASOUND

I was shown to a bed of familiar blue paper towel by a nurse in mid-blue and told to lie on the slab.

I was amazed – yet pleasantly surprised by the hot gel being squirted on me. The last time I had an ultrasound and had gel on me, I was around 30 weeks pregnant and bursting for a wee, having drunk a bath full of water. The gel on that occasion and all other previous occasions were most memorably cold. That feeling of bursting at the seams was so uncomfortable, and yet while you were at your fullest, a nurse would press down on your bladder, and you were supposed to remain calm and still. It was an uncomfortable experience.

PROBABLY, MOST LIKELY

A nurse in navy came into the room to do the ultrasound and after some sliding around with the probe, said it was 90% likely that I had cancer. The 10% margin of error was for a possible infection that would show up in the same manner, and the only way of finding out was to do a biopsy then and there on breast tissue and the lymph nodes.

I was remarkably calm, or so I thought. There were no tears. It was all a bit surreal. There was a whole rainbow of nurses in the room including a new one in sea-green. I hadn't gone with a friend, and a part of me wished a friend was now right there with me.

I wiped the slime off me and began lacing up my boots. I hadn't apologised for the two odd socks that I had shown, and as I covered my Kermit the Frog sock with my boot, it was I who felt like a bit of a Muppet.

THE WAIT

I had to wait a week for the results.

Although only a week, the days passed so slowly. In this day and age of instant gratification, I was guilty of not being able to wait for long. Everything is geared around to make life simpler and quicker. There are apps available to ease the burden of waiting; food delivery, paying bills and even dating. I think I was used to getting things straight away.

I am quite an impatient person. I always have to multitask. I can't eat my cereal without reading the back of the cereal box or watching TV or going on my phone. I hate queuing, and I most definitely hate waiting.

I had to return to the hospital a couple of days later for full blood tests. I took my paper ticket at the phlebotomy department and waited for my number to flash up. Unfortunately, I wasn't waiting at the deli counter for some nice cheese, or for my child's shoes to be fitted.

It took seven attempts to get blood from my veins. I did have tricky veins that opened briefly and then suddenly snapped shut. It may also have been because I was stressed. If I drank anything, I felt I would have been a walking sprinkler system!

The waiting for results continued.

THE BALLOON

I had done some long waiting before, alongside my then four-year-old daughter H. She had been picked to go on stage at the local pantomime to fill the time while the cast changed into their finale costumes. The comedian Kev Orkian had got her to sing Twinkle Twinkle Little Star on her own and had presented her with a goody bag and a pink balloon. H. was to look after this special balloon, and when it had deflated, she was to put the pieces under her pillow. When she woke up in the morning, apparently a £10 note was to be there!

H. waited so patiently for this balloon to go down. She didn't poke or prod it, and it sat wedged in a plant pot on a shelf. It was an ordinary air-filled balloon, quite small but it didn't seem to change; it just did not deflate. H. would check it every day, and it looked the same. At one point I even considered sabotage. Finally after six months and a few days, in June, the balloon started deflating, and when it was just a limp pink bit of rubber, she put it under her pillow. Magically ten pounds did appear. That was a long time for a four-year-old (and a 34-year-old) to wait, but we did it, we waited.

NOT THE SAME

Had I got cancer?

I was looking at people and objects and the house differently. As I passed people in the street, I thought how many others had cancer too? No signs were hanging around their necks. What do I say to my parents? Should I tell my daughters? I had so many questions, yet had so little time in the day with a full-time job to be worrying about the answers. There was plenty of time for worrying during the sleepless nights that were soon to come.

I was told not to go searching for answers on the internet. I didn't. Well, at least for the first few days I didn't. I then had the urge to search the breast cancer sites and then after looking at statistics and survival rates; I got it into my head that I might not see Christmas. I convinced myself I only had months, if not weeks to live. That was ignorance on my part but also some of the recommended online sites for checking the prognosis needed more data.

I began blitzing the house.

My possessions were just stuff. It wasn't important. The family was more important than things. I saw the furniture and ornaments in my house as extra things that I could walk away from. I let go.

I started organising bags of "stuff". There were bags for charity, bags to throw out, bags to keep to sell at a boot sale, bags for eBay and bags of personal objects that I wanted to give personally to different people. I started at the top of the house being ruthless and worked down, giving everywhere a spring clean too, in October!

I struck up a bizarre conversation with a buyer on eBay. It started with a question about the length of a soft toy, and then the questions got personal and sentimental about why I was selling childhood toys. Internet safety at its worst, but it was signal of how vulnerable I was if I was talking about my situation quite openly with strangers, yet keeping it incredibly close to my chest with friends and colleagues.

Apart from a Facebook hint that something was awry, I hadn't said anything to anyone.

A LONG ROUND ROBIN LETTER

I bought, wrapped and labelled Christmas presents – it was still October. I packaged and addressed parcels and had them all ready to go. I addressed and wrote Christmas cards but then left the envelopes unsealed. If things were to get tricky around December time, then I would be all prepared, and if I weren't around, the family would still get a present from me. Bizarre I know, but that was how I was thinking then.

What about my traditional included Round Robin letter? What could I write? I was still mindful of the time I sent my Robin letter flying way too early a few years back.

I am always quite organised when it comes to Christmas, and by the summer before the December I knew who was getting what and apart from the gift tags, most presents were ready and wrapped. It was partly a time management thing but also fun to be thinking throughout the year what to buy for different people rather than buy the wrong thing in one big frantic rush in December.

I also sent out along Round Robin letter to friends abroad who weren't on Facebook or email.

In October 2007 I started early and had my printed letter all typed and photocopied. I had written sentences like. "What a busy Christmas week at school!" and "The Nativity again brought a tear to the eye". I also knew which pantomime I was chaperoning and mentioned how tiring it was working behind the scenes, yet how proud I was of the girls performing up on the stage.

All of this at the beginning of October!

I was also organised in that I bought the stamps early to save queuing later in December. That day I weighed nearly thirty different letters all going around the world, and the lady in the post office was diligently collecting them and putting the airmail stickers on. We were chatting for a bit as there was no queue. After paying, I waited for my letters to be returned to me. The lady looked blankly at me. What did I want?

The letters had gone, over five minutes previously.

They had been collected while we were chatting. My friends in Hong Kong and the USA were to get a Christmas card with my letter full of future news, at the beginning of October!

GETTING ORGANISED

I had no idea what was going to happen between October and Christmas 2017. I certainly wasn't going to write about the future, so I left the box of addressed cards downstairs to be a "work in progress".

I did, however, start hand drawing a set of personalised snowmen cards for my Year One class. It kept me busy in the evenings; I needed to be busy. If I was busy, there was less time to dwell on things.

However, I lay awake most nights dwelling on things, my mind churning over and over.

2

CHILDHOOD MEMORIES AND NO FASHION SENSE

I had a great childhood, living in Kent in a typical suburban cul-de-sac with two younger brothers. Dad went to work, and mum stayed at home. It was a life very much like the Ladybird Peter and Jane stories, but without the dog.

However, it soon became clear that my parents had wanted three sons. Why else would they dress us all the same? Every family photo the same, dressed in matching home knits and C & A pretend denim shorts, even down to the same knee-length stripy socks.

Maybe due to this or something else in the water but I soon realised I was happier as not a follower of fashion, but a creator. I have my "whatever is ironed and nearest" philosophy about what to wear each day.

FASHION

Browsing through photos of pictures of me in pink rara dresses, corduroy pedal pushers and Wham Choose Life t-shirts, it did appear as if I followed some trends, but a Frankie Say t-shirt with a purple pinafore skirt and lace-up shoes were not and still not a good look. It's a photo that my brother has over me!

The Wham t-shirt did not, however, distract from the one neon towelling pink sock and one green one that I was wearing in another photo. Neon was such a big 1980s thing. I had even given the remaining pair of neon socks to a German friend for his birthday in the hope it would strengthen Allied- German relations.

Soon I was to discover the joy of the elasticated waist (I still enjoy it) and in particular a pair of men's purple, paisley print pyjamas. I can't believe people frown nowadays at women shopping in pyjamas, in 1990 I wore pyjamas everywhere! I wore them teaching international students English in Edinburgh, I wore them skate-boarding, and I wore them mountain climbing. I wore them inter-railing to Italy too.

One evening in northern Italy, I was slumped with my rucksack in a doorway waiting for a youth hostel to open, wearing said pyjamas, when a passerby threw me some Italian LIRE!

I was also wearing them the day I met my future husband.

Traumatically the pyjamas came to a tragic end.

While living through a freezing winter in Italy 1991, I put my washed pyjamas on the line to dry. Overnight they froze solid and then snapped. The fibres in them just broke. The pyjamas were no more, and to this day I mourn their loss, especially as that particular range was soon discontinued.

So fashion was never my strong point but nor was make-up. I suffered severely from eczema and reacted to cosmetics badly- still do but there was a certain trio combination that I thought I rocked in 1985-6

- Pink eye shadow
- Electric blue mascara
- Turquoise eye-liner

It was my signature "look". That was until the following year when I had one of those mad impulses and shaved most of my hair off, dyed what was left burgundy (I was too afraid of what my mum would think if it was coloured black),got two more piercings and entered my "I love The Cramps /Gothic" phase.

And I wore a lot of hats.

BARROWLANDS GLASGOW 1988

I went with the masses to watch Jesus and Mary Chain, and although the blonde hair was now showing through, I had done an excellent job of dressing down into some black netted number and had abused the black kohl eye pencil. It was standing room only and the queue -as is typical for the ladies -was long. When I returned the Chain had started, and there was a significant surge of people pushing, body surfing and the like and a fight broke out.

I was trampled on, although there was more air on floor level and the spilt lager swilling around the floor was quite refreshing to lie on. I heard most of the rest of the concert from the St. John's Ambulance pen. I was fine, just trampled. The thing was, my friends hadn't even noticed I was missing.

DRESSING UP

The Gothic phase was just that, a period, but it was around that time – 1988 that I realised that I wasn't going to be preoccupied with clothes labels.

As a student, I had no money anyway and could think of nothing worse than spending time in a hot sweaty changing room trying on clothes and telling friends that "no, their bum didn't look too big" in whatever they were trying on. We had our student uniform anyway of oversized sweaters and jeans, and for a change, we borrowed each other's clothes.

I adored dressing up parties. With the popularity of Children in Need and Comic Relief there became possible more opportunities to be a different character. I suppose for me it was like acting. I've been many characters and animals over the years, but these are some of my most memorable outfits:

The Gruffalo – Infant Enchanted Forest party- originally a monkey one piece, I sewed on knobbly knees and purple spikes all down the back.

The Headteacher at the school said he was interviewing a member of staff when they both looked out of the window and unexpectedly saw me walking across the playground as The Gruffalo. The vision broke the ice!

Little Red Riding Hood - World Book Day- A red gingham dress, cloak, picnic basket of goodies and hair in bunches. That year there were about seven or eight little girls dressed like mini versions of me. It was ever so sweet, and not a wolf in sight. We even made it into the local paper. In the picture, I was reclined at the front surrounded by all my clones and a random Cruella de Vil.

Tap Dancing Panda – What I remember most about the day dressed as a panda is the expression of a postman as he crossed the road in front of my car. He gave a double take, and a slight jump and my kids in the back burst out laughing. I suppose he wasn't expecting a panda to be driving.

The Great Fuzzy One- Wearing a black cloak, big wig and a curly moustache, I entered the school talent show playing the piano in a "Les Dawson" fashion, ending up with an audience participation version of Barry Mannilow's 'Can't Smile Without You'.

The Bad-Tempered Ladybird – My favourite costume- a large one-piece babygro with a zip up the front and padded feet, complete with matching reading book for World Book Day.

THE CROW 1985

Although mainly positive experiences, there have been times when I wasn't so pleased to be in fancy dress. Bridget Jones pleased her parents wearing a home knit jumper at Christmas, but there was someone else at the party wearing a similar jumper which eased her pain. In 1985 my friend and I went to a Mormon Halloween disco dressed as crows, to find no one else dressed up. It didn't ease my pain. I remember trying to dance to Pointer Sisters "I'm So Excited" with my wings on my back flapping about and this little tail. I even had straw stuffed in my socks that was moulting everywhere.

I had no change of clothes with me, but I did manage to dispose of the beak at the first opportunity. Whenever I hear that song, I don't think nostalgically back to the 1980s. No, I think of straw all over the floor and the sweaty black Lycra balaclava I was wearing.

THE SCHOOLGIRL 1987

On a school choir trip with over 150 of my friends to Germany, about six of us had planned to wear our school uniform St Trinian's style as we got off the overnight ferry. The other five didn't pack their clothes in their hand luggage. It was a bit awkward at breakfast as I faced the teachers wearing my version of the school uniform. (So much for strength in numbers).

I have vivid memories of me walking the streets of Heidelberg in broad daylight in a mini skirt, school-tie, fish-net tights and bunches, doing very little to fly the British flag. By then I had managed to rub the freckles off.

THE MILK BOTTLE 1987- RAISIN WEEKEND

Later that year as a first-year University student, I was a milk bottle in white tights and a card body, tied to other "milk bottles" on a cold November morning. I was then dragged through the freezing streets of St Andrews to be pelted with food by older students -all part of the traditional Raisin Weekend celebrations. Nice.

Recently the Raisin Weekend tradition has stopped because of the abuse of alcohol and mess left all over the town. It was a shame it didn't finish before I went there. Two 3rd year students would choose you in your first few weeks to be your academic mum and dad. It was a nice idea to mentor and look out for new first years, but Raisin Weekend was more of an initiation.

It started with an alcoholic, 'academic tea party' hosted by your mum with all your brothers and sisters and lots of spiked foods-vodka jellies and shots. Your mum would then present you with an object or toy that you would hang on your red academic gown called a Raisin String.

In the evening your father took you on a pub crawl (more alcohol) and gave you a Raisin Receipt with a Latin inscription on. Mine was a Victorian bathtub which I had to carry around with me. The idea was to give your child an unusual and awkward object to carry. I saw traffic cones and bins and all sorts of silly things being carried.

The next morning and a bit worse for wear, all the children were dressed up and paraded to the Quad where they were then subjected to the slime fest. Tradition or initiation? I'm not surprised it was stopped.

Whatever would William and Kate had made of all of that?

THE COCKROACH 2015

I managed to pick up a fabulous giant cockroach costume from a boot-sale, complete with legs and antennae. It had its first outing on World Book Day. I searched in vain for a storybook about a cockroach, so went as a non-fiction book instead "Cockroaches and Other Pests". The kids and parents at the school I worked in seemed to enjoy the costume, and all was well until I got a call from my daughter saying she needed ballet tights urgently for a ballet exam as she had just laddered hers.

I spent an awkward lunch hour dressed as a cockroach buying the tights in the town, although as I passed a few pubs and restaurants, I was daring myself just to run in one door and out the other to see if anyone would notice and call the Food Hygiene people. I didn't.

THE OFFICE PARTY

Staff night outs were also a chance to buy something sparkly and new and dress up differently. I didn't particularly like getting all dolled up so tried to initiate people wearing funny things- a colour scheme for example. One Christmas we all wore wings, another night out we all wore neon tutus.

However, one Christmas no-one seemed in the mood to be silly and were talking about their latest sparkly number and new shoes etc. I really couldn't be bothered that year being sensible and sitting down having a serious meal and ending up talking about work, so I wore a Mrs Santa costume. It was not an Ann Summers one; it was large and made of felt and covered a lot of me. I was more comfortable wearing it and warm as it came with a cloak than if I had worn a little black sparkly dress.

I liken how I felt that night to sitting on a sofa. It is possible to sit nicely on a couch, knees and feet together, sitting upright. But it's far more comfortable to kick your shoes off and tuck your feet beside you. I was most definitely the latter.

On another Christmas night out, my heels were too high for dancing, so I took them off and put them in the middle of the dance floor. A lot of other women followed suit, and we danced the night away quite comfortably. It was a change from dancing around your handbag. I had a sensible dress on, but when I danced, it started gaping at the top. I felt very self-conscious and hadn't got a safety pin with me. It stopped me performing some of my more adventurous dance moves!

While pulling the crackers and distributing the foil party hats, I found a perfect solution. I wore two gold flat coned Chinese style party hats under my dress. They looked a bit like the Madonna cones that she wore, but less pointy. There was no danger of any fall out with those on, and I danced the night away quite contentedly.

Talking of things falling out, at a work's party in the early 1980s, I was boogieing the night away wearing one of those Lycra body tops that usually had poppers down below to fasten. Mine had a set of hook and eye fastenings that were on their last legs that night having been stretched all over the place. Having progressed from the dancing around the handbag, we were now dancing around a panty liner which had escaped possibly during Wham's "Wake Me Up Before You Go Go"! A number of us looked at the said item in the middle. I watched in horror and then thought it best just to scoop it up, leave the dance floor and put it in the bin.

THE PUT-DOWN

Just this last October 2017 I wore the ladybird costume to the Primary school on Children in Need day and a beautiful pair of yellow Pudsey Bear ears. One of the year ones I taught as she came into school, put her hands on her hips, looked at me up and down and in front of several adults exclaimed a single word;

"Seriously?"

I had been put down by a six-year-old.

Would I have had the confidence to speak to my teacher quite like that at aged 6?

Possibly.

3
THE C - WORD

It was diagnosis day, D -day, or rather a 40G day. October 17 2017 My mum and I went to see the consultant. It was a coincidence that my parents were visiting from Scotland on that day, and as I sat in the Breast Care Clinic at the hospital, I wondered what my mum was thinking.

I was called to a small room full of an assortment of nurses- a burgundy one, a blue one and a plainclothes one. My consultant was straight talking and confirmed what I already knew.

I had grade 2 invasive lobular cancer. Grade 2 meant that the cells look less like normal breast cells and the tumour is growing faster. Most cancers are invasive. Invasive cancer has the potential to spread to other areas of the body.

Unfortunately, it already had. It was confirmed as in at least one of the lymph nodes. Breast cancer can spread when cancer cells are carried away from the breast through the lymphatic system or the bloodstream. Those cancer cells can then form secondary cancers elsewhere, which was a frightening thought.

The biopsy revealed that my cancer had receptors within the cell that bound to the hormone oestrogen. It was oestrogen receptor positive cancer or ER+. It was also a progesterone receptor positive. When oestrogen binds to these receptors, it can make cancer grow so I needed a hormone therapy would work against this type of cancer.

I was started on Letrozole 2.5mg tablets which would hopefully stop the production of any more hormones and stop the spread of the cancer. I had read that there were a number of side effects associated with taking the tablets including intense hot flushes, fatigue and insomnia, but that wasn't anything new for me!

I was introduced to a team of Macmillan nurses too. They are specialist breast care nurses who will be a support and a bank of information during these early stages. A lot of the information the consultant told me seemed to go in one ear and out the other, and I was glad I had my mum with me. My consultant was also my surgeon, and I did remember him saying that he could perform breast conservation surgery- a lumpectomy. However, I was told that my 40G breast would result in being slightly smaller after surgery. (He would make sure the other would match).

I'm sure my consultant could see me stifle a smile. Inside I was shouting, "Yes, yippee, result, smaller!" I also caught my mum smiling and nodding in a jealous sort of way at the burgundy nurse.

THE REALISATION

I had cancer, the C-word. It was confirmed.

How do you tell people? You can't slip it into the conversation:

By the way...

Oh, you'll never guess what happened last week...

There is a gap in the market in the card industry. There needs to be two sorts of cards; one to send out to family and friends, a bit like birth announcement cards or new address cards but announced in not such a "ta-da" dramatic way, and another that could be sent to someone. 'Get Well Soon' isn't the wish and 'Thinking of You' is the only sentiment that comes anywhere near.

I was able to announce my cancer on Facebook and lots of my friends sent messages of support. I could, however, sort everyone into roughly five groups.

1. The first group of people all seemed to know someone who had had breast cancer and were now fine or perhaps they had had it too. It was a group that I could go to for advice and to answer any little questions. However, I was well aware that everyone had different and very individual experiences. Everyone's cancer is different. It was reassuring to know that the lady in the shop's brother's friend's wife had cancer and now she's doing well. That was lovely for her, but I also know a lot of people or their relatives who unfortunately didn't win their fight.

2. The second group of people haven't contacted me. Not even a Christmas card. I know some of them didn't know/don't know what to say or maybe didn't read my posts on Facebook, but how can you truly be a friend of mine yet say nothing if you knew I had cancer? I had even personally messaged some people, and I could see that they had read my message and however I had no reply. Finally after four months and not a single "How are you?" or "Thinking of you". I had to unfriend some people from Facebook and take some others off my Christmas list. If I couldn't rely on them during this awful time, then they weren't real friends of mine in the first place.

3. The third group told me right from the start that I would be fine and that it was just a cyst or at least benign and not malignant. They are eternally the optimists and have lots of data and information at their fingertips. They are such sweeties to give me hope but keep playing the disease down. They very rarely say the word 'cancer' out loud and try and think of positive distractions.

4. The fourth group comprised mainly of the friends I have made on online American support groups. They tell me that my disease is a gift (not all of them) and bring religion too into the equation. They tell me to embrace the future and not dwell in the past. They are praying for me daily and believe that I have been chosen especially to fight this fight.

5. The fifth group comprise mainly of my family, friends and colleagues and this is the best group as they don't compare, or preach and are genuinely interested in how I am and that I get better. I get regular text messages and calls, and even if they didn't regularly get a text, I knew that they were there and could be relied and called upon whenever needed. Genuine offers of support were given.

I didn't want sympathy. I didn't feel ill either. I half wished I had a plaster cast on that people could notice and ask what had happened and they could see when a sling had replaced it and then maybe a bandage, and then a plaster when that things were getting better.

In the media, I had seen all the fantastic cancer fundraising activities-the Race for Life, the Pink shirts, the Moon Walks. I had attended coffee mornings and cake sales before. I had a few pink ribbon pins in drawers somewhere at home. What else could I do?

I seriously wondered why people suddenly started running when they got their cancer diagnosis- particularly breast cancer, and not just sufferers, friends and relatives too. It wasn't just a little jog either. It was half marathons and full marathons and walks right through the night. I may have had a spring in my step, but I certainly wasn't going to start running. I couldn't think of anything worse. I know everyone feels compelled to do their little bit, to raise awareness and to fundraise, but to run? I certainly wasn't going to start running and although there was a big TV and radio Breast awareness campaign coming up, I thought just by my talking would spread awareness to others. I decided then and there to:

"Tackle my tumour with humour."

I joined a few breast cancer forums and groups online and read survivor stories and blogs. One comedian named Tig Notaro claimed she had badmouthed her small boobs so much that they had tried to kill her! I liked that humour. My mum and her mum had always been big, and although in some circles it's nice to be well endowed, I didn't find many positives. Not many high street stores stocked 40G bras, and if they did they weren't pretty, lacy and feminine, they were more of the hard, wired scaffolding type. They reminded me of what a Stone Age bra —an over shoulder boulder holder, may have looked like!

It was a while before I told anyone that I had cancer and then slowly I dropped it into the conversation.

If the reaction was "I'm so sorry", I would ask why they were sorry. Sorry? What did they know that I didn't? And then when I had milked their worried feeling enough, I would laugh and say it was fine. It was fine. It hadn't sunk in, and although I was not in denial, I wasn't actually fully aware of the implications and blissfully unaware of what was to come.

The teacher in me was powerless to change anything. I was not able to control the cancer, so there was no point trying. It was the same with car mechanics and computers- I have no control of them either- I can take steps to make the understanding and troubleshooting of them better, but there is very little understanding on my part.

There is no trouble-shooting cancer.

I began posting on Facebook. I found some funny cartoons and came up with a few of my own too. I even Googled if I could skip the queue at Disney! Surely there must be some positives to having cancer? Was it all doom and gloom?

Oddly there were still no tears.

NEVER HAPPY

If I lost my hair with possible chemotherapy, did it mean I could wear a wig? I'd always wanted straight hair or a little pixie crop. I was stuck with the 1970s fro. I fantasised about possible hairstyles. I had had the same one for nearly 35 years!

They say those who have straight hair want curly hair and those who have curly hair want straight hair. It takes a very long time to cut, dye and straighten my hair. When I was younger, I never had the time or money to spend all day in the hairdressers. Many people have "had a go" at straightening my hair. I bought the fancy hair-straighteners, but as soon as there is any moisture in the air, my hair frizzes up big time.

I bought a few products to try out on my hair. One time before a party I worked what I thought was hair mousse into my hair only to realise it was shaving foam. The smell gave it away, but I was in a rush.

I have tried gel, mousse, wax and even mayonnaise in my hair in the attempt to make it more manageable. Some people are never happy with what they have.

My daughter didn't like her hair at aged four. It was Christmas Eve, and as I was getting her ready for bed, I noticed a significant bit missing from her fringe. She had cut it as it was going into her eyes. When I write cut, I should have written hacked. There was a large stubbly bald patch right at the front of her head.

I was surprised how upset I was, and she was sent to bed in disgrace on Christmas Eve without leaving a carrot for Rudolph. I think I may even have said that Santa may not even come. (I feel guilty about that now). It was so apparent that she had cut her hair herself that after a while I didn't mind. It wasn't like I had taken her to a salon and she had had a bad haircut. It was a learning curve for my daughter. Already incredibly vain, she never cut her hair again.

THE FUZZ

My hair has been referred to as 'the hedge' 'the bird's nest', 'the blonde afro', 'the Fuzz', 'Brillo' and 'the Fluff' amongst others that were never said to my face. When I had my long blonde hair cut off at the age of seven because it was a nightmare to brush, it then all sort of fuzzed up. If I left it to grow, it grew out like a lion's mane or even a hedge, and if it was cut short, it grew back even bushier. There was no taming it. Now I resign to the morning ritual of taming the fuzz, after going through gallons of conditioner when washing it and smarming it down with some sort of wax. There's not much I can do with it, and when very unruly, it's best tied up with a scrunchie into a fluff ball. I have even contemplated going regal and asking the hairdressers for a "topiary" style cut, and I also went to Big Mamas Afro Salon locally, but their products made it wilder still. B & Q haven't cottoned on to the market yet for the double use of their hedge trimmers!

When thinking about going to get my haircut one day in the 1990s, I first thought of a new hair salon that had just opened. I couldn't for the life of me remember the name, but it was so clear in my mind, and they were advertising offers. I then realised it was the salon in the soap opera EastEnders that I was referring to! I watched too much TV.

ALDI AUGUST 2016

Standing in the queue in Aldi, the man behind me tapped me on the shoulder and said: "Excuse me, madam, I think you have something in your hair".

I reached up expecting to find a bug or a leaf or even a bit of fluff, and instead pulled out a razor, complete with pink plastic handle.

Now, you may have expected me to run out of the shop in sheer embarrassment, but although relatively embarrassed, I took it in my stride. After all, these kinds of incidences occurred regularly and more often than not involved my hair. "Thank you," I said and removed the offending object from my hair. I said nothing more.

The razor in the hair story was just last year and what was even funnier was that only a few days later I was watching my heroine Bridget Jones in her latest film at the cinema and she had a toy train stuck in her hair without knowing. The loud snort of a laugh that I uttered in the auditorium seemed to last for a tad longer than I had hoped. Time enough for the few others in that matinee performance to turn round and look at me sitting there on my own, with my hand over my mouth. It was then that I honestly did feel I was Kent's very own Bridget Jones. It seemed to me some sort of secret seal of approval. Except Bridget Jones didn't have fuzzy hair.

The fuzz has been straightened before, but the slightest moisture and I look like the cartoon character Crystal Tipps. It clogs up plugholes, it's broken the Hoover mechanism, and it's almost been used as nesting material by a crow that came within an inch of a sunbathing me (I have photographic evidence). It's been used as kindling on fire, it has been the cause of my husband's toe going septic (the less said the better) and it has been the subject of a game for bored students while at school.

SCHOOL 1982

Unbeknown to me, pupils sitting behind me would hide things in my hair- biros, rubbers, paper balls, anything. They would score points and lose points if items dropped out. I was merrily oblivious until I moved suddenly or something poked accidentally into my scalp. I was only a game. The girls I sat next to had Thomson Twin style long bits at the back, and I'm sure one got cut off or something tied to it.

That hair "Buckaroo" story does link to a more recent one.

HUMAN BUCKAROO 2016

While a friend of mine was sleeping, another friend and I decided to take turns in balancing items on her sleeping body. It's a great game to play and involves a steady hand and the right objects. Compact mirrors are good, and so are pens and tissues, lots of folded tissues.

4

AN MRI NOT A KFC

I needed an MRI (magnetic resonance imaging) scan to check that the cancer had not spread to the right breast. I would have far preferred a KFC (Kentucky Fried Chicken).

I had gone for this MRI appointment on my own. I had to wear flowing clothes with no metal, and so I swooshed into the waiting room. I wondered how many people would notice I was missing from work. Not many teachers at work knew I had cancer; I hadn't said anything. I had set supply lessons, and the classes too would be merrily oblivious.

I entered a room in which there was an ominously huge machine. I had watched Casualty and Holby City on TV often enough to know the process, but I had never seen a bed to lie on with breast holes in. It was quite comical. I dropped into position and began listening to the standard tunes that came through the headphones. It wasn't exactly uncomfortable but lying on my front meant that my breakfast kept repeating on me and I was desperate not to pass any trapped wind! The music was Britney Spears. Don't get me wrong, I do like a bit of Britney, but I'm sure there was something wrong with the playlist as I had three songs on repeat. The nurse's voice came through in the headphones checking I was OK. I didn't have the heart to say could they play something else, but as I came out of the machine, "Baby hit me one more time" was so ingrained I could only offer a weak smile to the gorgeous male nurse that made sure I dismounted the slab safely.

A couple of weeks later I was back for another MRI with contrast. They had fun and games finding a vein that worked and squirted a blue dye into me to make the pictures better. Some women nickname themselves "Blue Tits" because of this process or adopt the bird as a symbol of their struggle. I just looked down and hoped I wasn't going to turn into a Smurf!

This time they were checking if the cancer had spread to the spine or the brain. This was the scan I was most worried about as I did have some symptoms I thought, that could indicate a brain tumour.

The slab was hard, and despite a pillow under my knees, it wasn't the best place to remain still. At least I was on my back, but this time there was no Britney, and the machine was so loud that I could hardly hear the music through the headphones. As I gazed into the mirror above me, I could see that my eye-liner had begun to smudge.

It was cold in the machine. I had been offered a blanket but thought I would be fine. The thin hospital gown with the back open to the elements didn't provide much warmth. I had left my faded red university hoodie on the chair.

I thought of my daughter finishing her first term at University, and I thought back to my University days- the best years of my life. The tears fell freely.

THE UNIVERSITY OF ST. ANDREWS
I went to the University of St Andrews and read history. It was an hour away from home- far enough to be away from the family but close enough to pop back home.

The MA Honours course would take four years, and in my first year, I took Modern History, Ancient History and Russian Language.

SKINNY DIPPING
There are several beaches at St Andrews including the magnificent West Sands where they filmed Chariots of Fire. I remember that

beach for the night I lost my clothes. Well, they weren't even my clothes as I was borrowing a friend's. A girlfriend and I had decided to go skinny dipping. We were careful to put our clothes away from the incoming tide, but it got dark, and we got out of the water, only to have no idea where the piles of clothes were. In the days of no mobile phones, we couldn't call anyone and had to wait shivering in the dunes until we heard people coming and then ask for help. We found our bags and shoes further into the dunes and the golf putter belonging to my friend, but the underwear jeans and tops had gone- possibly taken for a joke, but we never got them back.

It was a ridiculous thing to do, but we had not been drinking, it was just something on our bucket list that we wanted to do, and it went horribly wrong.

MAY DAY 1989

I went into the sea again at 5 am, but this time I'd been singing madrigals on the beach with a group of friends and wearing a red gown- the university red gown. I was sober, and this was a University May Day tradition. The North Sea was cold at that time in the morning.

Whenever I feel cold, I think back to the North Sea. That was cold, the cold that makes you want to cry out.

Lying shivering in an MRI machine was peanuts compared with those days!

ROYAL STUDENTS

Prince William and Kate were just five years old when I went to St. Andrews, but I was excited when walking in St. Andrews to see Prince William walking along the street on a visit back to the town. It was agreed in the time he was a student to leave him be. I believe he was known as 'Steve' when he was there.

However, as a future monarch, I thought it rude not to say hello. I could just cross the street and smile as I accidentally on purpose walked past him. At that moment a seagull with an upset stomach deposited its load on me. I didn't cross over the street.

I didn't feel very lucky either as I tried to scrape it all off me in the town's public toilets.

GRADUATION BALL 1991

I graduated in 1991 with an MA but the Graduation Ball to celebrate was just so expensive. I had stayed up in St Andrews the weekend of the Ball but didn't have a ticket. Together with some friends, we decided to gatecrash the Ball.

The tickets were white and had rounded edges. We tried various ways of getting in.

Through the main entrance saying we had forgotten our tickets didn't work.

Climbing a wall in a ball dress, tights and heels were hilarious, but there was security on the other side. That plan didn't work.

Carrying a real harp through a door pretending we were the entertainment got us to the main marquee, but we were recognised and escorted out. That didn't work.

There were various entrances, and we weren't upset as our plans were foiled. It just made us more determined. It was hilarious.

We tried one at a time, then in couples pretending we had lost our tickets, but each time we were escorted back out.

I almost got in on the arm of a friend but was recognised at the bag check and waved back to the starting position.

A little frustrated we decided to have a Chinese takeaway and discuss Plan Z. Taking the foil card lids off our dinner, we realised they were white on the reverse and with rounded edges. Perfect. We waited until it was dark and then ran; passing the invites to the security and just running in saying we were late for the show. What show? It worked. No one escorted us out. We were laughing so much. I'm sure we were spotted, but I reckon they were tired of turfing us out, knew we were students and not any threat to the flow of the show and just turned a blind eye. I want to think it was because of our cunning tactic. Whatever the reason, we had made it in. We joined in the ceilidh until the early hours of the morning and then did the traditional pier walk down by the harbour and watched the sunrise.

One of my partners in crime that night is now the editor of a prominent British fashion magazine and online partner magazine. It was this friend that introduced me to the gorgeous Mr Bingley. The boy in question was Crispin Bonham Carter who later did play Mr Bingley alongside Colin Firth in the BBC drama Pride and Prejudice; A Bridget Jones reference? Crispin studied in the Ancient History building, and I would often bump into him. Always a bit flustered (he was incredibly handsome), I would smile and wave and then gaze at his long blonde curly hair which he often tied into a ponytail as he walked away. He wore the traditional St. Andrews green waxed jacket and a particularly memorable tan suede tasselled jacket. He also spoke very nicely.

SALAD DAYS

They say your university years are your salad days. They were more my "tuna on rice, Chinese takeaway and cider with blackcurrant "days. If I could go back and do it all again, I would do, like a shot.

Since the William and Kate story, the university is even more 'English' in make-up, and a lot of students are there looking for future prospective wives and husbands of a certain calibre. When I was there my goals were to get my essays submitted in on time, buy a fudge doughnut from a famous patisserie in the High Street when I could, make it home to watch Neighbours on TV and find a good excuse twice a week why I couldn't go to aerobics. The boys I met there were friends, not really boyfriends. The town and University were too small I felt, for a relationship to work. I had plenty of ball dates, dinner dates and flings, but nothing serious.

THE OLD COURSE

St Andrews is the home of golf. My flat in the 3rd and the 4th year 1988 overlooked the 17th and 18th hole, and I often took a short cut over the iconic little bridge on the golf course that is always in pictures of St. Andrews. On one shortcut from the pub to home, a couple of friends and I had the sudden urge for the loo and nipped under the bridge. Nowadays that is a public order offence, and we are genuinely sorry now, mainly as the floodlights came on, and the groundsman calmly said,

"I don't think Mr Ballesteros would be pleased with you lot."

REMINISCING

I had to wait again for the MRI scan results. I just wanted them to come back clear. I knew I was facing a large tumour or several tumours- I could feel it now, and the dimpling was obvious when I did look in the mirror. I still had a bit of a suntan from the summer left- I had dared to bare the flesh, and I had worn a bikini.

I let my daughters feel the lump too. I wanted them to be aware of the symptoms. The whole of October had been Breast Awareness month at school, and they had been buying cakes and wearing pink with their school uniform. We didn't talk much about cancer at home- preferring to keep to normality as much as possible.

It was harder for my other daughter away at University because communication was all by phone.

As I went to bed after a face-time call with her, I could sense in her voice she was worried. Should I be concerned? I had been putting a real brave face on things and of course- fighting the tumour with humour. I was too young at 48 to be taken by this illness and I had no idea that all this would happen as I was growing up.

5
GROWING UP

I wasn't a naughty child but aged six, my Reception teacher had to continually pull me up about my offhand manner and for not listening to instructions. My parents were called in. It turned out I wasn't deliberately rude; I couldn't hear. I subsequently had grommets put in my ears and my adenoids out. My parents had a giggle at my consultant's name- Dr Lobo- particularly apt for an ear surgeon. That was my first time in the hospital.

What I remember most are the presents I received in the hospital from the school dinner ladies. I was one of those children that walked around the playground holding the dinner ladies' hands and chatting for England. I still have the little book given to me by one dinner lady, and I remember also getting a small net bag of glass marbles from another.

How times have changed. Dinner ladies- or Mid-day Supervisors as they are now known -have a tough job in schools today and probably dream about walking around the playground or school building idly chatting to children. Buying presents and sending cards to individual children is a definite no-no. The laws relating to working with children have been tightened up dramatically.

As a teacher myself I know I have to be so careful what I say and do both in and out of school and remain as professional as possible at all times. I'm having to be mindful of this too while penning these stories.

It's now the world we live in that we can't hug a child when they're feeling down or have fallen over and that if they ask you to do their shoelaces or buttons up you have to check someone else is in the room too. There are risk assessments for this and that, school visits to the beach cancelled for health and safety reasons, party games banned because of competitiveness, mats taken away from PE apparatus because it encourages jumping and even today (12/12/17) some schools have closed because the playgrounds have iced over after some snowy weather. Children were likely to fall over. Soon there will be no running allowed at all on a playground in case of injury!

I was always careful about running in the playground. It had something to do with witnessing my best friend run, fall and break her leg in a horrific way aged only six.

I worked hard at school and won a few prizes for academic excellence. I was reasonably good at French and Music and extremely competitive. I enjoyed my school days.

I am an associate member of the grammar and spelling police, and I find it sad that adults still muddle 'their', 'they're' and 'there' and misuse apostrophes. Once a teacher, always a teacher and I can't switch off when I spot a poor spelling out of school. I have always been like this. Apparently on my very first day at school I pointed out to my Reception teacher that the name on my peg was incorrectly spelt. It was.

I did, however, get a punishment at secondary school with a friend in the form of an essay to write titled: "Why it is inappropriate to hum the instrumental break from Nik Kershaw's 'Wouldn't It Be Good?' during a Physics lesson. The best essay I have ever written!

Quite proud too to boast that I never, however, received single detention.

MAKING A SPLASH

I was lucky enough to have a mum and dad that took me to various after-school activities in the evenings. I tried trampolining, swimming, Brownies, gymnastics and ballet.

Our family sport was swimming. I got to district level winning the Medway Championships in 1980 and then in Scotland swimming at the school district level. My youngest brother was the most successful. At 13 and 15 he broke the British junior age group records in breaststroke and represented Scotland at the national level. However, he then chose his studies over swimming. It was only later that I truly understood why people laughed when my mum shouted: "C'on Dom" (come on Dom- condom) from the spectator's gallery!

EDINBURGH 1986

In 1986 the Commonwealth Games came to Edinburgh. My friend and I were lucky enough to be helpers. In fact, it was a family affair with my youngest brother performing in the opening ceremony, my other brother working on poolside and my dad officiating at the pool. Only my mum was left out. But she was lucky; she didn't have to wear the hideous red BHS tracksuit with green piping and white lace-up shoes, nothing like the smart uniforms the Games Makers wore at later Commonwealth Games. The only positive this awkward tracksuit with an elasticated waist and ankle cuffs had was that it made us look like competitors.

I had great fun swapping badges and pins with other athletes in the streets of the city and also signing autographs. I was allegedly a "swimmer in the freestyle relay".

I was a VIP Steward. My job was to direct celebrities, dignitaries and Royalty to their seats – a bit hard not to find the royal box but also if, in that short 50-yard walk, they were to ask any questions about swimming, then I would be on hand to answer. I knew a bit about swimming.

A VIP steward was a great job as it meant I got to watch the racing and also talk to famous people. I had a massive crush on the English swimmer Andy Jameson who was due to race in the 100m butterfly oh and all the girls liked Mark Foster (Strictly Dancer famous for taking his shirt off).

I showed Prince Edward to his seat and was told to address the Queen as ma'am if she spoke, but when she attended, I was pushed out of the way by bigger wigs than me.

My friend was working on the poolside collecting swimmer's clothes in boxes as they began their races. When Prince Edward walked past her on the way to present the medals, she couldn't help but get my attention by surreptitiously waving. But the moment he walked past her she began pointing to his head and trying to get my attention again. It was fairly obvious why she was smiling as an HRH Prince Edward had a little bald patch and she had just seen it up close and personal. I couldn't wave back or acknowledge that I knew why she was smiling and "doing the circular finger thingy," as the world's TV cameras were on us. I was also really hoping we hadn't been caught and broadcast anywhere!

I showed Prince Charles and Lady Diana to their seats in the Royal Box. They came in the evening, but Andy Jameson was swimming. I took them the long way round to the box as I wanted to see what was going on in the pool. I had my priorities.

Andy J went on to win the gold medal for England. I got some excellent poolside photos, and he signed my autograph book:

"Andy Jameson xxx (claimable) "

Although happily married now and working with Adrian Moorhouse as part of a successful swimming commentary duo, I do still wonder if I can play the cancer card and get ever to claim those "xxx"!

I had been to the Royal Box before the previous year, but that time it was fair to say, more embarrassing.

THE WALK OF SHAME

I worked as a medal bearer at the Scottish Swimming Championships in 1985. Dressed in the sponsor's white t-shirt and a kilt, I wasn't particularly a figure of glamour and definitely not scantily clad or heavily made up, but I led the winners to the waiting dignitary in the royal box and carried the medals. The girl at the back of the procession would then collect the cushion ready for the next ceremony.

On this occasion, it was a packed venue, and we walked to a clap and loud music to the Royal Box. It was then I realised I wasn't carrying the cushion. I walked up the stairs, pretended to put the cushion down, told the dignitary in no uncertain terms to "hang on a sec" and walked fairly calmly down the other steps and back to the start to the bemusement of the spectators. I collected the cushion and did a procession of my own to my private applause, but no music. I didn't wave to the crowd like the winners. It was a long walk of shame.

NOT SO DAINTY

I went to the Joy Waite School of Dance, but I was no ballerina. Ballet for me was a social to see my friends. It was also a complete nightmare to get my fuzzy hair into a neat style, let alone a bun.

Ballet for my three-year-old daughter in 2002 was also social. She liked to chat and disturb her friends with very little patience for the ballet steps. She was eventually asked to leave her first dance school because of poor concentration and behaviour. Her next ballet teacher said she would never 'make a ballerina'. She wasn't put off, she persevered. At the age of twelve won the U/18 Open Entertainment trophy at Disneyland, Paris.

On the day after our house had flooded, after having no sleep, she took a ballet exam and was awarded distinction and in the evening won a scholarship to perform with the English Youth Ballet. In 2015 she performed at Sadler's Wells with the National Youth Ballet, and in July 2017 she passed her ISTD Advanced 2 Ballet Exam. (I just had to get that paragraph in). So much for not being a ballerina!

Possibly she gets her dogged determination from me.

I wasn't a natural ballet dancer. I took long toilet breaks and was bored doing repetitive movements and didn't really like being told what to do. I didn't understand why all the commands had to be in French, and I wasn't flexible or dainty either, but I did like performing in the big shows.

HAZLITT THEATRE 1980

Backstage before a dance show, I was nervous and couldn't get the Tarantella steps right. I didn't have good coordination and struggled to bang and shake my tambourine in the right place and in time with the music. I ran off in a huff and wrapped myself in a large red velvet curtain. I remember twisting around and around until there was an almighty crash.

The curtain rail came away from the wall along with a lot of plaster. A lot of adults came over and shouted at me, more in frustration I think. No-one had been hurt. I was extricated from the curtain and later shoved on stage.

I got away without severe punishment, but some of the money raised for charity had to go on repairing the theatre, so I wasn't particularly flavour of the month.

At home, the naughtiest thing I had done was put my brother in the laundry basket and then sit on it. He was not allowed out until he had recited the whole of the alphabet.

Kids can be cruel.

R.E. CLASS 1982

Teachers at school fell into two categories. The ones you liked and the ones you didn't. No one liked our R.E. teacher. She had a monotone voice, did not inspire us and we didn't learn anything. We did a lot of lying on the floor with our eyes closed, trying to short circuit our bodies with the power of the mind.

She was one of those unfortunate teachers who had wild hair and dull coloured clothes. Everything about her was boring. But she certainly didn't deserve to be shut in her store cupboard one day and not let out until she had sung Baa Baa Black Sheep.

We weren't punished for some reason. At the time I remember it was incredibly funny but still my ambition was to be a teacher, I had no other career in mind.

I apologise now on behalf of the class, and I have learnt as a teacher, never to go into a cupboard in a classroom without a key.

6

LOVE 'N STUFF

JUST GOOD FRIENDS

I was totally in love with Paul Nicholas from the sitcom Just Good Friends. I had his pictures on the wall alongside Jesper Olsen from Man United, the swimmer Andy Jameson and Nick Heyward from Haircut 100.

I had written Paul a letter and even sent him a birthday card for his 40th. I was so chuffed when he replied with a signed photo. I wrote to Jim'll Fix it to see if I could meet him. If only I had had Twitter or Instagram or Facebook then as I could have followed my crushes instead of spending a fortune of magazines just because there was a tiny picture or article in one.

I did however eventually get to see Paul Nicholas in real life, albeit briefly when he was a compere alongside David Soul in an Ira Gershwin Concert that I was performing in at the Royal Albert Hall. I didn't get to speak to him. That perhaps was a good thing as on the train home I realised I had my white concert blouse on inside out!

As a teenager, I had lots of crushes- on pop stars, celebrities, the French assistant, my maths teacher and a boy who was a boy three years older. My first two boyfriends now have husbands, and a third crush is living with his male partner. I used to like boys that were in touch with their feminine side and not all hairy, muscled and tattooed.

I did have an ideal man profile though- dark hair, gold-rimmed glasses and possibly from another country. I remember writing that in my diary in 1983.

SICILY 1990

There were plenty of dark-haired boys wearing glasses in Sicily and they all spoke Italian. I jumped at the chance of working my University holiday as an au-pair in the tourist resort of Taormina. I was to look after a five-year-old girl, but it wasn't the ideal holiday job I had hoped. I began to feel like Rapunzel trapped in the tower. The girl's family owned a hotel at the top of a mountain -except I had fuzzy hair and not long golden hair. I worked 9 am-10 pm every day. The little girl was very spoilt and did not like me at all and did not do anything I asked her to. To be honest, I did not like her either.

At five years old she was a little princess. She was in charge, and when I tried to talk to her parents about our relationship, they told me my job was to do whatever she asked me to do.

The little girl didn't like the sun, so we stayed indoors on hot sunny days, and she watched cartoons all the time. I couldn't persuade her otherwise. I think that's how I learnt most of my Italian.

One evening when sitting in the hotel lobby, the girl threw a pen on the floor in a rage that her drawing wasn't going well. I asked her to pick it up, and she went into full screaming meltdown. It was a public place.

The mother came running to her and asked whatever had happened. I felt a bit silly saying she had thrown the pen on the floor and not wanted to get it. The mother looked at the pen on the floor and looked at me.

"Pick it up," she said.

I'm sure that little girl smirked at me from the arms of her mum.

Needless to say, neither of them are friends with me on Facebook.

I wanted to stay in Sicily, yet I had no visa and no money. I was working in the hotel in return for my airfare, food and lodging. At 10 pm there weren't many places to go especially at the top of the mountain. There were 436 steps in different flights down to the town if you wanted the long scenic route or you could take a special shuttle bus. The bus was for guests only; I wasn't allowed.

With the backdrop of Mount Etna and the twinkling lights of the town below, it was a stunning setting for a hotel, and the town was equally as beautiful. Rich Sicilian women adorned in gold wandered the streets and Sicilian men also adorned in gold and opened necked shirts, hung around the street corners. Once the cafes and restaurants had shut and the tourists had returned to their hotels, it wasn't a safe place for me really to explore at night.

The only young people I knew were the boys who worked in the ice cream parlour. Sometimes I was allowed to get ice cream for the little girl- never for me, and the boys would give me an ice -cream 'on the house'. My favourite flavours were lemon and apricot, and I dreamed then that one day you could buy ice cream in loads of different flavours by the scoop in England. (Nowadays every high street seems to have an Italian themed ice cream parlour!)

One morning I was sent by shuttle bus (officially allowed) down to the town to go and get ice-cream. I met the boys from the shop and their friend N. in the street. I was wearing my signature pyjama trousers. N. spoke Spanish, French and a bit of Italian but not enough to have a proper conversation and no English.

In my schoolgirl French I chatted, flirted, and we got on well. It was either the fuzzy hair, the pyjamas or my charm, but whatever it was, a holiday romance ensued. I saw him late at night when he and I had finished work, and I had made it down the 436 steps. He would escort me back up the steps for safety- or to make sure I didn't collapse in a heap at the top. The summer nights were hot, humid and full of mosquitoes. As we had absolutely nothing in common, we got on. I liked the fact that we were so different; opposites did attract.

AGE NO PROBLEM

Living in a hotel and working long hours was quite a lonely existence. I wasn't allowed to talk to the guests, and apart from the little girl who wasn't one for having long chats, I rarely spoke to anyone. But I didn't want to go home.

One day while supervising the little girl in a park I struck up a conversation with an elderly gentleman (G). It was nice to practice my Italian, and I thought G. was sweet. He was 82 and lived alone in a neighbouring town. G. walked with a stick and enjoyed strolls around the tourist town.

Every day when I took the little girl to play with her friends, I spoke to G., and I enjoyed his company. He would occasionally buy ice-creams for us and tell me stories of the town. G. spoke with lots of dialect words and mannerisms, and I quite looked forward to our little chats. G. bought me a Sicilian bracelet, but I innocently thought it was just a cheap souvenir to remember Sicily. I later found out it was 18 ct gold.

I didn't talk about N. to G. or even mention N. as it was personal, but one day N. had a day off, and I had asked him to meet me in the park. N. was not allowed to visit the hotel where I worked and lived. I introduced N. as my boyfriend to my elderly friend. I wasn't prepared for what happened next. G. freaked. He was so cross. I thought he was going to use his stick. I had no idea why until in a verbal tirade G. referred to me as "his girlfriend."

I wasn't aware of some Sicilian customs and although I was well aware of the dangers of talking to strange men, let alone on a park bench, I honestly never thought that G. would believe our age gap of 63 years to be no problem. It all got really awkward, and I had to take the little girl other places and not visit the park anymore.

ARABIAN NIGHTS

I remember trying to work out where Morocco was precisely. I knew my family were there on holiday, but I was somewhat ignorant of the country and hadn't heard Arabic being spoken first hand. N was from Morocco. I assumed at first it was near Saudi Arabia, part of the ancient Persian kingdom, but no, it was in North Africa. I knew Casablanca was in Morocco but thought it was the capital city. It's actually Rabat. Despite an honours degree, my geography was still fairly shaky.

When N. began talking about the wild animals in Morocco and those he had seen in the wild, I listened incredulously. We spoke about squirrels as they didn't naturally roam in the wilds of Morocco and also it was a hard word for N. to pronounce. Because I was teasing, he began talking about the day he encountered a tiger. I was not falling for any of his tales. I knew my Monty Python sketches, and there were definitely no tigers in Africa!

N. worked long hours in a restaurant at the lowest level for one of those Sicilian men adorned with gold with an equally adorned woman on his arm.

"One day I will live in England and own a restaurant," N. said.

I admired his ambition.

The Gulf War broke out.

I returned to St Andrews for my final year.

"Come for Christmas," I wrote in a letter to N. merrily oblivious of home office immigration rules.

The computer said no.

I can see now why my family were concerned that the holiday romance hadn't ended. Well, from my end it hadn't. But I was relatively headstrong and knew we could talk about rhubarb yoghurt or Bruce Forsyth or Hallowe'en together, and his Italian was improving. I had begun Italian at night class on top of my degree work and had met a group of Italians at university so was getting the practice in.

It was at that time that I look back and wish I had a mobile phone or a computer with email. We corresponded by letter and brief telephone call at 8 pm every Sunday. We spoke in "Fritalian"- a mixture of French and Italian.

CANTERBURY CHRISTCHURCH COLLEGE 1992-93

I started Arabic classes and a PGCE in Primary teaching at Canterbury and spilt my heart out to my best friend, Cheryl. I missed N. terribly.

It was hard living in one country yet wanting to be in another.

It was also hard pretending to be in one country when you were actually in another.

FEBRUARY 1993

I missed N. terribly, and Cheryl lent me the money (I was a student again!) so I could fly to Italy for half term. Only Cheryl knew I was there. I felt a bit guilty not letting anyone know, but I think people had hoped the relationship was over.

I had to pretend the line was terrible when calling home. I got away with it though.

Long distance relationships are tricky but made trickier when N. held a Moroccan passport. The only way of being granted a visa for the UK would be if I kept a job and had somewhere to live. I was a student; there was no chance of that happening soon.

It appeared this was the only way, so I attended interviews.

I found a permanent full-time job in a multi-cultural school starting in September, and the plan was to go together to Casablanca at Easter to the British Embassy and apply together for a VISA. We would both have to make it to Morocco.

In a world without email or mobile phones yet, it was quite an adventure for me to go from Canterbury to Morocco and for N. to travel back from Italy to Morocco with the possibility of him not being able to return to Italy. It was scary yet exciting.

APRIL 1993

The week before I was due to fly, my housemates and I caught scabies. We all felt very sorry for ourselves but spent a brilliant few lessons off college, caked in "sheep dip", in pyjamas just watching rented videos. We had a few real girls' nights in. I was so worried that I would not get to go to Morocco, but fortunately, the scabies cleared up fairly quickly, albeit uncomfortably.

We also scrubbed, cleaned, scoured and washed the house thoroughly. Something that only happened when the landlord was due to visit!

Casablanca has that image of being a romantic yet exotic city. There had been change since the change of King but you crossed the road at your own risk, and the sights and smells were quite overwhelming. It was loud, dusty, colourful, vibrant, manic, chaotic and fascinating but I felt very insignificant and not covered up.

The British embassy was closed for the Easter Holidays. It had been a wasted journey. We couldn't apply together for a VISA. Now N. was stuck in Morocco.

I returned to Canterbury to do my eight-week teaching practice and cried my eyes out on Cheryl's shoulder. I found the strength from somewhere and immersed myself in teaching. Cheryl was a good listener and a good friend, and she had kept my spirits high from the first day I met her. She hadn't been feeling well for a few weeks.

She died of liver cancer the week before the "telephone call".

WELCOME TO ENGLAND

The telephone call was to say N. had been granted a Visa thanks to some faxes between my dad and the British Embassy. He was coming in three days to London. When my mum found out on the phone, she was so excited that she flooded her bathroom by leaving the tap running!

Emotions cancelled out each other. Cheryl would have been so happy for me. I wanted her to meet him. He would never meet her.

I didn't grieve properly for Cheryl.

N. arrived at Heathrow with two bags to his name.

My parents were worried that N. was going to distract me from qualifying as a teacher - I only had three weeks to go, and so my dad drove from Edinburgh to Canterbury to collect him and drive him back up to Edinburgh to stay with them and my little brother.

Despite no English, they seemed to get on. Mum taught N. his first English words- colander and frying pan, and once again I communicated long distance by phone.

My first birthday card from N. bought in the UK said:
"To my Wife
Happy Diamond Wedding Anniversary
Celebrating 60 years of married life together."
I didn't have the heart to tell him!

It was a difficult summer, signing on, having no money, living with the parents, but we did it. I started a new job in September and life began to be very busy.

HALLOWE'EN 1993

I held a fancy dress party for Hallowe'en and introduced N. to the bizarre traditions of 'dooking' for apples, eating marshmallows from flour and piling over to the local restaurant for a fancy dress party. A friend, N. and I had dressed in black and had taped life-sized card skeletons on to ourselves.

Covered in flour and still dripping wet, we went into the crowded pub to find no one else had dressed up except the barman with a pathetic Freddie Krueger mask.

Imagine a saloon in a western film when the baddie comes through the swing doors, and all goes quiet with every eye upon you. Yep, that summed up the room at that moment.   I remember N. at the bar subtly picking at the tape that tightly wound a card tibia to him.

I think fondly back to those days. I was determined things would work out. It was hard, but I ignored the warnings from friends and family.

7

SURGERY IS LOOMING

MY IDEAL FUNERAL

As I walked back to my parked car after the MRI in November 2017, I imagined the world going on without me. Where would my children live? Who would miss me? What legacies would I leave?

In the next few days, I spoke to my lawyer about making a will, and I started putting down some ideas for my funeral.

I want a cremation with my favourite hymns intermingled with some speeches- some funny anecdotes such as those contained in this book. First it has to be L'Aurora by Eros Ramazzotti and then in the middle during the serious part- Beati Quorum Via by Charles Stanford and as the coffin disappears behind the curtain it has to ABBA -Dancing Queen then to end on a cheerful note when everyone was filing out I would like a Muppets song or Sesame Street song to be played- possibly Boogie Woogie Piggies!

If it were allowed, I would be buried in my ladybird onesie. I would love it too if people wore fancy dress costumes and not black, but it wouldn't be respectful to other mourners and visitors to the crematorium if the mourning party were dressed as Spiderman, Minions and French Maids, let alone cockroaches. So 'bright colours' it would have to be.

MASSECTOMY/ MASTECTOMY?

Amongst all my "Thinking of You" cards on the shelf, there was not one there from N.

In these few weeks, I realised exactly what was meant by "scanxiety" (scan anxiety). It was a worry that was always there and as soon as you thought you had taken your mind off it, bang, the anxious feelings were back. The scanxiety didn't leave until the letter arrived on the doormat and even then is always bubbling away ready to rear its ugly head.

Fortunately for me this time the MRI scan came back clear; the cancer had not spread to the right breast. This was good news, but the hospital wanted to run some more blood tests still. I was still having some worrying neuropathic side effects, and the Letrozole tablets I was on were causing horrendous hot sweats at all times of the day and night and extreme fatigue.

I continued working full time.

The surgery- a mastectomy or massectomy as I commonly spelt it, of the left breast and all lymph nodes removed –also known as an axillary clearance, was pencilled in for December 1st. I would then be out of action until the beginning of Term 3 in January 2018 and not be able to drive for 4-6 weeks.

It was all so inconvenient. Why now? Why Christmas? It was just my luck that out of 52 weeks in the year; surgery had to be at this magical time. I would miss everything- The quiz night, the Cabaret night, the Carol Service, the school fair, the staff night out and the Nativity. I would have no time for any last minute present shopping, let alone savour the Christmas atmosphere with the lights and the hustle and bustle.

I can never understand why people fly to Barbados or similar country. Christmas is about the frost and the cold and woolly scarves in my eyes- not sipping cocktails on the beach.

THE NATIVITY

Like Marmite, you either like or loathe 'The Nativity'. It depends if you are the proud mother of the child in a white t-shirt, white tights and sheep ears or the father of the child in his dressing gown with a tea-towel on his head carrying a sheep.

And what's not to like about recorders playing the tune of Little Donkey over and over again with the occasional clip-clop from the halved coconuts? But if you are a teacher, Christmas you know, already started in August with the planning and ordering of resources and then continued in September with the making of the Charity Christmas Card and then peaked in October with the learning of the Christmas songs for the Nativity. November and December were usually just a stressful blur. Teachers were on their last nerve and generally frazzled- I didn't miss that bit.

I wrote a comedy Nativity play that the school staff acted out in front of the children in 2002. We had bored angels not wanting to hold their arms out, and Narrators that read in staccato voices from A4 pieces of paper stuck on to the shiny card. We had Kings delivering Amazon parcels and an Inn Keeper that welcomed everyone into his abode for a party.

I've written a few similar scripts and monologues but have never really had anywhere to showcase them; except at the girls' Annual Dance Choreographic and Drama Show.

Each year I would write a comedy piece or monologue, and one or both of the girls would perform them. My favourite was a Nativity monologue that I wrote from the donkey's point of view. My daughter aged twelve had squeezed herself into an old 3-4 donkey one-piece costume which kept riding up at both the front and the back. Her delivery of the monologue won her the drama shield.

A DONKEY'S TALE by Emma Sheils

DONKEY: *Coming to stage centre and brushing himself down.* Oh, get me out of there!

Ahhh fresh air. Sheep, oxen, cows, more sheep, horses. What a smell! Bleating, braying, neighing, and whinnying, a baby crying. I can't stand it! *Hands over ears*

How can a donkey get any rest?

Noticing the audience. Oh hello. Hang on, give me a mo. Brushes himself down a bit more.

What a night, I say what a night. You'll never guess what's been going on here. Points to stable.

Well, it all started a week or so ago. I was hoicked out of my beautiful field and told I was going on a special journey. There was a lot of commotion, and finally, Mary was loaded on to my back. Now don't get me wrong, I love Mary to bits, but my goodness she was heavy. She was with child.

Joseph, her husband, walked alongside, holding onto my reins. As if I was going to run off. I could hardly walk, let alone run. It was hot and dusty, and the track was bumpy and stony.

And strewth Mary weighed a ton!

It turned out the Emperor had ordered a census. Everyone in the land had to return to their birthplace and sign a form. I've no idea why they couldn't have just signed it in Galilee Town Hall, Ha! Those Romans with their big ideas, what have they ever done for us?

So I had to take Mary to Bethlehem, the town of David, where her husband Joseph was born. But did Joseph think to book ahead? No, he didn't. The traffic was a nightmare. Donkeys lined the route both ways and when we arrived yesterday, everywhere was full. We tried everywhere — not a Premier Inn with a vacancy for miles.

We knocked on a lot of doors in the hope there was a room at any Inn but nothing. Everywhere was full. It was all getting a little desperate when a kind man said we could stay in his stable. I had slept in worse places, and the food situation for me was really good, but you could tell Joseph wasn't happy. There was hay everywhere, and the smell of animals was pretty bad. Mary put a brave face on things. She had started feeling a few twinges and needed to get off my back and rest. The hay wasn't too bad actually for her to rest in.

Everything was OK for the first few hours and Joseph had gotten used to the smell of animals by then. Mary then gave an almighty shriek and scared the living daylights out of me.

Joseph was scurrying around like a demented ferret.

The baby was coming.

Joseph didn't know what he was doing, but Mary was pleased he was there at this end stage. (Apparently, he wasn't around at the beginning!)

After a lot of pushing and shoving, a baby was born, a little boy.

I gave three brays and had a wee look at the bairn. I was a bit squeamish, and I hovered at the back. He was a handsome chap.

The baby boy was laid in a manger and wrapped in swaddling clothes, and for a while, it was all quiet; but not for long. The baby then howled solidly for an hour, and just as Mary had finally settled him, the most bizarre series of events happened. You could not make it up.

Three shepherds arrived at the door and greeted us like long lost friends. They barged in and made so much fuss of the wee nipper that Mary didn't have the heart to turn them away. They brought sheep with them, a lot of sheep. There were sheep and lambs everywhere... and the smell! Hand on the nose.

Just as Joseph had seen the shepherds off back to their fields, three bearded old men dressed in finery turned up. They said they had followed a star to find us. I reckon they had been at a fancy dress party and had one too many if you ask me! Joseph was polite and invited them in. They also were interested in seeing the baby and presented him with gifts they had brought- gold, myrrh and some frankincense. I saw Joseph looking at the bottles. I knew I'd be carrying them back home.

They stayed until the early hours of the morning, chatting and laughing. Talk about outstaying your welcome. Mary couldn't keep her eyes open and had retreated to another part of the stable. I hung around in case I was needed, and I reckon I may have got a 20-minute snooze. I feel like death warmed up now.

Oh, how my bones ache. Hold back. My eyes can hardly stay open. I just needed to get a bit of fresh air.

So I'll love you and leave you. I'm going back now to see if I can rest a little bit more...

8
ALMOST TIME

It was hard carrying on, as usual, knowing I was about to have major surgery. I attended pre-op appointments in November 2017 and a talk on how to empty the plastic drains that would be sewn into me. I was presented with a "Cumfie" or "Foobie"- a fake soft fabric boobie and a hand-sewn roll that was to go under my arm. Having all the lymph nodes removed would reduce my immune system. I also had to be prepared not to lift heavy objects ever again and to protect the arm from trauma. I got myself a silver health warning bracelet to wear at all times because of the risk of lymphoedema. I could never have blood pressure or bloods taken from the left arm either.

I finished the personalised snowmen cards for my class and handed them out. The children appreciated them, but I did smile to myself as one child handed their card to their mum who exclaimed: "Bloody Hell, it's only November!"

I went into the loft to get a small suitcase. I had no idea how long I would be in the hospital for. I was cautious about climbing the ladder.

LOFTY ADVENTURES

Dance classes and school was out for summer in 2014, and I was putting all the children's costumes up in the loft. We had recently moved house, and I had only been up there once before. I piled the clothes up at the bottom of the ladder and took the boxes up first.

On top of the pile was a giant apple tree costume. It had a big, green, foam head part complete with lots of soft red apples.

The box I was taking up wasn't heavy, but as a habit, I used to lean back on to the bathroom door frame when I got to the top of the ladder to get a better grip and to turn on the light. I leant back, but there was no bathroom door. The bathroom hadn't moved, but the loft in the new house was in a different place. There was no door frame.

I fell back from the top of the ladder into the arms of the apple tree. Thankfully I wasn't hurt; I had just banged my elbow. I lay there in the tree and thought perhaps it wasn't such a good idea to go up into the loft when no-one was home. An inch or two to the right and I would have fallen down the stairs.

BOXES OF MEMORIES

I packed my small suitcase for surgery and put my new book in it, hoping for some time to start it. It had all been so busy lately that some quiet time with no kids or work or dog sounded just perfect.

My mum had come down to stay and help with my daughter and dog while I was away. She presented me with a pair of fluffy bed socks with a cute rabbit on. My mum hadn't noticed that the cute rabbit was the Playboy Bunny! I was grateful regardless. Naivety ran in the family. My daughter had made an Easter card two years previously using a collage of playboy bunnies! I was packed, ready to go and my house had been tidied.

My cupboards had never looked so organised. I had large storage boxes full of school resources and memories from the past. My favourite box was the clothes: the leotard with the BAGA awards sewn on, my Man Utd satin football shorts from 1985, a long purple floral homemade dress with smocking for a childhood party, my black and white stripy school tie, my christening gown, my Danish 1986 Football top, my daughter's first shoes and my Brownie Guide tunic.

THE BROWNIE YEARS

I was a Brownie Guide; I loved the uniform with the brown bobble hat and pockets full of random items: a 2p for the phone, a clean hankie, a safety pin, and even a piece of string. A piece of string? I can honestly say that apart from stringing some conkers, I have never used any string in 50 years, yet have a great big unused ball in that overfull kitchen drawer that most people have. But points were deducted from your "Six" if you didn't carry your pocket objects and disaster if you didn't have any string.

Nail inspections, however, were the worst. I didn't bite my nails, but they didn't grow. Later I was to find out that I suffered from a severe Vitamin D deficiency, but at the time I had to endure the weekly lecture from Tawny Owl of not picking or biting nails and those little girls should have beautiful, pretty nails. Points were always deducted.

It was also a challenge to have the most triangular interest badges sewn down your arm. For the Writer's badge, I had written a story about a scary person. It was a mixture of truth and fiction about a real neighbour that I didn't know well. To my horror, she turned out to be the external examiner, and I had to sit cross-legged on the floor while she obliviously read my story about her to the brownie pack! I was convinced she had guessed the story was about her.

Two weeks later she was back on pack night and those Brownies-including me-taking the Hostess badge, had to serve her a cup of tea and a homemade cake or biscuit. I felt that made up for the story. I had gone to much effort to make my cakes.

I passed both badges

LONDON ZOO 1977

My Brownie pack went to the London Zoo in 1977. Salome the Gorilla had just been born a few months earlier, and we were all excited to see her. I remember knocking on the glass and then being forced to hold Brown Owl's hand for misbehaviour. Luckily my behaviour improved and for a mere 30p, we could ride camels- not a crash helmet in sight!

When I returned home, the trip talk was about the shop and the coach as always, but my younger brother had been taken to the hospital with a concussion. Visiting him, I was so jealous. He was on Rooster ward in bed 3 and had this giant teddy bear on his bed and a table that you could put your books on. It was quite unfair.

The following day I went with my mum to the allotment. I was bored- I didn't do gardening and went and climbed a tree.

I fell out of the tree, on to my head.

I got my wish and spent the night on Rooster ward, in bed no. Three but it wasn't the fun I had imagined. I felt nauseous all night, and that big teddy bear was made of that horrid itchy fur.

I think that was the day social services investigated our family!

9

ALL THINGS FOREIGN

My hobbies apart from swimming and supporting Man Utd were writing letters to pen pals. I was interested in other countries, and I was an avid stamp collector.

One of my first ever trips abroad was to Calais on the hovercraft with my dad and brother. I was about six and apparently when asked what I thought of France I replied, "Even the children speak French!" I was also horrified by the two stone step public toilets, but that's another story.

I remember in 1987 vividly all the girls crying when we went to a school in Italy because the boys were so much better looking in Italy than in Edinburgh! I agreed, but I didn't cry about it. I just noted Italy as a return destination for the future.

I also loved watching American soap operas. I loved Dallas, Dynasty, The Colby's and Knots Landing and when the English actor Michael Praed went from being the dashing Robin of Sherwood to playing the handsome Prince of Moldova on Dynasty, I couldn't miss an episode. I would tirelessly set the video recorder to record and then pray that there was enough tape left to record the whole programme. No Netflix or I-player or digital TV's in the 1980s.

I managed to see Michael Praed in Nov 2017 in 'War of the Worlds'. At stage door, while my friend was taking a photo of us, I said, "I had you on my maths book." There was an awkward pause. My friend was horrified.

"That's nice," Michael said and moved swiftly away.

What I meant was that my maths book was covered in a poster of him as the dashing Robin of Sherwood. It was a welcome change from the loud Paisley or floral swirly 1970s wallpaper that covered the other textbooks. (My Jesper pictures were too precious to use).

I wrote letters to pen-pals nearly every day. I collected scented, novelty erasers and a sheet of writing paper from different sets that I had ever had. I liked writing gossip, hopes, stories and events and around 1983-4 I started keeping a diary too. I liked sending stickers and reprints of photos to my pen-pals abroad, but they were expensive.

TECHNOLOGY

Cameras too in the 1980s were quite complicated devices. Even to take an indoor picture you needed a flash cube with four possible flashes. What teenager now would wait a couple of weeks to get your developed film back only to have four or five good pictures just out of 12, 24 or 36?

They will never experience that joy or getting an extra picture from your roll or that feeling of despair as the camera back opens before you've manually wound on your film, flooding your film with light!

I do look at smartphones nowadays and wish I had had one as a teenager. But then if I had, I would never have experienced that feeling of excitement when a letter arrived on the doormat and the anticipation when the large film envelope finally did come.

Polaroid photos were even more precious, and even though they briefly made a comeback in 2016, there was still the five-minute wait while the picture appeared. I remember the anxious yet awkward silence of all involved peering at a blank square, eagerly anticipating the colours to reveal themselves. Perish the expensive thought of pressing the button a lot of times by mistakes.

GERMAN SPAM

I do remember some early spamming though when I eagerly awaited my film's return after a school trip to Germany in 1987, only to find it full of pictures of bottoms and genitalia. I had left my camera on a table in a Beer Garden while I danced on the tables and a group of drunken strangers seized it.

LETTERS OF COMPLAINT

Although most of my letters were sent to friends, I have written a few letters on a more serious note.

One evening I was watching BBC TV, and a new program came on. It was called Mrs Brown's Boys, and the main character was a man dressed as a woman with an Irish accent. I didn't get it. There was a live audience laughing and shrieking. I didn't find anything funny. I found it foul and offensive. The F- word was used freely, and although it was after 9 pm, the content was disgusting.

I was so furious at what my licence fee was being spent on, that I wrote into the BBC. I got an email back. I was in the minority, and they had had so many positive comments, reports and feedback about the show that they would be continuing with more series. To this day I don't find it funny, mammy, and I only watch it when it's been left on the TV in the background, and I've been too lazy to change the channel. I still don't recall ever laughing.

COTTAGE CHEESE PACKAGING

While my husband was working evenings, I would busy myself with crafts of some sort, apart from book-marking, and in particular cross-stitch sewing. I took it somewhat seriously and have sewn one of the hardest patterns in the cross-stitch world. I've ruffled a few W.I. feathers by winning several trophies and rosettes for my work at the local craft festival.

Anyway one night I had the nibbles and tried to open a tub of cottage cheese. I sliced my thumb badly, and it meant I couldn't sew that week. I decided to write a tongue-in-cheek letter to the supermarket where I bought it, about how I'd been injured on the cottage cheese packaging and I may have psychological repercussions. It was worth it.

I didn't receive a lifetime supply of cottage cheese, but I did receive a £10 store voucher.

THE CINEMA

Another hobby was going to the cinema and watching films. The first film that I remember watching was Star Wars in 1978. Those were the days when you had a small trailer film before. Because my brothers collected the figures and the toy, I grew up knowing my Boba Fett from my Jawa.

The first film I watched without an adult was Grease. The cinema was full of excited teenagers I remember and when the music started people were clapping and cheering. When the camera first focused on Danny- John Travolta, the whole place erupted. Girls were screaming. At age 8-9 I didn't see the attraction, but I did like the movie and the music and practised Grease routines in the playground. I also had the poster on the wall.

The cinema was a safe meeting place when I was younger, and I grew up watching the Brat Pack movies.

In the winter of 2017, there were lots of good films out; lots went on to win Oscars. I had overheard some ladies talking about the movie 'Lion' and that it was weepy. I had entirely no idea what it was about and had read no reviews. I bought the ticket and was told screen 3.I bought my nibbles and was a little surprised to find the film had already started. It was dark, and I had to disturb a few people to get to my seat. The film featured two Indian boys on a train with subtitles. I looked around. There was a mixed audience, but I thought I was watching the wrong show. I honestly thought I was watching a Bollywood movie. I waited another ten minutes, and it was still set in India with subtitles with no sign of a lion. I hadn't a clue what was going on.

I made my excuses and disturbed the people in my row to get out. I left screen 3 and looked at my ticket. The man had said screen 3. My ticket, fortunately, said screen 5, and according to the timing, the show hadn't started yet either.

I took my seat and Lion started, set in India with subtitles for the first part!

Sometimes it's nice not to know any spoilers or what a film is about, but in this case, it was rather funny that I was blissfully ignorant.

The film was weepy. I was distraught, mainly as it was a true story. I exited the cinema with tears streaming down my face right into the centre of Leicester Square. Chinese New Year celebrations were in full swing. The Square was swarming with people, and there were giant Pokémon characters and good luck mascots wandering around in soggy fur. It was also pouring with rain.

It's an odd feeling wondering through crowds that are happy when you are incredibly distraught. You feel lonely and isolated. However, I made a couple of phone-calls, bought myself some chocolate and was soon alright. The magic of the cinema is that it can take you to places you've never been to and that film deserved all the awards it was to get.

Browsing through Netflix today there seems to be so many films with cancer as the main plot- The Fault in our Stars, Beaches and Steel Magnolias to name some of my favourites. Maybe they had always been there, but there seemed to be lots of cancer storylines on soap operas and TV series too, they just seemed to be more frequent, and everywhere I turned. Celebrities were baking cakes and even baring all to raise awareness.

I had been aware, aware of self-checking and aware that cancer affects 1in 3 of us. 1 in 8 women faced a breast cancer diagnosis in the UK, and all of us would have a relative diagnosed in our lifetimes. I didn't think it would be me.

10

LIFE'S A SONG

My escape from being bullied at secondary school was to join the music department. Like HSM (High School Musical), our school had its different groups. I loved singing, and I played violin, piano and trombone, and I soon joined the choir and orchestra. I adored music, but my taste was (and still is) very individual. My first cassette was ABBA Waterloo costing £6, and my first 7" was Roland Rat the picture disc of Love Me Tender/ Pink Bucket Song. I remember proudly buying it for 99p in the new Virgin Media Store. I think I had made a name for myself in that shop as looking at my record collection now I was soon to buy Renee and Renato's "Save Your Love", Michael Jackson's "One Day in your Life" and The Herreys' "Diggi Loo Diggi Ley".

I was a big Eurovision fan (and unashamedly still am) and had learnt the whole routine of the Swedish winners (The Herrey brothers) in their golden boots!

I had quite a cassette collection too. I used to listen to my cassettes on a huge stereo player with big earphones.

For Christmas 1982 I got a Walkman complete with smaller headphones and an auto reverse button, so I didn't have to turn the tape over. There were cries of "Emz gees us a shot" as everyone wanted to borrow someone's Walkman. No split dividers or earphone each in the 80s.

Kids today don't know the precise art of how to start recording the top 40 tunes without recording the DJs' voice and perish the thought of getting the tape caught in the machine, twisted or mangled. There was a scene in Billy Elliot the musical that involved Billy asking or a pencil to rewind his tape after it had unravelled. That scene was lost on anyone who never owned a cassette. It was traumatic when it happened, and you held your breath as you wound the tape in.

MICHAEL JACKSON

In 1984 Michael Jackson released his Thriller album. Everyone was looking forward to this extended video, and the video was to have zombies dancing in it. I wasn't a fan, but I was swept along with the excitement and his moonwalk and his white sequinned glove.

At night I would listen to the radio for a bit on my big clock radio that emitted a loud beep for an alarm and could almost tune into five or six good channels and a French one.

I must have snoozed off before the radio had turned off as I awoke to hear a man talking in my room. He was talking about things waking from the dead, darkness falling and things terrorising the neighbourhood. I was so scared. I was still half asleep, and I didn't know that this was part of the Thriller song and the manic laugh at the end almost finished me off.

I was lucky enough to watch Michael Jackson live at Wembley in 1996. It was an incredible night, and he wasn't scary at all. We all had a bit of a cry especially at Heal the World and The Earth Song, and there was not a lighter in sight. I wasn't even a fan, but after watching him put on that show, I bought the CD and DVD but not the t-shirt.

I was a sensitive soul and not good with blood, gore or fish. I could never put bait on a fishing line or take the hook out of a fish's mouth. I was very squeamish.

BABYSITTING A BURGLAR

I call this story the Scooby Doo story. In Scooby Doo, they hear a noise and rather than run, they go and investigate. This is what happened, although in hindsight there were a few things that I should have done differently.

It was 1986, and I was babysitting a four-year-old girl. I wasn't driving yet, and I was dropped off and picked up by my parents. I'd babysat for the family before and wasn't scared of noises when it got dark. I had put the little girl to bed. A couple of hours later I heard noises upstairs. I shouted up the stairs that she ought to get back into bed, and it went quiet. I then decided to double check she was OK and I went upstairs. The noise of someone searching through drawers was coming from the master bedroom, and I could see the little girl asleep. Eek, we had a burglar!

I went quickly downstairs and phoned 999, but I had to hang up promptly. I had no idea of the street name, let alone the house number. I had been dropped off, and I didn't pay attention to those sorts of things.

I ran out of the house leaving the door wide open and knocked on the door of the neighbours to find out the address and to use the phone. She seemed more interested in where the little girl was than the fact there was a burglar. I didn't understand why but then I hadn't any maternal feelings. I wasn't a mother.

The police soon arrived, and it had appeared that the burglar had climbed up at the back of the house and got in through an open window.

Some jewellery was taken, and that's all. I had disturbed them. It's an odd feeling to think back. I wasn't scared, but I should have known where I was (good old Google maps now), and I should not have left the little girl- her safety was far more important.

AWAKE ALL NIGHT

Travelling all night on a train without a booked cabin was both uncomfortable and exciting. While inter-railing in 1991, my two girl-friends and I took many overnight journeys to save on youth hostel fees. The knock-on effect was that we were exhausted during the day.

We would take it in turns to:

1. Look for food
2. Sleep
3. Guard the rucksacks.

The summer days were hot, and after a long journey from Bologna to Munich, we found a beautiful park to have a snooze in. When we awoke a bit later on that morning, we didn't know where to look. We were sitting in the middle of a very popular nudist park!

We funded our trip for a month by busking. The three of us sang barbershop style acapella songs and didn't make too bad money wise. We sang for our supper and the youth hostel fee.

We had a couple of dodgy moments when our cap full of money was stolen by someone watching, and we didn't get the chance to run after them and then on the Ponte Vecchio, Florence, our tuning pipe was stolen. We needed the metal tuning pipe to get our starting note. There were a team of small non- Italian girls who distracted us with newspapers and put their hands into one of my friend's waist bag and stole it along with some money. They saw us coming with the word MUG on our foreheads.

I had joined a barbershop shop style choir at University and liked how the close harmony worked. I belonged to a four-piece and a piano group called "Rice in the Device" that sang at balls and small functions. I was also a member of the chapel choir and requiem choir. I love singing and have been lucky enough to sing in a supporting choir at the Albert Hall for the likes of Ruthie Henshall, John Barrowman and Lorna Luft and also sing with Harry Secombe on the religious programme 'Highway'. That's the extent of my singing. Now the only singing I do is in the shower or along with the school assembly songs with the cheesy backing tracks.

PARTY YEARS

Friends turning 18 and the last year of school meant lots of parties. 1980s party music was great - lots of Stock, Aitken and Waterman, Duran Duran, Wham! And Madonna.

Edinburgh city centre like any city centre is only as dangerous as the people who roam it. Mainly it was people drinking too much that made tempers fray. After one 18th party, a fight broke out outside a chip shop. I saw one of my good friends on the floor getting his head kicked in by older men. My instinct was to shout, "He's only 12!" and to lie on top of his head. I got kicked, but they soon ran off and fortunately, my friend who had been in the wrong place at the wrong time, was OK. It's strange what you do and say when the going gets tough.

SAY YOU, SAY ME

Parties also took a similar format of lots of music, long queues for the loo and then two slow dances at the end when everyone either grabbed their partner or grabbed their coats. One party I was dancing to Lionel Richie's 'Say You Say Me'. I hadn't heard the song before, and we were doing the awkward slow dance in a circle thingy. Towards the end of the song, the melody turns upbeat. I thought that was the end of the song, so I broke away and started to do this sort of boogie dance move. Everyone else was still slow dancing, and my partner was staring at me. It wasn't until the song reverted to the familiar slow "Say you, Say me" bit, that I realised it was still the same song playing. I had just done a funky dance break in front of all my friends and the potential new boyfriend. I wanted the floor to open up and swallow me whole. My dance partner was quite intrigued by my outburst, and we became boyfriend and girlfriend for a whole six months.

PLAYLIST

A lovely teacher friend of mine had made me a compilation CD of Italian songs to take into the hospital in December 2017. I had created a small playlist of songs that would cheer me up. In my eyes, I was going on a mini weekend break to an all-inclusive retreat. I was going to be able to relax, read and listen to some music.

I packed my suitcase and filled it with some midnight feast treats, some sweet juice and mints. I bought some new slippers, and although I was going to be having major surgery, I was surprisingly, looking forward to December 1st.

I asked for some help on Facebook with a possible "Mastectomy Playlist".

These were some of my suggestions:

Bye Bye Boobie- Bay City Rollers

Blame it on the Boobie- Michael Jackson

Any song by Michael Buble

Breast of ABBA or their Greatest Hits (Greatest tits?)

Friends then suggested me:

Tina Turner- Simply the Breast

The Breast Things in Life are Free- Janet Jackson

Boobs Up Side Your Head- DJ Casper and the Gap Band

Tit Willow- Gilbert & Sullivan

Thanks For The Mammaries- Fall Out Boy

Wooden Tit be Nice- Beach Boys

Hit Me Booby One More Time- Britney Spears

I had a few other sillier ones, although I did find myself singing "Now you've got the breast off me, come on and take the rest of me, oh baby," rather a lot!

11

"BYE BYE BOOBIE"

DECEMBER 2017

I know my work is a professional job. I am meant to be a role model and facilitator of learning. I have even signed passport applications and attended a meeting with families and social workers. I cannot afford to have any lapses in professional judgement, at any time, but I wanted a memory of what I looked before-before my mastectomy surgery.

There was a fair bit of giggling coming from my room as I took some pictures of my breasts for posterity. Of course, I was alone, but it was funny, I felt ridiculous. Very carefully I saved the pictures and then sent them to a safe place. I then deleted all record off my phone and nonchalantly came out of my room whistling a merry tune. It would be terrible if those pictures got into the wrong hands and I was notorious at sending the wrong text or picture to the wrong person.

DENTAL EXCUSE

I once texted my dentist to say I couldn't come to her 30th meal as I had a terrible toothache. It was very short notice, and I didn't want to turn up. The thing was, my friend's name began with D, and I had texted the dentist by mistake. I didn't want to go to the meal as I didn't know that many people and it had been foggy that night, and I didn't want to drive. My dentist shortly texted me back saying they would fit me in for an emergency appointment the following morning. Sheepishly I had to text back and explain I was fine with no toothache and had texted her by mistake!

SURGERY DAY

I was looking forward to getting started on my cancer treatment. I had immersed myself in my teaching and had told very few people. The sooner I had the surgery, the sooner I could get back to some normality. I arrived early and suitably hungry as had to fast from the night before.

At the hospital, I changed into a glamorous back opening hospital gown and was mildly amused at how many times different nurses checked and cross-referenced the name on my wrist and ankle bands. There is most definitely a gap in the fashion market for a design of hospital gown that doesn't make you look like a frumpy old woman or a 1930s Co-op worker. The designs make coach seat patterns look trendy.

The anaesthetist spoke to me to go over a few things. On my mind and his was the fact that I had had a failed intubation in the past, so a lot of what he was saying was going in one ear and out of the other. I did note that he had nice teeth and smile though. I was to be first to be cut up, and so there was a lot of people scurrying around and looking in on me. The surgeon in green came in and drew on me in the fluorescent light with a black felt-tipped pen. It was all getting a bit real and a bit surreal. I was sober and awake and standing there topless being drawn on with a pen.

A nurse in white asked me for a sample to do a routine pregnancy test. My word wasn't enough. It was hospital policy; I had to do it. I joked that if I were pregnant, then I wouldn't be breastfeeding. There was an awkward pause. I had heard that story recently and thought it rather funny, perhaps not the first thing in the morning.

I hadn't eaten or drunk anything for over twelve hours, and I was going to struggle to do the test. I ran the taps in the toilet, and I tried to go. I thought of waterfalls and rivers. Nothing. A nurse in blue hurried in and turned the tap off. She asked if I had 'done' and that they were waiting to take me to the theatre. I could hear two blue nurses impatiently waiting for me outside. That did the trick, and I conjured up a sample.

I walked down to the theatre.

I felt like a criminal being escorted down to the cells or up to the gallows, flanked by a couple of stern-looking nurses in blue. For some reason I thought I would be wheeled in a bed- obviously, I've watched too many hospital programmes. I was finding it hard to walk in my slippers as I was sporting a very slippery pair of surgical stockings. At least if I did twist my ankle, I was in the right place.

Members of the public and other workers passed me by, going about their business, oblivious that I was being frogmarched down to the abattoir.

Finally, I got to go on the trolley, and like a ghost train, I was wheeled through one set of double doors and on through another set. We were going to pause on this ride here for the anaesthetic, and as the double doors opened in front of me, I could see a flurry of activity. The last thing I saw was the clock.

When I came around, I was attached to oxygen and had two drains. I stayed calm, and I propped myself up on a mountain of pillows. I was in a side room, and I felt remarkably chipper. A nurse in mid blue came and took my blood pressure, and temperature and a nurse in darker blue told me things had gone well.

My small suitcase was next to me, but I couldn't reach it, and even if I did, I wouldn't be able to lift it. It was a bit like 'Mission Impossible ', and I inched closer to my case and strained for the zip. I had supplies inside- chocolate and sweets and other edible goodies. The exertion wore me out, and I left the case half opened where it lay.

I was given a bowl of soup. It was a small bowl of soup and very lovely, but that was it. I thought perhaps after my surgery I wasn't supposed to eat or drink much. I had told my mum and daughter not to visit on the first day as I thought I wouldn't be compos mentis, but I was fine, and they came up in the evening. While they were visiting, the dinner lady came into my room to collect my dinner things. She was surprised to see only a soup bowl and realised I had been forgotten.

Had I been forgotten? Well, that was a good start, but I was given a plate of chilli con carne and sticky toffee pudding, and I sat munching and chatting to my mum, friend and daughter.

A nurse in blue came in to give me an injection in my stomach to prevent blood clots as she went in with the syringe she stabbed my finger by mistake. It was quite comical and rather than an apology I was given a bit of tissue to mop it myself, and she went in for the second stab again. I was too stunned to say anything!

I was dosed up to the eyeballs on painkillers. Mum went home to attempt to put the Christmas decorations up.

It was too noisy too read my book and too light with no blinds, bright lights outside, in the corridor and on in my room every time someone came in to empty my drains or take my blood temperature.

A nurse in sea-green hurried in and hurried out, a nurse in blue gave me a sidelight, and a buzzer (no real rush then) and the cleaning lady exclaimed that someone had used the loo and not flushed. Well, it wasn't me- I couldn't move.

I was secretly smiling. This was the perfect material for my book.

The night was noisy. There was a nurse's station outside my room so I heard all the gossip and who was getting who what for Christmas. It was almost enough to send me to sleep.

A night nurse in royal blue came in to do my checks and kicked my suitcase. I apologised that it was there but explained I couldn't get to it. She wasn't impressed and ceremoniously picked it up and put it way out of arm's reach. My midnight feast would have to wait.

Throughout the night my blood pressure was checked. A nurse in blue cane in around 2 am, and I strained my neck to look at the readings. I imagined the light flat-lining. The nurse turned the machine away from me. I asked if the readings were ok and she said "shhh". I felt like a naughty schoolgirl.

A few short hours later a nurse in mid –blue retook my pressure. The nurse brought her face right up close to me and said: "Do you feel dizzy?"

"Well it is the middle of the night" I replied. It felt like it.

"No, it's a quarter to six," came the reply. She redid my pressure shortly after and it was fine.

A lady in turquoise put my breakfast tray over me, and I listened out for the familiar rumble of the trolley bringing breakfast. The previous night I had heard the trolley carrying hot drinks and had thought they were bringing my baby to me. It was a sort of a "tired, hallucination déjà- vu, kind of feeling". I wasn't sure if I was disappointed that I was only brought a cup of tea. I know I could not have looked after a newborn at either that moment or later.

There was more chance of catching MRSA in the hospital than at home, so I was taken home after just one night. I had to measure and empty my drains and keep a beady eye on my arm. My arm was now not protected against trauma, and forever more I can't have my blood pressure taken or bloods taken from the left side.

DRAGGED THROUGH A HEDGE BACKWARDS

My hair hadn't seen a hairbrush- it was typical bed head. However, the phrase "dragged through a hedge backwards" was particularly apt. I have been dragged through a hedge backwards, twice. The first time was when I was about nine years old, and I had a stye in my eye. The ointment hurt so much that I would rather hide than have the ointment. I had run out of good places, but the hedge in the garden was a great time-killer. I could hear mum calling and getting crosser. She must have had x-ray eyes because I soon found myself unceremoniously pulled back from the hedge, being scolded at the same time and dragged to the "light" in the kitchen window to have the ointment put in. It's funny what memories stay with you.

The second time was during a big game of hide and seek in a friend's back garden. As an adult, there weren't too many places to hide, but I had managed to step into a hedge. It was great, concealed all of me and despite the few creepy crawlies, I was quite comfortable. I could also peer out and see what was going on. I was the last to be found, and when the novelty of finding me had worn off, I thought I would come out; except I couldn't. My hair mainly, but my clothes too were trapped amongst the twigs and leaves. After a fair bit of shoving and lots of laughter from the lawn, I eventually reversed out taking out a lot of hedge with me. Fortunately, it was pre-mobile phone days.

A UNIBOOBER

It was odd looking in the mirror at myself. Part of me that had always been with me was gone. People said I would mourn its loss, I did.

I was now officially a "Uniboober"! My clothes half fitted. I did wish that they had taken the other breast off as it was all so uneven. It did look weird.

I didn't want to see under the dressings, but I knew there was no longer a place to rest my cup of tea! There had been several tumours in one place, and they were now on the way for testing. I wondered whether I could keep any bits as a souvenir. In some religions, I read that the placenta was retained after birth and sent to friends and relatives to eat or keep. I imagined the look on my friends' faces if a little bit of breast tissue arrived in a box- possibly dried out first, with a wee gift tag reading;

– 'To my Bosom Buddy' or
"Don't Eat It" (Don't eat tit?!) or just
'With Love from Em xx.'

My brother had a tube containing his ingrown toenail at home; I had a glass vase ready!

Surely I could also make some lava lamp or snow globe with a bit of glitter in from some breast tissue and water?

Alas, I was not able to keep anything for a craft project or even as a souvenir.

THE PLASTIC GONDOLAS

I am a bit of hoarder. I don't like throwing anything out if I can use it again or if it holds memories. I have scrapbooks of cuttings and events, and I have plastic memory boxes filled with souvenirs and objects from over the years, the kind of things you don't want to have on display or to dust- a clog from Amsterdam, a ceramic tankard from Munich or a plastic gondola from Venice.

Having fallen in love with all things Italian since school choir trips, I spent a lot of my holiday time from University in Italy.

I'd spent the day in Venice, and the same evening I was watching a film with a friend. The family told me I was staying with which bus to catch home and I knew it was a few minutes' walk from the end of the line. I'd had a great day as a tourist, and I'd managed to buy ten plastic silver gondolas as tacky souvenirs for some of my university friends. Although not particularly big, they were awkward and not easy to put by your feet in the cinema.

I watched the film, and as I was walking to the bus stop, I saw the bus coming. I had to catch the last bus and ran like a mad woman to catch the bus, gondolas bashing into my side as I ran. Relaxing on the bus, I think I may have fallen asleep. It didn't matter I thought as my friend lived at the end of the line.

I jumped off the bus expecting to see familiar landmarks except I was in the middle of nowhere. I'd caught the bus 45 minutes in the wrong direction. My Italian wasn't particularly great; however, I managed to find out that there were no buses back until the morning. The bus driver called me a taxi, and I spent an awkward journey home with my bag of gondolas. The fare was higher than I had with me. I knew I had money in my suitcase squirrelled away but trying to tell the taxi cabbie that I had money in the flat and I would be back in a few minutes was getting me nowhere and getting him very irritated. This was 1990 and pre-mobile phones.

Eventually, I gave him my passport as security and said: "per favore, aspettami" (wait for me please). I pressed every buzzer of the flats to open the door, wedged my sandal in the door so it wouldn't shut and took the lift upstairs. I ignored the angry wails of the Italian mum and rushed to my suitcase. I think she had thought I'd met someone and was leaving again.

There was no way she was going to let me out of the flat. I had to wake my friend and get her to convince her mum to let me out and that I would explain. I eventually returned to the taxi to find the fare had increased substantially. From that day I was determined to learn Italian properly.

My friends liked the plastic silver gondolas.

I was glad the gondolas were not made of anything more valuable than plastic; they may have been stolen that night. Perhaps I then could have paid the taxi fare with them instead? Fortunately, I had chosen these gifts myself, and they were not a present given to me. I remembered Bridget Jones's luck when she brought a 'present' back from someone else. I didn't fancy a visit to the prison. Maybe it was a good thing I had chosen them myself and had escorted the precious cargo carefully home and into safe hands!

I never got to keep any part of the tumour as a souvenir; it was sent off for some serious testing.

RECOVERING WELL

I did as the doctor ordered for the next few weeks. I was already prepared for Christmas, so I added some stories to this book and allowed my mum to run around after me. I felt like 'Lady Muck' at times, and all I had to do was keep healthy, recover and look after my stitches and drains. I couldn't believe how much the removal of lymph nodes would affect my arm though- it was both hot and cold, and it was both numb and sensitive. I wasn't prepared for my arm to have so little movement, although as a right-hander I was glad it wasn't the other arm affected. I could barely lift my left arm above my head even though I was doing my set exercises. I had to prevent something called axillary web syndrome or cording too. That's when you can feel ropes or cords under the skin of the inner arm, and it feels tight, particularly when raising the arm.

I was touched how many messages and cards, flowers and presents I was sent, including a hand-made quilt sent from abroad. I tried to keep people informed, and it seemed social media although not very personal, was the easiest and quickest way to let people know how I was getting on. Sometimes it was news for everyone or a joke, and sometimes I sent private messages, not wanting everyone to know absolutely everything. After all, not all your friends on Facebook are your closest friends.

I was most definitely "Tackling the tumour with humour".

I was on top of the pain, but it was just more comfortable some days to relax and wear pyjamas as they were loose fitting. I don't think my postman has ever seen me fully dressed!

I sprayed dry shampoo into my hair as I wasn't allowed to shower properly just yet, just flannel wash. I was cultivating a superb bed head. My mum looked at my hair and asked" Do you want help with that? 'That'!

A lot of giggling later and we had washed my hair in the kitchen sink. It had been a while since I had had it cut or styled, let alone cleaned and washed by my mum.

THE C –CARD

Everywhere I went or turned on; there were references to Cancer. There was more awareness in the community and TV, and radio adverts offered support and helplines to the phone. I didn't feel the need to ask for assistance just yet. I thought I was coping. It hadn't sunk in yet, possibly because I hadn't really cried.

Friends had started saying I was an inspiration and such a strong person and I was humbled. I must have got the strength from somewhere. There was nothing I could do to change anything. The cleaner in the hospital had said: "why worry about the things you can't worry about?" She was right, and I thought even if I sat in my room sobbing my heart out and feeling miserable and sorry for myself, it wouldn't change anything. I still hadn't taken up running!

I was taking each day as it came. I did contact Eros Ramazzotti and Andy Jameson on Twitter, but I didn't hear anything back. It was worth a try, but I was a nobody to them, and I'm sure they received hundreds of requests a day for pictures or autographs or the like.

My mum was then given the news that she too had cancer.

Cancerous cells had been found in her uterus; she had endometrine cancer. She was to have MRI, and CT scans too in the New Year and a hysterectomy, but the good news- if there is good news re cancer- she could come and celebrate Christmas with us and go on a scheduled family holiday in January. A few days delay wouldn't make any difference to her treatment.

Naturally, I was upset, but I was more worried and cross even that this C. had crept up on and got another person in my family and I felt sorry for my dad now trying to be the patriarchal pillar of support, with his daughter and now wife fighting cancer. It made me more and more determined to get the awareness out there even more.

• To get women (and men) to check their breasts for any changes.

I posted cartoons and pictures on Instagram and Facebook-including dogs and cats complaining that they had six breasts to check and funny references to cancer to spread awareness, never to jest about the illness. I wouldn't wish it on anyone.

I seemed to grow in confidence in talking about a subject matter that I may have been both shy and awkward talking about previously. I could even say 'boob' and 'breast' without smiling, and I perhaps had said the word nipple more times in two months than in 48 years!

"With cancer, you need to have a sense of tumour"!

I had taken the dressings off too and looked at my scar. The stitches weren't exactly neat, and it was more a jagged line going straight across my chest and up under my armpit. I didn't feel a loss either. It was odd to look at, but it wasn't hideously ugly, and if anything it was a reminder that the cancer had been taken away.

I had a lot of extra skin in odd places like a lunar landscape, to be used for a possible reconstruction perhaps or just because I was overweight! The nurse said later it was normal and the skin left was what used to hold the whole weight of the breast. The flaps at the side of my chest were commonly referred to as "dog ears"!

I wasn't embarrassed either about my scars. I thought it was quite funny how I now had a half suntanned bit and a half that had never seen the light of day.

I would have no problem talking to other women either who were about to have surgery. I chatted openly on online forums and Facebook groups and was able to offer reassurance to other women who were just a few weeks behind me in the stage of things. I was also able to ask questions to ladies about what was likely to come next in both the healing period and in my treatment.

For the first time in a while, I didn't mind people talking about or discussing me.

I also didn't mind how I looked, and sometimes I went out with the knitted boob in and sometimes without. It wasn't important to me.

15 MINUTES OF FAME

How you look shouldn't matter.

That's what I said to my two teenage daughters before a quick shopping trip in 2013.

I was choked up with cold, complete with a red nose. All three of us were feeling rather sorry for ourselves, and we needed cold remedies ASAP and comfort food. As soon as the girls got home from school, they put their pyjamas on, and I suggested a quick trip to the supermarket. We wrapped up with coats and thick jumpers and scarves and even hats. "It doesn't matter what you look like", I said to my eldest, "you won't see any of your friends at this time". As we entered the store, there were lights, cameras and people everywhere. As a flagship store selling Comic Relief merchandise, the supermarket was being used as a setting for filming some footage for the Red Nose Day evening later that month.

We didn't hang around but soon filled our trolley with lots of foods containing vitamin C and some comfort food. It was in the fruit aisle that a producer descended on us and said we looked like an ideal-typical family and asked could Alexander Armstrong (of Pointless fame) film a small scene with us as we browsed the watermelons.

We were talked into it as I had said we all had colds and had to load some things in our trolley- nothing too taxing. I removed my fingerless gloves, held a watermelon aloft and there was polite applause. We didn't have to say anything, just be interrupted by Alexander who would come over and say "Thank you". The thank you was to families like us who shopped in that store and bought the Red Nose merchandise. We filmed a short scene in just one take, and the lighting was fine.

On the night of Red Nose Day, I sat praying our clip wouldn't be used. We had all pulled on the nearest hats gloves and scarves. Surely someone high up would realise that our "real red noses" would defeat the object of buying a charity one.

My prayers were answered. Our scene wasn't used. It was a lucky escape.

But it wasn't my first lucky escape from being humiliated on TV. There was another time nearly thirty years previously.

ORVILLE THE DUCK 1983

The producers of the BBC programme Take Two filmed a few of us at school talking about current television programmes and personalities. During my interview, I happened to mention that I liked Orville the Duck – Keith Harris, the ventriloquist's sidekick. After all, he was a cute big green bird in a nappy.

I was filmed singing the duet "I Wish I Could Fly" with a friend. But a week before the programme was due to air; I received a letter from the BBC saying they were ever so sorry but due to time constraints could not broadcast the song. Although I was shown numerous times talking intently about 1980s TV programmes, with hindsight, I am so, so pleased the song was not aired.

12

THE HONEYMOON PERIOD

"AMOR VINCIT OMNIA"

In 1994 I married N.

No relatives were able to get visas, and we had a simple registry office wedding.

What we hadn't noticed when taking all our wedding photos in front of a brightly coloured mural, was the now infamous hidden phallus! It could not be unseen.

We didn't have a professional photographer, just a friend and we asked our thirty guests to send us any nice photos they had taken.

On active service in Bosnia, my brother missed the wedding, but he sent flowers coincidently that matched my bouquet. My Reception teacher and close family and friends were there only, around thirty people. We had a toast to absent friends and family, and I remembered Cheryl.

I had made menus and printed "amor vincit omnia" on the back, Love conquers all. I was determined from the first weeks of meeting N. that our relationship would survive even though the odds were stacked massively against us. We had come this far and now had our whole married life ahead of us, in England.

I wore a dark green velvet dress from Laura Ashley. I hadn't heard the superstition about being unlucky to marry in green. I had a professional do my hair and make-up, and I had no flower girls, page boys or bridesmaids. I knew all of the extra things- ribbons on the car and favours etc. we would do, but a lot of the customs associated with an English wedding are western and not Moroccan. We both wanted a simple wedding with minimal fuss.

My mum had ceremoniously frogmarched N. out of the restaurant the previous night quite late, saying to the owner that she was taking him as he was getting married in the morning and even though the Reception was taking place where he worked, N. shouldn't be preparing the food for his wedding!

The wedding went without any "You've Been Framed" moments. N. wasn't confident in English enough to do a speech, so my brother who was the best man and my dad told a few tales about me, and soon it was time for us to say our goodbyes. I wanted the bouquet, so I didn't throw it!

We spent the weekend in a hotel in London, but for some reason or other, the hotel had lost our booking. We were put in an annexe that you had to walk outside to get to, in a room with no window and no bath. I remember stealing the rose from the table at breakfast and dropping petals on the floor of our cell like in the film "Coming to America", except I was no royalty, to try and make it more romantic!

The weather was cold and wet, and there were flakes of snow in the air. It was Chinese New Year, and all the other rooms were fully booked. We said we had just got married, but there was nothing the hotel could do at that moment in time. Looking back, it wasn't a great start, but we had each other.

We started saving for a proper honeymoon.

ECZEMA

Unfortunately, my eczema became terrible at the end of the 1990s. I was under St Thomas' hospital and on steroid tablets and steroid creams. My weight increased, and I felt a bit sorry for myself having to sleep in wet wraps- cream impregnated bandages. After bathing I had to put on cream and the bandages, then dry wraps and then pyjamas. I looked like the Michelin Man. Not the best look really to feel feminine and sexy!

It's a hard illness to cope with. You don't want eczema on your face or visible to others, yet when it can't be seen you feel you are battling an illness without anyone knowing and in a way you want people to know, to understand, to sympathise. You constantly itch or feel your skin crawling. There is no, and the urge to scratch is just overwhelming. Occasionally I'd rub my hands on the steering wheel or carpet until they bled. Then there came a brief period of relief before the pain set in.

I joined a support group and went to a conference in London, but when I was there, I saw people entirely covered head to foot in eczema. I felt a fraud, and it made me feel worse. I was complaining about my 40% body coverage, and they had almost 100%. I bathed in slime and coated myself in slime yet; I was still continually getting the sores infected. They were dark times, and I didn't see an end to my suffering. No one truly understood how I felt. The pain was 24 hours a day, and although eczema is a physical illness, the mental and psychological stress on me was immense.

CHECK YOUR YOGHURT

Constant infection of my skin meant constant antibiotics and constant antibiotics indicated a side effect of infections "down below". I had heard an old wives' tale that plain yoghurt was good for soothing the itching and burning, but it made things ten times worse. A note to all women reading- Do not apply vanilla yoghurt, it has to be natural yoghurt!

DISTRACTIONS

To try and minimise the risk of infection to my hands, I went to school with polythene surgical gloves on my hands and sometimes white cotton gloves. At a private school I worked in from 1997, the girls wore white gloves to go home in the summer, so I matched.

I began staying at home rather than going out, and the doctor recommended sewing or drawing to avoid scratching and act as a distraction. I tried both until there was no wall space left to hang or display my creations. I enjoyed art rather than be any good at it, and I was creative, so I managed to enjoy what I did.

The sewing came naturally and sometimes I would prefer to sew than answer the door, the telephone, or even eat. As it got dark, I'd move towards the window or sit under a bright light and then invested in a blue daylight simulation bulb. It was a very sedentary lifestyle, but I was happy as my husband was away in the evenings at the restaurant, it was something for me to do. I developed a bit of a phobia to crawling insects like ants. I felt like they were continually crawling all over me- especially at night. For that reason, I rarely go camping and have great admiration for any celebrity that appears on "I'm a Celebrity Get Me Out Of Here". I joined a sewing group with some older ladies and met at each others' houses each month and just sewed and chatted. I was their surrogate daughter.

I began watching a lot of TV like an old lady with a cotton duvet or sheet on my lap as I needed the feeling of cotton. I wasn't exercising just sitting sewing and eating, so my weight started to increase. I got addicted to lots of soap operas including a weird American one called Sunset Beach. When it disappeared from a terrestrial TV channel, I even went and bought the digital box too so I could continue watching it. When it did finally finish, there was a helpline to phone for those who would miss it. I called the helpline; there was a recorded message from the Queen (a joke) urging the caller to be healthy and British and keep their chin up. What would I know do on a Sunday afternoon instead of watching a three-hour omnibus edition of the show?!

PESTS

It was a good thing I only suffered from mild eczema in July 1979 during the greenfly plague, as I would have hated the feeling of hundreds of flies all over me even more.

We shared our caravan/beach holiday with a plague of greenfly. The whole of the south shared their airspace with this phenomenon. They were everywhere, and I remember we weren't even safe in the car as they crawled through tiny holes. We were re-enacting the film 'The Swarm'! The greenfly were particularly attracted to the colour yellow, and I squabbled with my brothers over who carried the yellow rubber dinghy off the beach at the end of the day. It was ladybirds a few years later too I remember.

It was only when I moved jobs that my eczema got better, and it turned out that I was reacting badly to the formaldehyde that was being produced in a local factory and the fumes that were in the air. I should have realised there were chemicals in the air, as on the first Wednesday of the month at school we had a chemical drill. An alarm would go, and we would assemble in the hall, closing all doors and windows. Why on earth did I question this?

Wrapping myself in bandages was my first artificial experience of being a mummy; my first real experience came in 1999.

13

A PREGNANT PAUSE

As a teacher, I was frustrated that my pregnancy wasn't exactly going by the book and I wasn't in control. I had worried and fussed almost the entire time and was thoroughly exhausted. I had an emergency caesarean and my daughter, and I spent a couple of weeks in the hospital. It all went wrong at the last stage, and I didn't see the baby for 24 hours.

I found out what had happened from two nurses gossiping outside my door. Imagine the two Les Dawson ladies in his famous sketches:

"Ooh, you'll never guess what happened with that one in there. They opened her up, and the smell was awful. Everyone jumped back, and there was pus everywhere. We nearly lost both of them."

The official version told me was, "there were some complications".

I had had a failed intubation, and my throat had swelled up. I also had septicaemia. My waters had burst a while before, and things were going septic nicely.

Not much about the birth was funny apart from perhaps throwing up on the shoes of the very moody consultant, who when I said the pain 'wasn't quite right' he very arrogantly said how would I know, I hadn't had a baby before. Karma!

There was more to this consultant and apparently after losing a patient the week after me, he skipped the country.

SPARKLY DOWN BELOW

But a couple of days before being admitted I went for a cervical sweep. If anyone offers you this to induce your baby, trust me, say no. I mean it, take my advice, and say no.

However during my sweep when the doctor said: "It's not a good idea to use any of those products downstairs." "OK," I replied, not knowing what he meant. I thought he was being funny. It was only later, on finding I had sparkly underwear, that I realised then-horrifying then, what he had meant. I had flannel washed by mistake with a flannel I had used to mop up a broken snow globe -complete with glitter.

WHAT'S IN A NAME?

Choosing baby names occupied a lot of pregnancy time. What would sound good with an Arabic surname? I had spent six months debating whether to change my name or not. Generally, the kids cope well. It's adults that can't pronounce it. Occasionally I use Smith over the phone to order a takeaway or in surveys, but one evening when ordering a Chinese and saying Smith for ease, I got the reply:

"Smith? How do you spell that please?"

I'm used to people reading my name and then just calling out "Emma", but one day I had been stopped by one of those street survey takers. Normally I look at my watch, avoid eye contact and pretend I have somewhere to go every time I see one. On this occasion, I felt sorry for the elderly gentleman, and it was beginning to rain, so I stopped to answer his survey. He asked me my name, and I said, "Emma, my second name is too hard."

I tried not to giggle when I saw him write on the clipboard: "Emma Too hard".

I had another run-in with a lady taking another survey. I didn't mind taking the survey if it helped them, but I didn't want to give my personal information as then you would get constant phone calls.

When she asked me where I lived, I just said the name of another random road, not my own. The lady looked at me and said, "Really? so do I, which number?" I then had to guess a number hoping that;

1. The numbering did indeed go up that far
2. That it was nowhere near her.

I tried number 7. There was a pause.

"Oh the other end," she said, and I unclenched my fingers. That was close.

My husband found traditional English names funny to hear like Richard or Charlotte, a little bit how I felt about Abdul or Khalid-they were too Arabic sounding to me. We had to rule out names we both couldn't pronounce or that translated poorly into Italian or Arabic. I liked Robert or Andrew, but the shortened Bob or Andy didn't sound quite right to N. Also as a teacher there were a few names I had called out a little too often in the classroom and across the playground so couldn't possibly use!

After a lumbar puncture and some other tests, my daughter was declared healthy.

I was told I was scarred badly and had endometriosis and that it was unlikely I would fall pregnant again. In 2003 I proved that theory wrong and desperately hoped things wouldn't go wrong again. It did. I had my second daughter seven weeks early weighing 6lb 2oz. I had spent the whole pregnancy worrying and getting fed up with the "no two pregnancies are the same" type comments. In hindsight I'm glad I didn't carry her until full term, she would have been huge!

The birth was fun. I had been rushed in earlier in the week with bleeding, and on the day of my daughter's 4th birthday, I discharged myself against doctor's orders with the promise that I would take it easy. I couldn't be in the hospital on my daughter's birthday, and I wasn't coping very well on my own. My brother was on active service with the Royal Navy, and a 13-year-old girl I had been privately tutoring had been tragically killed the week before. She had been hit by a remote-controlled aeroplane in a park. It had affected me severely, and I just wanted to be at home.

Three days later in the middle of the night, I started haemorrhaging. My mum was visiting for my daughter's birthday party, and she called an ambulance. They had a tricky time lifting me on a chair downstairs that turned-I was heavy. I felt like I was the piano in the Laurel and Hardy sketch of the same name. It would have been far easier and quicker if I had just walked down the stairs. I remember a very bumpy and worrying ambulance ride.

It turned out I had "Placenta Praevia", and the plan was to do an emergency Caesarean. Things didn't go well in theatre. My mum was allowed in with me, and I remember watching the heart monitor beeping and moving across the screen and waiting for it to flat line. I also remember my mum making small chat with the anaesthetist. Then she was suddenly told to leave the theatre, and I heard the staff call for a senior consultant as they were' losing her.' The "her" in question was me. I was aware of everything that was going on, and I knew we were both in trouble,

My daughter was born at 10.32pm and taken to the Special Care Baby Unit, and I was wheeled off to the High Dependency Unit. I was OK physically (in the grand scale of things) but mentally all over the place. Same staff, same machines, almost four years to the day and all despite being continuously told that I was worrying too much and everything would be fine.

No funny stories about the birth and recovery apart from a fire alarm a few days later and just as I was about to leave my room in those glamorous surgical stockings and backless gown, wheeling my drip, I was told to stay put. I wasn't a priority or a celebrity. Thankfully it was a false alarm.

MONGOLIAN BLUESPOT MAY 1999

I took my first baby regularly to the health clinic to get weighed and plot the graph and worry about which percentile she was for length and weight and head circumference. I didn't bother with baby number two.

During a baby weighing, I remember the health visitor exclaiming loudly, very loudly, that my baby had Mongolian Blue Spot and hurrying off to find her colleague. I watched the other mums in the room clutching their babies closer to them. Mongolian Blue Spot? Seriously?

It sounded like a fish disease! However, it turned out only to be a small bluish mark at the base of the spine found on some mixed-race babies. I did, however, take great delight in phoning my mum with a tearful voice and tell her that her grandchild had Mongolian Blue Spot. She wasn't laughing as much as I was.

I breastfed both babies. Apart from the normal embarrassing leakages, all went well. However, my husband did hand over a breast pad by mistake with all the documentation to a bewildered registrar when registering the name!

RED WINE 1999

On one of the rare nights I had a babysitter, I went to the restaurant my husband worked in and ordered the chicken in red wine sauce. After a while, the room was spinning. It had gone straight to my head. Unfortunately, I was driving so I had to wait a while until I had sobered up before I could drive home. It had been that long since I had drunk.

HEATED GLOVES 2001

The events of 9/11 somewhat overshadowed the next few months, but N. was working long hours in an Italian restaurant and coming home on public transport. If customers stayed on, then, he would get back in the early hours of the morning. My dad bought him a thoughtful present for Christmas; battery powered heated gloves. N. recounted one night when he was on the bus wearing the gloves with a large battery compartment and wires connecting the heat pads to big black gloves. It only took one look from a passenger on the bus at the gloves, and N. realised the days wearing those gloves out in public, unfortunately, were numbered.

Everyone was jittery and nervous although thankfully N. received very little targeted racism as an Arab living in Kent.

Bringing up the girls and teaching when your husband worked long hours including the holidays, were tricky, but I had great support from my parents despite them living 400 miles away.

NO SLEEP 2006

The girls were generally good, but one of my daughters went through a phase of not sleeping through the night and coming into us. We had a baby gate, but she was able to scale that. We had to leave the landing light on as I had caught her climbing the landing bannisters to get at the light over the stairs. I only just caught her in time before she may have fallen down the stairs. We tried reward charts, stair gates, late-night exercise, stickers and bribes, new pyjamas and stories, but she would still manage to come through to us around 2-3am.

One night before bedtime, I offered her gold chocolate coins in the morning if she stayed in her room. She came in at 3 am, woke me and said;

"You can have the coins; I'm not hungry!"

Fortunately, it was just a phase, and now as teenagers, I have trouble getting them both out of bed!

THE CARPET SHOP 2001

Both girls were confident and extrovert toddlers.

So confident was one daughter that she decided to play hide and seek in a carpet shop. My heart was in my mouth as I searched everywhere for her. An old lady found her holding her breath wrapped in a carpet and with a massive smile on her face. She had been peeping out watching us frantically looking for her. I had even told the security guard that I thought she had been taken. I was bordering on hysterical. I was so relieved to see her that I didn't punish her.

MINE

My daughter was fond of loading her buggy with goodies unbeknown to me, especially in a supermarket if I had a basket balanced on the top, as I couldn't then see what she was doing.

She was caught out in a little cross-stitch shop, which is no longer there anymore. As I was leaving having paid for my purchases, the owner stopped me at the door and said they had been tracking my daughter on CCTV and that she had stolen many items.

Sure enough, the basket had a few items, but she was two years old and not a cross-stitch fan and indeed not stealing to order as the lady was implying. It took a while, but I had to convince the lay that this wasn't a pre-planned operation. Luckily I was able to show her that the items were at pram height and it was an opportune taking and not something I had taught her to do. Nevertheless, it was all rather embarrassing, and I didn't take my daughter there again.

Dance and drama classes were a way of channelling their energy and confidence.

#PROUD MUMMY MOMENT

Both daughters went to the same local dance school and took up the tap, ballet and musical theatre. My younger daughter soon followed in her sister's dancing footsteps and was lucky enough to secure roles in the musicals Billy Elliot, Matilda and The Color Purple on the West End. They were terrific opportunities, and she has made life-long friends. I was now a seasoned "dance mum" and to be honest I enjoyed accompanying them wherever they danced. To date, the girls have danced on three European cruises, twice on stage at Disneyland Paris, twice in Disneyland California, in endless competitions, festivals, shows, school fetes and fairs and two big international competitions in Barcelona and Hollywood. Why wouldn't I accompany them?! I even had my personalised hoodie too with "FUZZ" written on the back!

HONEST QUESTIONS

I kept diaries and wrote down funny things the girls said and did as they grew up. Those notebooks have been handy when compiling these stories. These are a few of the best:

- The girls watched me annually put on my Pudsey ears and dress up for the Children In Need appeal. They watched as a lot of money was raised for Children In Need, and they took in their donation to the school. However, it was all very puzzling for my daughter, as at the end of the day she asked, aged four, "Where is Need?"

- On leaving a public car park, my dad said to the attendant "Thank you, kindly" to be asked by a little voice in the back: "Grandad, how did you know his name was 'Kindly'?

- When pregnant, my daughter asked me if I was having a boy or a girl. I said I didn't know yet. She replied:
  "Well, when you've decided, could you let me know please?"

- My three-year-old hurt her toe. I asked her which one she had hurt. After singing the rhyme to herself, she said:
  "I think it's the one that had the roast beef."

- It's adorable when a little one around the age of three uses a new word for the first time. My daughter had said "altogether" when counting so I wanted her to phone her grandma and tell her she had used a "big" word. I passed her over on the phone, and she said:
  "Grandma, apparently I've just used a big word!"

- My dad often answers the phone in many different ways. My daughter was phoning him, and he answered, "Chateau Sheils, with whom am I speaking?
  There were some giggles and then came the reply, "No it's not whom grandad, it's me!"

- I had both girls in car seats until a late sage- I took safety seriously, however, the one day that my eldest aged 3 managed to open her door from the inside was a day that you couldn't make up. I thought I had activated the child locks, but as the girls had never tried the doors from the inside, I had no knowledge they weren't switched on. We were stationary at traffic lights, and suddenly the door swung open. My mum was driving, and I had to run around and close the door swiftly.
  We were on our way to a safari park with a drive through lion and other wild animal enclosure!

IN ALL INNOCENCE 2005

If you've ever seen the film Polar Express with Tom Hanks, then you'll remember a little boy's journey on the Polar Express train to see Santa at the North Pole. I didn't realise the effect it had on my six-year-old daughter until I went into her room on Christmas

Eve. She was sitting upright having gone to bed a few hours earlier, dressed in hat, coat and scarf. She was waiting for the Polar Express.

It was both adorable and heartbreaking as I had to tell her it wasn't going to come and pick her up.

P.A.R.K.

So that my daughter would not get excited too early when she heard the word "park", we would spell it out in conversations, e.g. "If we get back early from the market we can go to the p.a.r.k."

One day around age three, my daughter asked if she could go to the p.a.r.k.!

I'm finding myself doing the same with the word 'walk' with my dog and even whispering the word in case she hears!

THE COLD INCIDENT

"Get off your mammoth and smell the generation of 2017".

That was my daughter's remark to me when I didn't understand her and her friends. It made me feel very old and out of touch. You want the best for your children, and you hope you have raised them well and you know deep inside when you talk that you've turned into your mother! But occasionally even they do things that to test you and to be honest the only thing you can do is laugh, afterwards of course.

Even at aged 16 when you have a common cold, you want your mummy. She had blocked sinuses and was rummaging around in the bathroom cupboard for something to take. On this occasion I was busy, and so I shouted to my daughter, "Take a Karvol decongestant capsule from the medicine box".

My daughter wasn't very good at taking tablets. I thought that if she squeezed some of the capsules on to a handkerchief or her pillow, it would ease her blocked up nose. She came into my room quite triumphantly announcing that she had swallowed it with no problem.

Swallowed it? Surely not. I paused for a moment and then I checked on the Internet what to do and then phoned the emergency nurse who as I suspected, advised going straight to A & E. The capsule was not to be swallowed.

Surely she had read the box? She had had these as a child on her pillow. Yes, she had read the instructions.

She had read: DO NOT TAKE ETERNALLY.

She thought Oh OK they're addictive; I'm not stupid, I won't take them forever (eternally), I'll take the one.

The box read: DO NOT TAKE INTERNALLY

We both spent a sleepless night in the children's ward being awoken every few hours or so by the beeping of the blood pressure monitor attached to her arm.

THE SHOULDER

Fortunately, to date, we haven't had many visits to the hospital, although in 2007 my three years old complained of a sore shoulder. There weren't any visible marks and so I took her to a soft play birthday party that day and swimming the next day. That night she still said it hurt, so I got it checked out with a late night visit to A & E.

She had broken her collar bone. It later emerged she had fallen (or had been pushed down a few stairs by her sister). Having a high pain threshold meant that when she complained, we knew something was wrong although I reckon she's milked this fact over the years!

HOSPITALS

In 2003 when I was in the hospital recovering after the birth of my daughter, there were no fancy beds that you could raise up and down at the flick of a control. There were no fancy televisions with film channels that you could subscribe to. Instead, you had to hire a TV on wheels by the day at an extortionate amount.

You certainly weren't allowed to use your phones; that is if you were lucky enough to own a mobile phone.

Flowers had been banned a few years earlier because of the risk of disease. You could take food in, but everything was checked and overseen to minimise disease or infection. Big signs were pinned to the entrance saying do not enter if you have or have been in contact with someone with the flu or Norovirus. It was all very real. As you ate a grape, you wondered whether it had been sprayed with disinfectant first.

14
OTHER C WORDS

"CHRISTMAS, CRACKERS AND CARS"

Christmas at my house always started early. I would put my tree up at the beginning of December and usually start wrapping around September. I had a bit of a name for myself for being organised, although this year (2017) I kid you not, I was handed a bag of Christmas presents by my sister-in-law in July- I couldn't compete with that.

Christmas 2017, my mum and daughter put the tree and decorations up while I was in the hospital and I came home from the mastectomy surgery to a beautifully decorated tree and house, and just how I liked it. I didn't change or move anything.

It had always been my job to put the decorations up downstairs, and the girls still had their separate tree in their rooms for tinsel and anything they had made at school. As they had grown older, their decorations coming home from school grew less, but they still wanted sparkly, so their decorations still stayed upstairs.

I had missed the staff Christmas night out.

I had seen a great "Reindeer Boob" costume where one breast is decorated like a reindeer with a red shiny nose and antlers, and the other is covered up, perfect for Uniboobers. It was a clubbing fashion that had started in Manchester, but I wound my kids up with the threat of appearing with one. I may like dressing up, but there's a limit!

NO JOKE

Crackers have been around since 1845-50 when the sweet maker Tom Smith introduced them to London. They have also been on our family Christmas table as long as I can remember. There is childhood competitiveness in grabbing and winning the more significant part of the cracker and the disappointment when the banger doesn't go off.

The paper hat never fitted over my hair, and for some reason, I always seem to get the orange one. It depended on which shop you bought the cracker set as to what toy you got, from plastic moustache that hurt after a while, to fortune teller fish with that odd word-fickle. As a child, I never understood that word.

The best laugh came last year with a cracker joke that I told and then laughed so much at because it just was not funny. It was a mistake, but we spent ages rereading it and trying to work out the meaning:

"What kind of cough medicine does Dracula take?"

"Con Medicine"

(The real answer to this joke is in a later chapter!).

CHURCH DECEMBER 2007

Sitting near the front of the church I was at the school carol concert. I had already played the recorder with the school orchestra. It was the annual event where I just prayed that I didn't get the giggles. From experience, it is impossible to play the recorder with the giggles especially when the person next to you plays the wrong note, or their recorder squeaks or they get the giggles themselves.

Fortunately, the orchestral numbers went well, and we were now onto the carol singing. I could hear sirens outside but carried on singing. A few minutes later a policeman interrupted the reverend. A voice on the microphone said, "Would the owner of LX51........."

He was reading my registration number.

"..........please make themselves known."

Oh my goodness, that was me. How embarrassing. Do I put my hand up or shout out or stand up? I left my daughter with friends and made my way out to the front. I then had to do the walk of shame accompanied by the police officer from the front of the church right to the back, with the eyes of every child in the juniors and the parents and all the teachers on me.

Outside, my parked car had been written off in an accident. Possibly it was the shock, but I wasn't worried about the insurance, or my car or how to get home. I wanted to run back into the church and clear my name!

PIECE OF FLUFF 2014

I'm always fiddling when driving – as well as concentrating of course. This day I was driving along, and I saw a bit of fluff or apple on the seat next to me. I pressed the electric window and reached over to get the bit of fluff with my left hand.

I have no idea how it happened, but the fluff was sticking to my fingers, so my hand was still out of the window when the window closed.

It didn't hurt, but I was driving along holding the wheel with my right hand and my left hand trapped in the window. OK so it was dangerous, but it was also hilarious especially when I was trying to pull my hand out and indicate at the same time. What may only have been seconds, felt like minutes. I yanked it out and changed gear in the nick of time.

I am quite a cautious driver. I'd been involved in a car crash on the freeway in L.A. 1988 and had passed too many accidents on the A1 to drive fast.

They say most accidents occur within a quarter of a mile of your own home.

LET THERE BE LIGHT 2013

This story started at home. It was a dark and miserable night, and as I started driving the children, I really couldn't see at all. I slowed down a lot but found even seeing the kerb on the left hard to do. I was pressing all the fans and buttons, but nothing seemed to clear the fog. I really couldn't see the road.

I looked for my demister sponge but only found an old bit of tissue. I had the window wound down too as I thought it would help the windows demist more quickly.

At the first set of traffic lights, we get to; I was frantically trying to wipe the window with a bit of old tissue. I was in the process of reaching for a school coat to try and use to clean the windscreen when I heard a man's voice shouting from the car next to me.

I looked over, and he shouted it again;

"Turn your lights on!"

I was trying to wipe the darkness away with a bit of old tissue when all that had happened was the automatic light activation had flicked to manual!

FLASHING LIGHTS

Whenever the car went wrong, I wanted an instant fix. I went to a six-week adult night-class on car mechanics but it was quite technical and all about taking bits apart and carburettors and the like. I just wanted to know what to do when lights on the dashboard started flashing or beeping. I stuck it out, but it was incredibly dull.

IS CANCER CONTAGIOUS?

My girls were worried that breast cancer was in our family or that it was contagious. Would they catch it? Apart from an aunt, no one else is known to have suffered from breast cancer, but now my mum had been diagnosed with cancer, it did play on all our minds.

My mum had the BRCA gene test done, and fortunately, it came back that she was not a carrier of the gene. This cancer I had was not hereditary.

But if the cancer wasn't hereditary then maybe all these little "life tests" or embarrassing incidences that were happening to me, were?

Looking at my parents' lives, apart from a grainy VHS recording of my mum shouting out random prices to her friend on ITV's " The Price is Right" and some dodgy footage of some accordion playing, nothing too strange or amazing had happened to my them- thankfully. We did, however, have some competing stories that we all as a family brought out on special occasions.

THE PRESIDENT OF GHANA

My mum's story wasn't a tale about her son being a helicopter pilot but involved the President of Ghana.

Watching the African Nations Football Cup on television, the President of Ghana was talking about how sport brings people together. My mum phoned me excitedly to turn on the tv and that she recognised the man speaking." That's John," she said, "I used to rub petroleum jelly into his son's face to make it shiny".

There was an answer to that, but it did emerge that she did indeed know Kofi John Kufuor, the president of Ghana. While he and his wife were studying in Oxford in the 1950s, my grandmother fostered his son and mum indeed rubbed petroleum jelly into his skin to moisturise and also make him look even cuter in a baby show that he was entered in and had won.

My mum wanted to make contact, but how do you contact a President?

She was successful, however, and with the help of the Ghanaian High Commission in London, she later received a letter on headed paper from the President saying he had fond memories of my grandmother and inviting my mum over for a visit. He also said he had just been on a state visit to the UK and it was unfortunate that they hadn't met. They are to this day penpals!

So my unfortunate luck was not directly hereditary, but what about siblings, were they to blame? Had anything unusual happened to them or had they any unusual tales?

AUSTRALIA 2005

My brother and his wife were looking for a beautiful beach to go snorkelling in during a visit to Australia.

They saw a lovely little beach from the road, but it was tricky to get to. Apart from the smell of fish, and the lack of a proper path to get down to, it was lovely, deserted and they spent a lot of time swimming and snorkelling.

Later that evening they told the owner of their Bed and Breakfast where they had been during the day. The colour drained from his face when they described where they had been swimming. They had swum in Shark Cove, a notorious shark feeding ground!

The sharks had just fed, hence the smell of fish. The "DANGER-NO SWIMMING" signs were there and clear for people to see at the main entrance down to the beach. My brother had taken an alternative route down!

15

COME FLY WITH ME

I love the excitement and the hustle and bustle of airports. I love people watching there too, but now I prefer to get through into the departure lounge and sit down without any hitches.

I used to like eating a second breakfast because everyone else was eating and also buying last minute doubles of things in panic from the shops. Now I say a little prayer before I travel that things go smoothly. You may be thinking why.

JUNE 2010

We were going on a family visit to Casablanca. Our luggage was well overweight as we were taking lots of clothes and presents for the family. My husband hurriedly repacked the suitcases and hand luggage distributing more by hand to even out the weight and avoid a fine. At security, I beeped through the door. I was wearing loose clothing and nothing metal but was taken to the body scanner.

Something was in Zone B that they didn't like.

Something was still in Zone B that they didn't like.

What was in Zone B that they didn't like?

They eventually gave up and let me return to my family who were having problems.

The girls' bags had yoghurts and cans and the contents of my fridge in that we couldn't take through, but had been in the suitcases. What was worse was that my husband's bag had been stopped because it had "traces of explosives "on it!

N. had begun talking to the officials and was getting nowhere which is why I possibly volunteered that the bag was mine. Not sure why I said it, it wasn't my bag, and I hadn't and idea what was in it.

I watched as they emptied plastic kitchen utensils and another tat from the cheap shop on the High Street that we were taking with us, onto the counter. The bag was 'of interest' to the security guards, and I was asked who I was, where the bag was kept and other similar questions. It was getting a bit scary, and I was waffling. Where did I keep the bag? It wasn't even mine. I said, "In the garage with lots of art products in and paints that I use for school" (I was the art coordinator after all).

Did I dye my hair?

"Err yes, and the peroxides are kept in the bag," I replied trying not to show that I was lying.

I was sweating profusely, but I remained calm. I was lucky. They gave me the benefit of the doubt and believed I was innocent of any dodgy activity.

They took my details and confiscated the bag. All the plastic utensils and placemats and things from the cheap shop were given back to us in plastic bags which we were allowed to carry on as extra luggage.

"Come on everyone; let's bomb it!"

This is what I said loudly as we emerged from the baggage check area. I meant let's run fast as we were very late to the gate. I momentarily froze. Had someone heard me? What was I thinking? But it was OK, no-one had heard, and we made the gate in time, just. We boarded the plane, carrying plastic spatulas and fish slices in neon colours and placemats of quaint country cottages in plastic bags, albeit later than planned.

Surely it couldn't get any worse? (Wait till you read the return journey story!)

MOROCCO

Morocco is an Arab kingdom in North Africa. Although primarily Islamic, I found it not as oppressive for women as perhaps some of its neighbours. My husband's family were very hospitable and friendly towards the girls and me.

I had to constantly try not to view things; however, with British eyes and not to compare. Morocco and England are worlds apart even if the King is trying to make changes. If you admired a painting or an ornament in a family home, they would give it to you. If you visited a house, then it was expected that you had something to eat or drink even if you attended late or night. If you had a photo of a grandchild, they would replace the one they had in a frame and put the other one in the bin!

I attended N.'s sister's wedding. It was a feast for the senses and full of tradition. The wedding presents were paraded through the streets on silver platters and guests, family and friends followed with singers and chanters and drums playing and a lot of clapping and cheering.

There was a cow on the patio of the house where we were staying.

Nothing now surprised me, but I did wonder how it had gone up three flights of stairs or whether it took the lift. It had a garland of flowers on its head, and at first, I thought it was a wedding present until I realised it was the dinner!

I visited N's relatives in the mountains. I struggled shelling peas and peeling potatoes without a peeler and had no idea how to cook a meal for so many relatives. There are no supermarkets up the mountains.

Even washing up I struggled with as there was a little tiny bowl with liquid in and you were meant to dab a small cloth in to and leave crockery to soak and then boil the water to rinse them. I realised I took a lot of things for granted.

I tried my hand at washing a step but felt entirely out of my comfort zone. I'd swept a step before but not scrubbed like Cinderella, and you don't scrub as that rubs the dirt in more, it's more of a sweeping movement. But I didn't know that. I also couldn't tell the family how we crop tomatoes in England or which pesticides we use on tomatoes as I got mine by the bowl for a pound at the market or the supermarket. I felt uneducated and ignorant.

When I first visited Morocco in 1993, I swear nearly every car would have failed its MOT in the UK, and seat belts were not important. I remember protesting at being made to get into a car with nine people in, including some kids in the footwells. Now with more Moroccans working in Europe and earning and sending money home, the cars were fancier, and laws were passed to try and improve road safety.

Kerbs had been built on the pavements, traffic lights worked, and taxis were only licensed to take three passengers only. This meant that we had to split up as a family when travelling. I wasn't happy about that especially as I didn't speak Arabic, but safer than maybe catching the bus.

N. and I caught a bus from Casablanca to Marrakesh. It was a country bus chock full with people going to market, a few chickens and fruit and vegetables. In my sheltered life, I had never shared a bus with chicken before.

I looked at some suspicious wicker baskets, praying that there were no snakes in them. It was a hot journey and how the bus got up steep hills, and around mountain corners without going over the side, I don't know. It stopped to pick up and drop off people at a watering hole, and N. got off to get water. My first Arabic phrase was, "Hada blaza am'ra" meaning – "this place is taken". I needed it as the bus was filling up, although looking out the window, I was more worried about the conversation N. was having with a herdsman. I'd heard stories about Western women being exchanged for camels. I'd watched that episode of 'Fabulous' when Edina and Patsy went to Morocco and sold Saffron! There were plenty of camels and donkeys outside.

It was exotic and traditional, yet downright scary.

Another bus journey taken in Morocco was one caught from the beach back home with the kids. I was wearing a denim dress, and it was sopping wet with sand all over it.

We had gone to a public beach, but there were hardly any women in the sea. It was so hot, and I wanted to go into the water. I went in wearing the dress, except it wasn't a particularly good idea as it billowed everywhere then got sand stuck to it.

It was very windy, so my hair was rock hard, salty and a blonde afro by this time. I was so uncomfortable standing on a crowded bus hanging on to the kids.

CAIRO

Cairo was behind Morocco on improvements to roads, kerbs and cars. On our first visit to Egypt in 2010 with N., we endured a perilous taxi journey from the airport to the hotel in eight lanes of traffic on the road made for about four lanes. It was horrific. It appeared that motorists had their own set of road traffic rules. The first evening in Egypt was spent with a bottle of water, sitting by a busy roundabout, watching the traffic. There were no set lanes, and at one point the cars were six abreast and stacked with all sorts of goods. We saw camels in pick up vans, wardrobes on bonnets of cars, no lights or one light working, and I swear none of the vehicles we saw either would have passed MOTs in the UK.

I had finally got to visit Egypt – our real honeymoon-and apart from the driving and the utter inability to cross a road; it was an unbelievable feast for the senses. The ancient architecture was magnificent, and I cried when I stood face to face with Tutankhamen's mask.

THE RETURN JOURNEY JUNE 2010

After a week in Morocco during the school half term, we were ready to go home.

Moroccan passports open from right to left and although mainly written in Arabic, the details are completed in French in felt pen and then laminated. In the hot sun, all the writing on my husband's passport had faded. In effect apart from the photo, it was blank.

Our suitcases were already on board. It was a Sunday; no embassy was open.

The blank passport was discovered at the passport control, and my husband was taken away for what seemed like ages. When he returned the airline had decided there would be too much paperwork and disruption so Heathrow could deal with the situation.

It was a very emotional flight home. We were going to be separated, and the house keys were in my husband's suitcase. I tried to fill in the landing card. It was also bizarre how rules between airlines could differ so much. I was used to tucking my bags under the seat in front of the overhead lockers, but on this plane, you could have your bags on the empty seats next to you. You were supposed to turn off electrical equipment too on takeoff and landing, but the man next to us was continually plugged into his laptop.

When we arrived at Heathrow, my husband stayed with us rather than joining the separate non-EU queue. We were all either crying or tear-stained. My youngest had a henna tattoo on her hand, and she held the three burgundy passports and the one green blank one.

The passport control person was concerned with my youngest's tears, and I said we were all exhausted. She was also intrigued by the henna patterns.

The official scanned the passports including the Home Office stamp in the green passport. She started opening the passports, but for whatever reason, she didn't open the green one from right to left. As she was flicking through the pages for the information, she was distracted by my girl's sobbing. She handed all four passports back without noticing the blank back page, and we walked. We just kept on walking. We didn't look back.

The very next day my husband went to the Moroccan Embassy and got the passport changed and started the process of gaining British Citizenship. They were astounded that in the current climate he could have got through passport control, but it wasn't as if he was illegally here. His documents were in order; just the passport was blank.

When I unpacked N.'s suitcase, there was an oil burning, metal, ornate, hanging light wrapped in newspaper that had leaked oil all over the suitcase. He had a tub of anchovies swimming in brine and two-litre cartons of my favourite apricot nectar. These last items had come through in hand luggage. I had had no idea any of these things were there, but more worrying was that nor did the airline, or if they did, they weren't too fussed.

BRITISH CITIZENSHIP

N. learnt the whole British Citizenship Revision book and passed the test gaining citizenship in a ceremony in September 2010. I, on the other hand, failed. I took the practise test online. Even with an MA honours degree, I couldn't tell you what percentage of Irish emigrated after the potato famine or who lived at 12 Downing Street.

I knew my patron saints and some local accents, but something has gone very wrong in the devising of this test. It's hard. It's not just general knowledge. However, had I revised, I may have passed, and I do understand why it is important to know about the history and traditions of the country you propose to live in. It just hasn't been thought through. However, it may well have changed since N. took it. I hope so.

16
MID LIFE CRISIS

My mid-life crisis came when I was 40. It began with a desire to be young again and then to change my appearance to be the Emma that had been lost somewhere in the transition into wife and mum.

The first stage of my "crisis" was to do all the things I used to be able to do- like stay out for a drink late without having to think of the children at home in bed. It was a desire to wear what I wanted and also a will not conform to what was expected of me as a middle-aged, professional mum.

The second stage of my "crisis" was a complete lack of self-confidence, a desire to be slim and a fear of growing old. These feelings were coming quickly, and it was somewhat scary. The last stage of my crisis was a determination to do all the things I ever wanted to do.

I was going to climb a pyramid if it was the last thing I did and I was going to learn to ride a motorbike.

BIKER GIRL

I rode a moped when I lived in Italy, but I wanted a burgundy and silver bike with cream upholstery. Of course, my family thought I was mad. How would I carry my school books? Did I know the death rate of riders? And how could I be so inconsiderate?

I started with the CBT test and passed, but that's as far as I got. It was liberating yet exciting.

I also got to climb a pyramid when my husband and I went on the honeymoon that we never had. Well, technically I climbed a pyramid as I got to go up one or two blocks. The Egyptian authorities have stopped tourists climbing any further now. It was just as amazing and breathtaking and magical as I had imagined.

THE BIG 40

I planned a big 40th birthday. Forty was apparently the new thirty. There was a local venue that played 80s music. Perfect. I sent out over 150 invites. It was an optional 80s fancy dress – I just wanted to wear my Frankie Repeat t-shirt and neon beads.

Nine people turned up.

One of those nine was someone I had never met and who had come with my friend!

That was harsh, but those nine people danced all night to Wham Rap, Duran Duran, Tiffany and Depeche Mode and we all had an enjoyable time. It was then I knew who my real friends were.

At forty I had a crush on a younger man, but it was not worth risking the breakup of a marriage. They never knew, and I was sensible enough not to act upon my feelings. However, the fact that I could have feelings for someone else meant that there was trouble in paradise.

It had started when I had gone to Italy for the weekend to watch my beloved Eros Ramazzotti in concert. While I was away, N. had ready all of my diaries from 1984-2009 and also my dream diary that I kept by my bed to record my dreams if I could ever remember them. I felt violated. It was such an invasion of privacy. Of course, N. did not see it that way.

GOALS

I set myself small attainable challenges and also some long-term goals. I thought this would put an end to this feeling that grass was greener anywhere else.

One of the challenges was to learn to tap dance. I enrolled in my daughters' dance school, and my teacher was also in the West End Show Billy Elliot. I found I wasn't a good student. I didn't like being told what to do, and also I didn't have a good memory. I couldn't even remember a short sequence of steps. Also, I didn't have much coordination either. I should have remembered that.

Earlier in 2009 while on a dance cruise, I had tried Rumba and Salsa class. Admittedly it did have something to do with the gorgeous Latino instructor, but I couldn't get the hang of it. I couldn't even blame the excessive swaying of the boat and horror of horrors it was captured from afar by a video which is still in circulation.

I'd put on a lot of weight. Not just because of the steroid tablets, but from comfort eating and the static lifestyle sewing or marking books or sitting around the dance centre waiting for one or other of the girls to finish dance class. I knew I wasn't fit and I decided to start dieting.

At first, I did the keep fit videos in front of the TV, but I kept skidding in socks and banging into things. I was also conscious of passers-by looking through my lounge window at me trying to squat, lunge or grapevine on the carpet! I'd also try and do sit ups and press ups on the bedroom floor. I'd lie there on my back thinking how stupid I looked and then one night my arms just buckled doing a single press up, and I fell flat on my face.

"Hey Em what did you do to your nose?"

"Carpet burn, don't ask."

Being a larger lady meant chafing of the thighs in hot weather, terribly uncomfortable although to my great delight I did see some lacy garters advertised online that could be worn in hot weather to solve the problem. At times I would start a fire with the amount of rubbing going on!

Miranda Hart on her TV show talked of the "boob clap "when rolling over; I had "applause"!

MENORCA 2012

There must be an elegant way to get on a plastic air bed. Climbing on one as a larger lady is just traumatic. Once I'd heaved myself up, I'd disappear over the other side with a splash. If I managed to get on a little bit, I would get stuck. The sound of flesh on hot plastic was grim as I tried to heave myself up a bit and then collapsed, half on half off with costume munched up at the back. I'd think of those glossy travel magazines with the model in sunglasses and hat and a cocktail in hand reclined on the air bed. How? They may well have been air-lifted on or photoshopped on to it.

There was also an art in getting out of a swimming pool elegantly. If it was deck level, then you had an advantage unless your sun lounger was at the deep end and you wanted to do a minimal amount of exposed walking.

Exposed walking: the duration spent on the show to the public during the walk from the sun-lounger to the pool.

If lots of kids did not hog your steps, then it was guarded by a man in Speedos. In that case, you had to heave yourself like a manatee on to the edge of the pool and then roll over on to the hot poolside and hope that your costume rolled with you.

And that was all before doing the exposed walking. Eyes from all the loungers and pool bars and from in the pool watched you as you walked back to your lounger, hair stuck to your face, costume askew and flesh wobbling like jelly, mentally undressing you and thinking "why would you wear that costume?"

Do you think Mediterranean look at women wearing large one-piece costumes in the same way as British women look at men in Speedos?

"Hey look, Carlos, here comes another Brit abroad. She's wearing a one-piece."

"Nasty"

"It's even got a modesty frill!"

"Do you think it has the huge foam removable cups inside?"

"Possibly. Why do they wear them? And why do they only come in black or swirly curtain print?"

"I don't know Carlos, but thank goodness they don't come in white!"

TRAPPED IN A DRESS

As mentioned before, I don't like the trauma of trying on clothes in bright lights and lots of mirrors, and this tale confirms why I hate it.

I was shown to the cubicle by the young perma-tanned assistant, and I began trying on the chosen selection. I then tried on a blouse that had a vest attached inside it. There were a lot of straps. Putting it over my head, the straps twisted and my arm went through the wrong gap. It was a bit too small.

I then got stuck. I couldn't take the top off the way I had put it on, and the straps had pulled tight. I was alone and needed help before the whole blouse ripped. Awkwardly I opened the door and stood awhile before gaining the eye of the assistant. She then set to work untangling the straps and me from the blouse. I didn't buy anything and made a quick exit. MEMORY GAMES

As a child, I loved playing the memory game with cards or electronic flashing colours. However, my memory seemed to be getting worse. We all go upstairs and think what have I come up here for? But this "stairs" feeling was happening more and more frequently.

It was June 2014, and even though my eczema had got better, my health seemed to be deteriorating. I seemed to be continually disturbing my doctor with complaints. My migraines were increasing, my eyesight was failing, my ears were so sensitive to noise that I had to wear earplugs, my ankles and wrists were burning, my feet were hurting, my nose was numb, and my short term memory was shocking.

The various doctors in the Practice that I saw could explain each of the complaints. The numb nose was from wearing sunglasses too long. The sore feet resulted from wearing flat shoes. My eye-sight was failing because of my age.

One day my heart felt it was making a bid for freedom; it was beating so fast. I got an emergency doctor's appointment. The doctor said I'd drunk too much caffeine.

My thumb went numb- I was using the phone too much.

I had a sore coccyx and had to sit on a cushion- no cure for that one.

Every one of my ailments could be explained away but not necessarily cured. The different complaints on their own were annoying, but when you had all of them going on and all of them invisible, it was so frustrating and upsetting. When someone asked me "how are you?" it was far easier to lie and just to say "fine".

The ailments kept on coming. My tongue started hurting as if I'd eaten a hot curry or sherbet lemons. My scalp was getting itchier and scabbier, and one day the glands in my neck just swelled up. I called NHS 111, and they said to go to A &E. I was scared and worried, but the doctor took one look at me and said to change my shampoo as it was an abundance of yeast- dandruff that was affecting this gland! I felt so embarrassed and yet frustrated. I also knew something else undiagnosed was going on.

A WORRYING TIME 2015

My eye kept swelling up too and felt like someone had scratched it. Even if I closed my eyes, you could still feel the scratch. The eyelid looked swollen, and it kept watering. I usually went to the doctor's first for a referral and then to the local eye hospital by bus and was given eye drops. After 2-3 days it went down, and I could carry on as usual with only some ugly selfies looking like Quasimodo as a memory.

One morning when I awoke, I couldn't see properly. My eye had swelled up quite badly. It was always frustrating as it meant I couldn't drive and therefore couldn't get to work. Also, it was very painful, so it meant I would not be able to do much that day. I saw the doctor first for a referral, but it was a different doctor that I saw. She seemed more worried than I had expected and asked if anyone could drive me or go with me and not to worry. She handed me a referral sheet and a leaflet which she said to read that night.

On the bus with my good eye, I read the leaflet. I had suspected ocular cellulitis. The first line read "Ocular cellulitis can be fatal."

Somehow, I would have remembered something like that had the doctor have told me. It was an anxious wait at the hospital, but thankfully my eye was treatable with antibiotics and steroid drops and soon was back to normal.

Those weeks were awful. My mind was playing so many games. I had already mentally planned my funeral and divided up my possessions. I genuinely believed something serious was wrong with me- possibly a brain tumour, but no-one is listening or taking me seriously.

I felt silly, but I knew something wasn't quite right, especially as my memory which as a historian I prided myself on, was getting worse.

B & Q AUGUST 2014

I lost my car.

I had parked it in B&Q car park, and after shopping, I couldn't find it. I reported it stolen. I was so upset especially as it was full of boot sale bargains. While I was waiting for the police to arrive, I suddenly remembered driving to another car park later as my feet were hurting and I didn't want to walk. I had to tell the very helpful assistant sheepishly that I wasn't even parked in their car park and I had suddenly remembered where my car was. But later that month I lost my shopping and never found it.

I had bought about four or five bags full of shopping, and when I got home, it wasn't in the car. I returned to the store to see if it had been handed in or was still at the till ...nothing. To this day I have no idea where it went, although the most logical answer is that I put it on the floor by the car and then driven off. I like to think that whoever stole my meringue nests, tinned mandarins and pasta, enjoyed a lovely feast.

THE GARAGE

The police knocked on my door one night too- I had forgotten to pay for my diesel. Fortunately, I was a regular at the garage and not a diesel thief, and they saw on CCTV that I had just bought shopping and driven off. It was the same garage that when N. first came to the country, told him that you couldn't haggle down the price of petrol. The petrol came to £40 and N. tried to give them £30. We were not in the Arab souk!

It was also the same garage that I nearly blew up twice before!

The first time was when I parked the car on a slight slope and got out. The hand-break didn't hold, and the car started rolling backwards. The pumps were only metres away when I got into the car and successfully pulled the hand-break tighter.

The second time I took my purse out of my bag near the pumps to go and pay and at the same time a "Snappy Snap" fell out of my bag with my purse and onto the floor. The kids had bought Snappy Snaps to throw on the floor with a bang. I was looking after them and forgot they were there. Luckily the floor wasn't covered with any spillages, and the snap didn't explode.

VISIT TO CONSULTANT NEUROLOGIST

I was convinced I had a brain tumour and I was prepared to hear the worst. My memory was getting worse. In the musical Billy Elliot, the grandma with dementia hides her pastie in the airing cupboard. I found my full cereal bowl in my airing cupboard. The thing is, I didn't even remember not eating it, let alone putting it in there.

With a bit of a fight and another visit to the doctor holding a written list of symptoms and things I had forgotten, I was finally referred to a consultant neurologist.

In the meeting with him, I told him all the strange occurrences and memory problems. I was a bit tearful. I had to look at a picture of a seaside scene, and there was a lifebuoy. I couldn't for the life of me remember the word when describing the picture, yet I was diagnosed with stress. Stress? I wasn't stressed. I enjoyed my job, and a lot of my paperwork and marking had eased. If I were any more laid back, I would have been horizontal. I had nothing to be stressed about. Finances were OK, N. and my daughters seemed happy. My youngest daughter had just been cast into a West End show. I wasn't stressed; I was excited and couldn't wait to start taking her to rehearsals. It would be a busy time, but I wasn't worried about travelling. More strange things then started happening.

WUDDLING MY MURDS

I started muddling my words, or "wuddling my murds," as I called it. I would look at something and momentarily forget what it was called. It had had briefly before while having a migraine headache, but this was happening regularly and not as part of a migraine. I was muddling people's names a lot, and then as I spoke, I would stammer and stutter and come out with a whole load of rubbish. I wrote down some of the weird things I said:

- Pass me the sugar" instead of ketchup.
- "Is that a plimsoll?" for "is that a splinter?
- "Please tear away the drapes"- Can you draw the curtains, please.
- "I'm parching for a tea-bag"- I fancy a cup of tea.
- Eat my face -for please come down the stairs
- Battle of the Pigs for the book Lord of the Flies

I tried to work out why I was saying such sentences. Sometimes there was a link between the subject and sound of the word or linked with a topic I had just been talking about. Sometimes it was just random, and there was no fathoming it out.

My head-teacher was supportive, and I didn't have to do assemblies for the time being that involved the whole school, as who knows what I may have said?

But I was still worried. I had not been sent for any tests or put on any medication.

GUIDE CAMP 1982

Getting stuck for words is embarrassing, but getting stuck in the toilet is everyone's worst nightmare. I once got stuck, but at least I can now look back and laugh. I was at guide camp, and the lock in the toilet just came off in my hand. I tried to crawl under the door or into the next cubicle but got wedged. I completely ruined my clothes. They were wet and contaminated. The floor wasn't very clean.

I reversed and then tried to climb over the top into the cubicle next door. There was an awkward moment when I was sitting on the top, and the pack leader came in to see where I had got to. But looking at the state of my clothes and seeing the locked door, she realised I was escaping!

Now I don't lock the door of any public toilet if I can help it, and sort of perch with one hand out in case the door is pushed open!

17

WHATEVER THE WEATHER

I found one thing that made things better was sunbathing. Lying in the sun naturally cleared my eczema and any spots, but I also seemed to feel better in the sun.

Thinking back, I had always loved the sun. At one point I contemplated buying a lightbox as I thought I might suffer from SAD-Seasonal Affected Disorder, but I was persuaded not to.

There was nothing like lying on a sun lounger and feeling the rays on your face and dreaming of being on a tropical beach. It was complete 'me time' and relaxation too.

If you parked me in the sun like an old lady in a wheelchair and left me, I would still be there when you got back. Unfortunately, nothing gets done when you're in the sun, and sunbathing was a rare, luxury occurrence with work, housework, marking and two children.

SUN

In the 1980s I experimented with the product "Sun-In" and had big bleach yellow tufts of fuzz. Lemon juice does the same job and makes your hair blonder in the sun.

I didn't have any lemon juice, so I poured undiluted lemon squash on my hair.

Don't copy me. Don't do it. The smell is horrendous, your hair is sticky, and it attracts every insect under the sun!

RAIN

A car driving splashes Bridget Jones through a puddle. I do make sure I drive carefully through large puddles (honestly) but walking through the market one afternoon in 2014, a stall holder wasn't so considerate and emptied his canopy of rainwater by poking it with a pole, just as I was walking past. I was drenched. I had a lot of shopping still to do and somewhere to go later as well. On a summer's day that drenching may have been refreshing, but not on a gloomy Saturday afternoon. I looked around for any sign of TV or secret cameras and then squelched away about my business.

The rain on a school walking weekend in 1981 was so bad that I still shiver now thinking of it. I was 12, and there were holes in my boots, and a cagoule was no defence in the Scottish lowlands. The cagoule had those elasticated wrists that dug in like needles but let the water up the arms. The youth hostel my friends and I stayed in had three showers, and I recall the squabbling over who went first to warm up. Later that evening, the two teachers looking after us went off to the local pub to warm up and left us almost teens on our own for a couple of hours. We were supposed to sit all and watch a video.

We didn't.

MUD

Looking for Easter eggs in the rain and the mud wasn't my idea of fun, but I had meticulously hidden the plastic eggs in all sorts of places in the garden. Overnight there had been a storm, and it was still bucketing it down. The girls were aged around 2 and 6 and were so excited. Dressed in welly boots and raincoats, they were oblivious to the elements. Driven by the reward of chocolate in exchange for plastic eggs, they ran around with their little baskets looking under and over everything. Of course, the older daughter was finding more but what she didn't realise was her sister was stealing the eggs from her basket and putting them into her own, all captured on a large old-fashioned Sony video recorder. They came in with no chocolate around their mouths, but mud.

SNOW

It was Mother's Day in 2010, and we were visiting friends 10 miles away. The girls were wearing thin, floaty dresses as where we were it was a lovely sunny day. As we drove out into the countryside, there was still snow. It hadn't melted from a couple of weeks previously. I have some great pictures of the kids' sledging in my friend's garden in summer dresses, pretty hair bands and welly boots. What they needed to be wearing were onesies.

The invention of the giant "Onesie" (trademarked) meant quick and easy fancy dress costumes. They were great to 'veg out' on the settee in and although like giant babygros they were both warm and cool. On snow days they were ideal because they let the air circulate, so are cosy.

I invented a game of biscuit surfing. It had begun as a hunt for a packet of biscuits hidden in the snow and then morphed into a giant slide down the garden, grabbing a packet of biscuits as you went. It was quite an art and great fun.

I also witnessed a playground of 4-6-year-olds in 2017 see snow for the first time. It was a mixture of screaming and shrieking and admiration and moments of silence. It didn't settle, unfortunately. At first, the children were getting reprimanded for screaming and then when someone said, "It's as if they haven't seen snow before," it suddenly dawned on everyone on playground duty that was probably true. We then let them scream and run around encouraging them to try and catch a snowflake on their tongue! No-one was able to make a snowball unfortunately as the snow wasn't heavy enough.

I can't honestly remember the first time I saw snow, but I can remember the first time it rained after a long period of dry weather.

DROUGHT

It was 1976, and it was raining. People were shouting and crying out in the streets of Kent. Everyone was shaking hands with each other. Old ladies were raising their hands to the heavens and squealing. At age seven I wasn't sure whether to stare or laugh or whatever. It didn't mean much to me but was very odd to witness. I remember only that we hadn't had a bath for ages, the grass was yellow and dad's car hadn't been washed for a long time.

HAIL

Hail the size of golf balls when dropped from a great height hurts. My daughters and I were caught in a hail storm in between a drama show in 2012, and although the storm caused considerable damage to roofs and conservatories, we got off lightly and ended up only wet and with a few marks on our arms. We ran screaming down the pavement looking for cover. I had never seen hail ever that size. The newspapers the next day were full of pictures of the extensive damage it had caused to property and car windscreens.

SAND

Having been on a tour of Luxor in Egypt, we stopped for mint tea on the top of a mountain. From high up, we could see dark clouds rolling in. They were sand clouds. It got very dark, and as the sand reached our tented cafe, the sand hurt as it blew against our bare skin and you had to keep your eyes firmly shut. We wore scarves over our heads. The sandstorm didn't last long, but in neighbouring villages, some elderly people died, and a lot of damage was done.

FOG

Edinburgh has the weather phenomenon "haar," which is like sleety fog that rolls off the sea. As the days got shorter, it wasn't much fun going to school or coming home from the school in the cold haar.

One night I was convinced someone was following me home from the bus stop and I hid in driveways and tried to use the lamp light to keep hidden.

The person was following me, and in the days of no mobile phones, it was pretty scary. It was a man, and he was carrying something. I started walking faster, and he started walking more quickly too. As I finally spluttered into my porch way and rang the bell, my next –door -neighbour came into view carrying a violin and wearing a long Mac and hat. His silhouette had looked scary. He shouted out "evening" and that he had been trying to catch up with me as it was quite unusual weather, but I had been too fast for him!

THE HOT AND THE COLD

I was used to the cold, after all, I lived in Scotland, but I wasn't prepared for the cold in Northern Italy in January 1992. I'd sleep fully clothed, in a hat with two pairs of socks and a sleeping bag and blankets and was still cold. A piece of tarpaulin at the window blocked a fair bit of draught out but winter nights were grim. We had a heater that N. poured Kerosene into, but that just made us sick and have headaches.

In the summer, the tarpaulin acted like a greenhouse, and the gaps just seemed to let every flying, biting insect in under the sun. Summer nights were grim too.

THE POTHOLE JUNE 2017

The dodgy Kent weather of hot, cold, ice, and sun had left potholes in the road and pavement. There was a huge one on the pavement at the end of the drive. I had punctured my tyre twice and had emailed the council to complain. In my letter, I said that an old lady was likely to trip over the pothole if it isn't repaired.

There was a church at the bottom of my road and a constant stream of old ladies walking up and down and especially on a Sunday.

It was duly repaired, but unfortunately, I returned home a couple of months ago to find that an old lady had tripped over the newly repaired pothole. She had cut her eye badly and needed to sit down and phone her sister. She was sweet and grateful and popped round a few days later sporting butterfly stitches and with flowers to say thank you. I didn't have the heart to say I'd got the council to repair the hole so no one would fall down it!

18

ALL THE WORLD'S A STAGE

My husband bought half of an Italian restaurant. Rather than cook the food, he started running the front of the restaurant as a manager. He said one day he would own a restaurant and he did. I was so proud of him, but it meant more responsibilities and more extended hours. My daughters and I saw him even less if that was possible.

However, N. being away in the evenings meant the girls could carry on their dancing.

I got my chaperone licence which meant I could accompany the girls to their shows and help backstage. When both girls were cast in the touring Joseph and his Technicoloured Dreamcoat musical, I chaperoned the rehearsals. When it came to the dress rehearsal, I found myself sitting at the side of the stage near the seated children. We had some very young children, and I was to keep them facing the front and sitting still. On the day of the first performance some scenery had been moved, and as the curtain rose, I could see the first two or three rows of the audience. If I could see them, then they could see me. I was wearing black sitting on the stage next to the children, and there was nowhere for me to move to.

I then had an embarrassing matinee show to endure trying to sing or mouth the words of the songs. The lyrics weren't too bad for the classic songs, but some had loads of verses! I had not been paying attention either to the actions in rehearsals, and there were some claps and "heys" and actions to do at certain key points. It was awful. I learnt live on stage. I was dreading the evening performance. As it turned out, we were able to move the giant cactus prop, and I could hide behind it yet sit near the children.

For six consecutive years, my daughters performed in the local professional pantomime. I was lucky enough to be one of the chaperones which was a fun yet stressful job, especially as I'm not very good at doing French plaits, but I can entertain bored children.

PANTOMIME TIME

As a chaperone, it was both exciting and stressful. Sometimes kids would throw tantrums and refuse to go onstage, and sometimes costumes ripped or tore and slipped down. We had to have a needle and thread constantly on standby if we couldn't nip down to the wardrobe in time. There was also more drama that the audience wasn't aware of:

- One acrobat's stunt went wrong badly, and he landed on his head. He had to go immediately to the hospital leaving a trail of blood on the stage. The children were very professional and despite a few questions, carried on performing as usual.
- An Ugly Sister broke their arm tripping over a dry ice machine in the matinee but returned with a full cast and performed in the evening show.
- Bobby Davro in a kangaroo costume took out props and small children with his tail as he swept by and then got into trouble for some vulgar jokes.
- Lesley Joseph complained that there were too many children on stage in her opening scene and ruthlessly had us cut two children out of every performance. It caused so much upset- parents complained, and the kids complained. I think she didn't like working with children and even came to the kids' Christmas party between shows in her dressing gown and hair rollers which meant the kids couldn't take photos.

- Craig Revel-Horwood deserved a medal for sitting through a kid's version of Snow White; they had made it up in the dressing room, and although very intimidating in his high heels and foobs, he made an effort to speak to the chaperones and was lovely with the kids.
- Anne Widdecombe presented all the children after the run, not with the usual chocolate but with House of Commons rulers. She was adorable and loved working with the children. In return, the children loved her.
- Steve McFadden starred in Aladdin and deserved a medal too for not revealing "Who Killed Archie?" from the current East Enders storyline, despite being asked by the kids every time they saw him.
- I had to shield the children's eyes from seeing the comedian Kev Orkian playing Muddles wearing a Lycra frog costume and a Union Jack thong each performance as his scene was before theirs. He was fabulous with the children and such a talented pianist.
- And finally, Joe Pasquale in Peter Pan made sure the kids were involved in the show as much as possible, valued their participation and didn't sing any songs that "got on your nerves".

THE CANDLE

As a surprise for my birthday in the summer of 2017 my daughter had bought a caterpillar cake and a fancy candle that once lit would burst into many little candles, spin round and play a high pitch happy birthday melody. It was great the first or second time. But the tune didn't stop.

Powered by battery, the tinny melody kept playing even when all the candles were out and had even been picked off. We put it in the bin, but could still hear it. We stamped on it, but could still listen to it. We gave it to the dog for a quick chew, but could still hear it. In frustration, I lobbed it down the bottom of the garden, but we could still hear it. I balanced it on top of the fence, but it dropped over into next door. We could still hear it.

At night when the air was calm, and the windows were open, we could still hear it. My neighbours were away. I kid you not, that candle played for ten days until I went on holiday and I'm sure it carried on even longer. That was one tune that did get on my nerves!

LA TRAVIATA MAY 2015

I too was lucky enough to perform on the same stage as the Christmas pantomime.

I won an opportunity for a friend and me on Twitter to appear in the opera ensemble in the Italian opera La Traviata. We were to mingle and socialise when the main soprano burst into song.

We went along to the wardrobe to get our costumes after having a quick rehearsal. It was a mainly Russian touring company, and they didn't have a dress big enough for me. I was a UK size 16, and I had to squeeze into a pink tiered taffeta number that did not do up at the back. I looked and felt like Miss Piggy. During the performance, I had to make sure that I never turned my back on the audience as there was a gaping hole. It was not the lovely experience I had hoped for. I was so embarrassed. I felt fat frumpy and forty-six. They couldn't do anything much with my hair either and just plonked some flowers in the fuzz.

This was it. I was determined to lose some weight, and I joined the gym two days later.

CHUB CLUB

Approaching 40 I did try to lose weight seriously before. I created a Facebook group Chub Club and weekly when the girls were dancing a few of us chubbier mums went into the costume room, and a friend weighed us. We paid 50p and the lady who had lost the most weight that week took the winnings. We even wore stickers if we had lost anything! However, we started making excuses and not paying the 50p and then not even turning up with flimsy excuses. Willpower was needed. Then Chub Club then became Grub Club, and there was no more mentioning of scales and stickers. Did someone say Chinese?

BETH TWEDDLE

In the same year, an Olympic gymnast visited our school along with a gymnast/actor who talked to the children and tried to inspire them to exercise. Beth Tweddle brought her medals, and the children were excited to ask questions. Later the whole school went outside to do circuit training-simple exercises that would make the children healthier and fitter if they did them regularly.

The whole school did spotty dog jumps and squats and star jumps and short sprints and obstacle races. It was a hot day, and the children were hyped up. They shouted and cheered in team events and fun was had by all, even I had a smile on my face. That was until all the staff were called upon to line up.

All of us including the headteacher and deputy's head and teaching assistants were lined up in front of the whole school (and my own two children) in the full glare of the sun. We had to do the same set exercises and star jumps and squat jumps. I had red underwear on, and every time I squatted down, I was aware my top was too low, so I had to keep one hand on my clothes for modesty. There is also nothing flattering about a larger lady doing star jumps. It was humiliating. It was even more embarrassing as I knew and liked the sportsman who was running the whole day as he had starred in the pantomime that I had chaperoned at. That ten-fifteen minutes was truly and utterly horrendous.

THE GYM MAY 2015

I think they saw me coming to the sports shop. I bought the leggings, the top, the socks and the trainers. I even had my running analysed and given the hard sell on the special posh shock absorbing supporting, all singing and dancing insoles.

I got on the treadmill at the gym and lasted 45 seconds. I thought I was going to die. I was seeing stars and horrendously out of breath. My legs had also turned to jelly. I wasn't fit, but I persevered, and after a few weeks I did get up to 12 minutes of running non-stop at six mph. It was an improvement for me, and the weight just dropped off.

DIETING

I had joined a slimming club too, so my diet was better too. I had tried various diets before, and exercise class worked for a while. But the day that my friend and I had been good all week and lost nothing ended those classes. We drowned our sorrows in a lovely carvery down the road. I had tried the cabbage soup diet too. It burnt most of my insides- If I even see cranberry juice which was part of that diet, I wretch with the memory.

SEATS

Occasionally if the tube or bus is busy, I hold my bloated stomach and pretend I'm pregnant. It works a treat. I almost always get offered a seat and almost always take it.

I first was asked if I was pregnant on a crowded airport transfer bus. I wasn't pregnant, but this little boy was insistent that I was. He didn't offer a seat, and actually, there were only about four on the bus, but he kept asking about the baby. In the end, for an easier life, I just said yes, and he soon stopped asking questions. I caught a side-view reflection of myself t in the window and perfected the hand on the back pregnant look.

When I was pregnant, around six months, I went with a friend to Wembley Arena to watch my favourite Italian singer- Eros Ramazzotti, in concert. Our seats were the highest possible, and even though I don't suffer from vertigo, I was distraught because I wanted to be closer to the stage. I spoke to an official helper and deserved an Oscar for my acting.

It paid off. My friend and I were upgraded nearer, and it was naturally a fantastic concert.

TREADING THE BOARDS

I used to enjoy being on the stage. At school and University, I have performed in many a play or musical theatre show, even singing in Gilbert and Sullivan productions.

I made my fairy costume in 1988 for Iolanthe and was quite excited to trip hither and thither. However, the director said other lights were picking up our underwear under our leotards, so we were told to take bras off. It soon became apparent in the tech run that all of us were not such dainty fairies and it was far more sensible to keep bras on. The instruction was then to wear flesh coloured bras if at all possible.

The following year I was a gentleman of Japan and sang tenor in the Mikado. It was such a fun show to be part of, but we had to keep bowing down to the Lord High Executioner and the Emperor. Our knees were bruised.

I came up with the idea of sticking large sanitary towels to our knees. It worked. Most of the tenors and basses stuck pads to their knees, and even stage door had pads on to muffle the sound of the door closing. There were pads everywhere, and they were even more useful to mop the brow of one of the main singers as he came off stage after singing one of his fast and furious comedy songs with loads of lyrics.

19
EVERYTHING'S NOT ALRIGHT

NOT EATING

I was still going to the gym every day, sometimes before work from May –July 2015. My sister-in-law was staying with us, and it was Ramadan- the Muslim month of fasting. I was still going to my weekly slimming class. It was easy to cheat and not eat. No-one in the house noticed that I wasn't eating properly because they weren't eating between sunrise and sunset. The more I didn't eat, the more my stomach shrunk and when I did eat I didn't have to eat much before I felt full. No-one at the slimming club realised I was not eating properly and awarded me stickers and prizes and praise for losing a lot of weight. I liked the praise and attention.

CAN IT GET ANY WORSE?

It was July 2015. My sight had got worse, the anxiety was worse, my short-term memory was at an all-time low, empathy had gone, and a great dark cloud seemed to follow me everywhere. I couldn't shake it. I couldn't work.

The insomnia was terrible, and my husband moved downstairs. He had had enough.

I went every two weeks to the doctors. They diagnosed depression, and I started CBT (cognitive behaviour therapy) sessions. Although the counsellor was patient and supportive, the counselling didn't help. It just made me more determined to prove I was not going mad and this was a more than just feeling down or depressed. I stopped teaching and nearly everything else- the washing, the ironing, the cooking, the cleaning and the looking after of the children. I felt nothing, no emotions. When my daughter's nose was running, I remember just staring at it and not saying anything. When my mum's feet were covered in sore blisters, I felt nothing. Those two memories were so vivid yet stirred nothing in me. It is hard to describe the feeling of emptiness of nothing, but I remember that feeling so well and can understand others who are experiencing this. It doesn't last, yet at the time you have no idea how long it will last, and you want it to stop. You continuously are questioning yourself and thoughts, ugly horrible thoughts are in your head constantly, and you want relief, for it to all go away. If I wasn't so strong, I could have easily succumbed to these negative thoughts and not be here today.

I had no urge to do any of the things I liked doing; going to boot sales, shopping, sewing, playing Scrabble, or visiting friends. I didn't even enjoy eating or even simple things like blackberry picking or reading a magazine. The days were empty, and I felt nothing at all.

BILLY ELLIOT

The only easy task I could do apart from shower and sleep was to drive to the station and catch the train to take my daughter to London Victoria so that she could perform in the musical Billy Elliot. I would then and either watch the show or chat to the mums there in a local coffee shop all evening. Maybe it was escapism or the fact that it was an incredibly long show so killed three hours of my time. I was tired of waiting to feel better. Three hours could disappear in the blink of an eye. I don't know, but I didn't have any feelings or motivation to do anything else. The mums of the children had no idea what I was going through. I kept quiet.

If you've not watched the film or the musical, Billy Elliot is about a boy who likes dancing- particularly ballet, hairy miners, the miner's strike, individuality, politics and it is set in County Durham. It wasn't a story that I thought would appeal to me so much, but it's about determination and prejudice. The music is catchy, and there are some fantastic solo dances and large ensemble dance numbers. There are some intense scenes involving riot shields and police sirens, and in contrast, there are some very quiet emotional scenes where you can hear a pin drop.

THE ALARM

Earlier in the year, towards the beginning of H.'s run, in one of the quietest and most important scenes in the show, my friend's son's mobile phone went off. We were sitting in the second row, and although the phone was switched off, it had an alarm to alert the user that the battery was low. The alarm sound was of cartoon cats and dogs fighting with each other, and it was loud. It was so embarrassing that it became funny. The conductor looked over, and later the actors said that they had heard it too. I remember shifting the other way as if I wasn't sitting with him or didn't know him. His mum was in tears of embarrassment. Nearby patrons were disturbed, but I think they saw the funny side, especially as it went off again a few minutes later.

Of course, I enjoyed watching my daughter and her friends in the show but during the summer of 2015 my health suddenly took a turn for the worst. The weight was dropping off too quickly, and I was starting to look gaunt. I didn't care. I had no energy to care.

I tried hard to try and work things out for myself and visited the doctor. He just said I had to wait and started me on anti-depressant tablets. I waited. I was getting no better.

My parents came down and took over, and I retreated to my room. I was tired but not lazy. It was tiredness that was worse than jetlag which I had had several times before. It was tiredness of the mind too. Everything ached, and it was easier to lie still and do nothing. The only thing that got me up was the knowledge that I had to get my daughter to the West End show in time. Even breathing was an effort.

NO SLEEP

As a student I stayed up relatively late watching films, chatting, partying or writing up an essay, but I still managed to get some hours sleep even if just a couple. There was one occasion when I had no sleep at all, and I felt genuinely dreadful the next day.

After an exhausting day in Marrakech, Morocco exploring the city my husband and I tried to book into a hotel. Unfortunately, it appeared that no hotel would accept us as a married couple unless they had a stamped copy of our marriage certificate. Luckily we had brought our certificate to Marrakesh along with our passports and had to go to the police station to get it stamped. It was a precaution to stop western women from getting into any problematic situations, but we got into our room late.

As I pulled back the bed sheet, I saw what looked like a beetle or giant spider. I screamed and asked N. to get it.

He couldn't find it.

I am generally not afraid of insects, but this one was huge and had a chunky body and moved quickly. We stripped the bed and looked everywhere. Nothing. There were only a few pieces of furniture in the room, and I lifted and checked everything. There was no sign of a beetle.

It was very late, and N. was pretty fed up. He hadn't seen the beetle and doubted its existence. I had seen it. I tentatively got into the bed but sat bolt upright. What if it came back?

N. went to sleep, and I stayed on the lookout. Directly in front of me was a mirror. It wasn't particularly a great sight, I'd burnt my nose in the sun, and my hair was a bit wild, but as I sat staring at myself, a giant beetle calmly came out from behind the mirror and crawled across the wall. N. has woken up rather abruptly, and the beast was sent on its way out of the window. My heart was beating fast. I was now looking for its brother or sister in the bed. I tried to sleep but kept imagining beetles in the bed.

Then the roosters started crowing. On top of lots of the houses roosters and chickens were kept, and as the window was wide open because of the heat, I listened to the crowing. It stopped just as quickly as it started.

I tried to sleep. Then the call to prayer started, but not just from the minaret nearby. There seemed to be a chorus of calls from all around the city, and it was loud.

Then the city awoke. Cars, delivery vans, crashes and bangs, people beginning their day. There were all sorts of sounds. The busy streets were filling.

The hotel was stirring, and then our alarm went off.

I felt like death warmed up.

SICILY AUGUST 1990

This story is about the sort of tiredness that is caused by heat exhaustion.

I had spent the morning on the beach in Taormina but had spent my cable car money to get back up to the town on a drink. I would take the road. Unfortunately, there was no pedestrian access to the road and the only way back up to the town if not going by cable car was a steep mountain path. In the midday sun, I stupidly decided to take the path. It was silly especially with no water, but I thought it would be quick, and I could go and get water from the fountain in the town square. Every bone in my body ached. My mouth was dry, and I felt dizzy. I have no idea how I made it up the mountain, but I didn't want to be found in a beach dress. It was not how I planned to exit the world! The sound of the crickets echoed in my ears, and

I forced one foot to go in front of the other as I climbed the path. I did make it, but it's all about learning from mistakes. I learnt a lot that day, not just about my stupidity but also about an inner strength that I seemed to have.

A MOOSE IN THE HOOSE AUGUST 2015

I had scary mood swings. My parents were worried. I had violent outbursts and wanted to stay by myself with absolutely no responsibilities. I saw a different doctor who ran blood tests. I was diagnosed with bipolar disorder due to severe B12 deficiency, but no extra medication was given. It was just a label. So basically I was no nearer getting better. It explained why I had outbursts though. I just had to continue on the anti-depressant tablets and give them time to work.

I thought I was safer in my room out of the way than annoying everyone. I felt completely numb and empty. The hallucinating at night was getting worse. I opened my bedroom window one night to let an eagle out that I thought was there and then I saw a moose.

When telling people there was a moose in my bedroom, I smile. It is so random and bizarre, but in my mind on that night it was true- a huge hairy Canadian elk like moose was standing looking at me by the window.

I had always been interested in dreams. I kept a dream diary from the 1990s, and as soon as I woke up, I wrote it down. I then cross-referenced themes and objects with my dream books. However, most of my dreams were adventures. People from my life were always in them, and I was the main character.

I had recurring dreams where my teeth crumbled or fell out, and lots of dreams where I was late for something or couldn't walk fast or was blind. Sometimes I would wake up and take a few moments to work out whether the dream was true or not.

The worst dream I had was a few days before my degree result, and I dreamt I had failed, with believable reactions from my friends and family. It took a while to realise it wasn't true and my mood was one of disappointment.

THE DARKEST HOUR

I went to watch Gary Oldman portray Winston Churchill in the film The Darkest Hour. It was such a powerful film, and I came away feeling very patriotic and wanting to give him a big hug. He had to make huge decisions in 1940 when the odds were stacked against Great Britain, and there was so much pressure on him from his fellow members of the War Cabinet and Parliament, but he came through, and he stood up to Hitler and led the Allies to victory. He did it going through depression.

Churchill referred to his depression as his 'black dog'. A lovely friend bought me the book "I Had a Black Dog" by M.Johnstone and the cartoons described how I felt. There was also a partner book of cartoons for relatives of people going through depression which explained again in cartoons what to say to someone with depression and what they were feeling. They were simple pictures yet scarily accurate. Obviously what I was feeling wasn't unique and others before me had recorded their mood. I identified with the black dog analogy. Sometimes there wasn't a reason why the "dog" or depression appeared, it just sort of came along and as it says in the book "Having a black dog in your life isn't so much about feeling a bit down, sad or blue. At its worst, it's about being devoid of feeling altogether".

A SAFE PLACE

I continued to go and watch Billy Elliot. To me, the theatre was another safe place. Unfortunately, people complained that I was watching the show a lot and saw me at the stage door a lot. I used to travel home with one of the cast members as we shared the journey. People thought I was weird.

My daughter had a 6-month contract with Billy Elliot which ended in September. Although disappointed that she was too tall for her character, she had been cast in the touring version of the show which was due to start rehearsing in December. She was so excited, and I thought I'd be better by then to take her to rehearsals.

I was told in November that it was for the best that she didn't go on the tour. My health was a concern. The company knew I was suffering from depression and didn't think I would be up to it. They also were concerned that I was watching the show a lot and didn't understand.

That day was the darkest ever, and I don't know how I found the strength to come home from London and tell her she wasn't going on tour. I sat on London Bridge desperately wanting and needing help. Not to make light of this situation but it was worse than telling her I had destroyed her amazing Hama bead design when the iron had stuck to it.

I could completely identify with people who just stood on rooftops or even took their children with them in a sad suicide. The person depressed knew that they would cause heartbreak and upset to their children and couldn't bear that, so took them with them to save them the hurt and the pain. It was the same in some shocking acts where gunmen took the lives of their parents. It wasn't necessarily a cruel, selfish senseless act, but one where they had considered their actions for a long time and to them this was the only solution.

Of course, I'm not condoning any of these people's actions for one minute; I'm just saying as I have been there and for a short moment I knew exactly what they were feeling. It is desperately sad and although not a cry for help, help is urgently needed at that stage. I didn't have help as such, but I texted and phoned close friends as I wandered around London. I found the strength from somewhere, and I did return home. A good friend came round for support, and I did tell my daughter.

There were checks about my mental state. Every time I went for a CBT session I had to tick boxes on a clipboard. But I was clever; I knew I would be sent away if I ticked the box that I felt I was a danger to myself or others, so I didn't ever tick it. It was all an act.

I then spent nearly three months hardly ever leaving my bedroom.

H. was my carer now, my parents had returned home, and I was left alone to try and figure out what was going on inside my head. I wasn't a mum. I just existed. Each day I would take took my medication as instructed and wait for a difference, some sign that things were going to get better. It came, but not until well into the New Year.

20

THE BUTTERFLY YEARS

I was still regularly walking round to the doctors. There was such a turnover of GPs in the practice that I saw someone different nearly every visit. On this occasion, in December 2015 a doctor took an interest in my case and sat quietly reading my notes in front of me.

"Have you had blood tests taken?" she asked still scrolling up and down the screen. She asked me about everything, eyesight, hearing, tingling feeling and ten days later sitting her in her practice room, she told me about Pernicious Anaemia caused by severely low B12 levels. I recognised the low B12 reference; this had been flagged up by the MIND doctor who had diagnosed me as bipolar, yet no medication was prescribed. No letter had been sent from MIND to my GP. Later when I followed this up, it was revealed that the MIND doctor that had seen me was just a locum and had only worked there a few weeks and although his notes had been sent to me, they had been lost in the system somewhere and therefore no B12 tests had been ordered nor indeed had any B12 been prescribed.

This new doctor was upbeat and positive and told me that the deficiency was caused by having Pernicious Anaemia. My body was unable to absorb B12 from food. But there was some hope and a way of alleviating this. I needed loading doses of six B12 injections over two weeks and then top up injections every 12 weeks for life. I was also prescribed strong vitamin D tablets, folic acid tablets, iron tablets and vitamin D sprays.

JANUARY 2016

Almost immediately after the first loading dose, my eyesight returned, and the shaking and tremors stopped in my arms. As quickly as my eyesight had deteriorated, it got better. It was unbelievable. It meant I could finally go on my phone and read, sew and even watch the television; although I had missed all my favourite soap operas and so didn't bother catching up with them.

My energy levels got better, and I was able to leave my safe place; my room, for more extended periods. I started meeting up with old friends and driving more. Things were definitely getting better but it was awkward, and there were still some friends that I couldn't face and some that I wanted to see but had not been in touch.

I felt like a caterpillar that had been in a cocoon for ages and was now a butterfly just learning how to spread her wings.

It took a little longer for my feelings to return, but they did.

MEMORIES

Spending so much time on my own gave me a lot of time to think. I liked my own company, and as my memories returned, I wrote them down and tried to remember the smallest of details. I also contacted people that had made a difference in my life and let them know.

I read my diaries, and I tried to relive funny stories. I needed to laugh again, to feel again. I had almost lost my children, and things were now very strained with N. There had been nothing to laugh about for months.

LAUGHING OUT LOUD

My funniest and favourite story has to be a day spent in Oxford while on a University Madrigal Choir Tour. We were a group of sixteen singers that travelled by minibus singing in cathedrals and churches. We performed a capella concerts of madrigals, part songs and sacred works wearing our red gowns and staying with host families.

On this day I was able to pop in and see my grandmother who lived in Oxford. She had saved and presented me a red and cream polyester dress with thick belt and fine pattern- very much like the ones they were in the co-op in the 1970s complete with little pearl buttons, a long collar and breast pockets. It was truly hideous but so as not to offend I tried it on. My grandma then gave me some 1930s black patent shoes to complete the outfit. They were so old that when you walked the shiny patent leather cracked.

I decided to wear the combo into the city centre to meet the rest of the choir. I wasn't embarrassed, and I remember my grandmother's happy face as I waved to her as I headed off down the street, shoes cracking as I went. The choir were not sure what to make of my outfit. I had a photo-shoot in front of some parked cars pretending to be one of the sexy ladies sprawled across posh cars in the adverts.

One of my friends said I looked so sexy he would like to take me for a picnic somewhere. We walked around the town centre but it was milling with tourists, and as students, we didn't have the funds to go anywhere glamorous. We bought a cheap sandwich, packet of crisps and a drink and sat in the middle of a roundabout on our own "private island". It was safe, and we weren't disturbed. It was a little bit of paradise for the 35 minutes we were there. Although possibly we may have distracted some drivers, there were "no picnics" signs on the roundabout, so we merrily ate our lunch.

That night I sang in a local cathedral with The Madrigal Group. As the conductress conducted an intricate part-song, her eyes travelled to my feet. I saw her clock my shiny shoes and then stifle a giggle. As the song finished and the sound of the voices faded away, I gave a little squeak from my shoes, and we completely fell about. I wasn't allowed to wear them for the second half of the concert.

Everyone has days that they look back on and smile- this is mine. I cried so much with laughter that day, and so did my friends. I didn't care what anyone thought of me, I sang beautiful music in a beautiful church, and I had lunch on my special island with a good friend. That was one of my precious memories that I had lost and now was getting back.

B12 DEFICIENT

Finally, I had something to explain what had been going on with me. I had a medical disorder, Pernicious Anaemia. If B12 levels are left undiagnosed to run low, they can cause manic depression, obsession and psychotic behaviour along with nearly every single other symptom that I had been to the doctors about for the past 11 years. Some vegans are warned of the dangers as their diet sometimes lacks B12. I had never heard of the deficiency. My Vitamin D deficiency was obvious- poor teeth, brittle nails, fuzzy hair and the love of the sun and tablets could replace some of the vitamins I needed.

I also read that common symptom of low B12 caused not by diet but by the body's inability to absorb B12 was tiredness and pins and needles in the arms and hands. I had these symptoms.

My long term memory returned within a few weeks, and my short term memory gradually got better though there has been neurological damage so some things won't ever be the same.

The pins and needles and sore tongue were better but still present. I was still "wuddling my murds" and the mood swings although better would sometimes come out of the blue and take over completely. I was sleeping for longer periods at night but woke with such extreme tiredness that sometimes I couldn't move. It was very hard not to feel bitter or angry, but I was just pleased that I could finally feel something. It was going to take a few injections and time, but definitely, my life was going in a more positive direction.

To this day I still say it was watching Billy Elliot and the friendships of some loyal friends that kept me going and gave me strength (and of course the strength of my character), but nevertheless some people will never understand what I went through or how I felt or even why I acted as I did. That's fine; I don't need those people close to me.

SEEING THE LIGHT

A return visit to Dance Excellence in California March 2016 had mostly been paid for before I became ill. There were times when I thought I would never be able to accompany my daughter and the group from her dance centre, but I fortunately I was.

I had a fabulous time going on all the rides and pretending I was five years old again. Disney is like marmite, you either love it or you hate it. I was a fan, and the day was made even better with the performance of my daughter's dance school on the Fantasy Stage and the bumping into Robbie Williams with his family. Although obviously on a private visit, I did manage to say 'have a nice day' as he went past and he smiled at me.

Returning from the Disneyland Park at 11 pm to the hotel I switched on my light up trainers. These were black shoes that flashed in different colours. I'd bought them myself a few months earlier for Christmas. I liked them. The adults I was with all laughed at me. They were embarrassed and asked why I was wearing them?

If you couldn't wear light up shoes walking home from the most magical place on the earth, then when and where else could you wear them? I wasn't embarrassed. I saw the light in those few moments. A real friend would laugh with me and not at me. I wasn't going to take them off. It made me more determined to do from then on what I wanted to do. I loved those shoes, and I still do. I felt confident enough to let them flash. No one was going to dull my sparkle!

TROUBLE AT HOME

My husband never understood my depression and wasn't supportive in the way that I would have liked. I lost friends and gained new ones. I must have been a nightmare to know in those few months, but some people stuck it out including my children, although they didn't get the choice. In March I was well enough to go to that American dance trip, and by June I felt ready to go back to work. It had taken a year, but I was ready.

Unfortunately, not everyone at my work understood what I had been through. Some colleagues-not everyone- had not even contacted me to see how I was. They resented me taking time off and going on holiday as they saw it when they were covering my classes. They told me posting my holiday photos on social media 'wasn't one of my brightest ideas'. However, I was on sick leave monitored closely by doctors, and other professionals and part of my rehabilitation was facing the public again and doing things for myself. The holidays weren't either in term time. Teaching is a team profession; I couldn't and wouldn't work there with people who thought like that, so I resigned.

I stifled my pride too and signed on at the job centre. I wanted a challenge, something different and I told the careers officer that although I was grateful for the jobs he was suggesting -in the local sorting office and the retail field, I would hold out and go for interviews in schools nearby. There weren't many jobs vacant as it was the wrong time of the year and it was difficult not earning. It reminded me of student days again, and we got by. By now the three of us were in a routine, and it was working.

My husband had moved out, and I felt free and happy for the first time in a long time.

A job opportunity did come up. I needed a challenge, and I got one, and to this day I still have that challenge with new and wonderful colleagues and amazing children.

My daughter was not too disappointed as it happened not to go on the Billy Elliot tour. She wanted her mum healthy more than performing. But things happen for a reason, and an opportunity did come her way. Bigger and better, she was cast in July 2016 into the West End musical Matilda as one of the children. Not working meant I could take her to and fro rehearsals and on the stage was where my daughter was happiest.

KILLING TIME

There were a lot of hours to kill in London. Fortunately, spending so much time in bed in 2015, I learnt how not to be bored and how to relax and pass the time patiently. Previously I could never sit and do nothing, whether it be reading the cereal box while eating breakfast or writing a shopping list watching the TV.

In London, I liked to sit, and people watch or walk through new streets. I took Phoebe with me most days and found lots of dog cafes. Wimbledon and the Rio Olympics were on, so on dry days, I sat with some of the "Matilda mums" in deckchairs watching the sport on big screens. I also did a lot of sunbathing- a great way of killing time. On the first day of meeting all the new mums I was lying on the grass, and a mum said to me,

"You're just like a hippo!"

There was a very awkward pause, particularly as I had just met this lady and we were about to spend ten long weeks together. She then suddenly looked very embarrassed and blurted out that she meant camel and not a hippo. The camel reference is due to the act that I hadn't moved from the grass all day and hadn't needed the toilet!

I also watched a lot of films.

LEICESTER SQUARE JULY 2016

On the day that I watched the latest Bridget Jones film, Leicester Square was getting ready for the film premiere of Girl on the Train with Emily Blunt. When I went into the neighbouring cinema, the barriers were going up, and people were starting to mill around.

When I came out, a train track had been built, and the stage and big video screens and lights were up. It was quite exciting. I asked the security guard if I could watch from the barrier and he said no problem.

I waited for two hours, and then the stars started coming down the red carpet. I had a perfect view and saw Emeli Sande, Stanley Tucci and various X Factor finalists. I listened to various interviews hosted by Edith Bowman and oohed and aahed at Emily Blunt's dress. I then needed to go and pick up my daughter from the Matilda theatre. The guard said I wasn't to move until everyone had come down the carpet. How long world that takes I asked. I had about 15 minutes before the chaperones would get cross.

"About an hour, hour and a half", he said.

I was trapped.

He wasn't going to change his mind, and I started panicking a bit. Theatre companies have a strict pickup and drop off times. I couldn't be late. I had to hatch a plan.

I texted a "Matilda mum" to phone me and then loudly pretended that I was needed urgently at the theatre because my daughter was ill. It worked. Once again my acting skills were on point. I was led through the barrier and down the red carpet. I was walking in my cropped trousers and flip-flops and carrying a plastic supermarket bag- tres chic.

I walked down the red carpet, occasionally looking up at bewildered fans trying to work out who I was and then rather than turn into the cinema I headed out through the barrier and bombed it round to the theatre- and got there in time.

A NEW YEAR

2017 started well with a new job in a grammar school teaching history. It was the dream job, and I was determined to enjoy every day. I made a new set of resolutions and was going to do my best to stick to them.

My B12 deficiency was being treated with injections, and although still was the cause of some symptoms, it was manageable. In an ideal world, I would get injections more frequently than every 12 weeks. My mood dipped a little bit around weeks 7-8, but in the UK the injections are only licensed for every 3months. On the internet, you could buy the kits to self inject, and in other countries, the injections were available in closer intervals. I was just wary about self-injecting and decided I would just put up with the fatigue and the pins and needles. After all, it was so much better than before.

I had to try and stop feeling so angry that my deficiency had not been picked up sooner. I had almost lost everything. The girls' schools were involved, and social services knew what was going on. Fortunately, they did not intervene. I had told every doctor that I had seen that I thought my condition was physical and not mental, but I wasn't taken seriously. I was continually told that it was depression and I just had to wait it out as my body adjusted to the different strengths of medication.

We all know our bodies and my eyesight had got worse "overnight". I can still hear the optician telling me that my sight had gone due to my age and that it would get worse as I got older. He didn't buy the overnight story.

My memory had returned, and I was more positive about things. I certainly didn't want to return to the dark days of autumn 2015. However there were still some little things that I was doing or saying that were a bit odd, but mostly things were going in the right direction, and I loved my new job. The murd wuddling was reduced to saying things like "par cark" for a car park, and I had just the occasional complete mind blank.

SNEEP ALEEKTION

Despite my returned memory, when an Australian teacher came into my classroom in the summer of 2017 as I was packing away and announced excitedly that there was going to be a "sneep aleektion", I was intrigued. I had no idea what that was. He asked the class to raise their hands if they hadn't heard of a 'sneep aleektion'. I hadn't a clue, but I'm so glad I didn't show my ignorance and raise my hand, as it soon became clear he was talking about Prime Minister Theresa May's call for a 'snap election'. I hadn't tuned in to his accent!

NO MORE N.

Although incredibly personal, my marriage ended in the arrival of the Decree Absolute on 10 July 2017. There is nothing funny or embarrassing about this. It is sad after all we went through to be together, but obviously, there's a lot that is personal and can't be put in print. It was for the best, and I was going to be just fine on my own.

21
WHEN PHOEBE MET FOOBIE

DECEMBER 2017

Full of white stuffing, my 'foobie' or fake boobie was a tempting target for my dog.

Phoebe, my two-year-old pug, planned her attack one morning, stole it from the table and proceeded to launch a full-scale attack on it. It went from being a G cup to more a D cup in five short minutes. There is also no bargaining with a dog when she has it in her mouth. The art is to try and ignore her as if you're not bothered; otherwise, she thinks it's a game, sins her teeth into even more and bolts for it. I've lost count the times I've had to think like a dog and identify the hiding places for a foobie around the house. Fortunately, Phoebe hasn't learnt how to bury it in the garden.

THE PUG LIFE

My youngest daughter was pug mad. Her room was a shrine to pugs and had wanted one for my five years. The day before her 13th birthday in May 2016, I was sitting in the garden and thought to myself, if we had a pug it would be me who would be looking after it. I wandered around the house seriously looking at our space and whether a dog could lead a happy life with us.

I phoned a local breeder who had pedigree pugs for sale and said: "talk me out of buying one of your pugs!" I wanted to know the advantages and disadvantages of owning one. The breeder approved of me, and despite it being a birthday present, she was happy to sell a pug to me the next day. She also gave me a list of things to buy for the new arrival.

I didn't think about how embarrassing it was to pick up your children from the gates of a secondary school. I was only thinking of how both my daughters would react to this tiny bundle of fur that I was carrying so proudly.

They were both speechless. It was the emotion when you are too happy and too shocked to speak. It didn't happen often. The puppy was named Phoebe after one of the US Friends' characters and was an utter joy to have at home. So not Monica or Rachel, she was to be named Phoebe. I smiled to myself as I remembered age 14 or 15 reading a whole set of trashy American High School teen romance books and one of the main characters was Phoebe; only I had never heard of the name and had read it as "Foeber" throughout the whole set of books!

I sat on the kitchen floor with Phoebe on my lap thinking 'what on earth had I done?' there was no midwife to call for advice. I had never been an animal person. We were going to have to make it up. The weather was ideal to start puppy training outdoors. I had to take my daughter to rehearsals in London for Matilda every day, and Phoebe was going to get her first ride on a train, and a tube, and a bus. Phoebe would also feature in some memorable embarrassing stories that summer.

BLACKBERRY PICKING

I love blackberry picking. It's so worth the nettle stings and thorn scrapes and stained hands for the tub of blackberries. While I was walking Phoebe, I came across a bush that no-one had picked already. The only thing I had to collect them in was one of Phoebe's unused dog poo bags. As I went around the park, I ate some of the berries. It was only later that I realised whey people were staring me. I was eating straight from a poo bag!

THE STATION

One hot summer's day I was dropping my daughter off at the train station to be taken to dance rehearsals by another mum. I had taken Phoebe with me for the company to ride in the car. There was a standstill on the motorway, and I ended up taking my daughter and the dog on the fast train to London myself. It wasn't ideal, but the children had to attend the rehearsals on time, and it would only be letting down the team if they were late. Purchasing an expensive peak time ticket and carrying a dog without a lead or treats or doggy bags, I made my way to London.

Fortunately, all went well, and Phoebe behaved. Walking back to my car parked in the furthest and cheapest car park, I put Phoebe down to walk next to me. It was a hot morning, and I was tired of carrying Phoebe. She began trotting nicely next to me up the road which was one long hill. When we got to the top, she turned around and started running back down the hill. She wasn't good at recall yet and certainly if you chased her she would run further away. She was on the road, although I was more upset possibly about the fact that she had gone down the hill that I had just struggled up! I panicked. What if a car came? I had to attract the puppy's attention somehow, so I lay down like a starfish in the middle of the road making a strange wailing noise with my eyes almost shut.

It worked. I opened my eyes and could see Phoebe was interested and coming my way. I closed my eyes again. When I could feel her right next to me, I pounced and grabbed her. I surprised Phoebe, and I also surprised a couple of bemused passersby further down the road.

I couldn't be cross, Phoebe was only a puppy, and as I sat in the middle of the road on that hot summer morning, I hadn't the energy to explain to the passers-by what I was doing so just smiled, got up and carried on walking, dog in arms.

ST. PANCRAS STATION AUGUST 2016

My daughter, Phoebe and I were walking through St. Pancras station on our way to catch the 5.10 pm commuter train back home. We were admiring the glass ceiling and the sparkly white floor. International students were sitting on suitcases and people playing the pianos on the concourse. Cafes were filled with travellers, and there was a general feeling of calm, in contrast to the underground. It was then that Phoebe stopped, squatted and 'exploded'!

My daughter was so embarrassed that she stood rooted to the spot. I looked in my bag for something, anything to clear the explosion up with. I had nothing. My daughter had nothing. There was no way that we could walk on. I looked around for any member of staff that could help. We were outside shops by now, not a pile of serviettes to be seen — no yellow warning sign to stand up. No offers of help from passersby either.

At that moment I made a split decision, possibly not one anyone else would have made, but I was both desperate and embarrassed. I took off my favourite cardigan and mopped the mess up as best I could in a big sweeping movement. I then quickly put the soiled cardigan straight into my bag. For security reasons, there were no bins to be seen. What else could I do? We did not look around us, just carried on walking to the platform.

The commuter train home was packed, standing room only and very hot. I was carrying a bag that slowly everyone on the carriage became aware of. I was so embarrassed that I was crying with laughter. It hurt with crying. As people got on the train, you could see them sniffing and grimacing. The smell was truly horrendous. I should have binned my cardigan, but it was my favourite.

Luckily it came up like new, after a wash or three.

THE RECOVERY

I was recovering well from my mastectomy but unsure whether I still had cancer. In just a tiny amount of skin there are over one million cells, so in all likelihood, at least one had escaped. I was to have another type of treatment. The question at the back of my mind was what?

I joined a few Facebook groups and internet Forums which gave me some answers and some strength in the small hours of the morning. The members were mainly American, and I was now a Powerball, a Pink Sister, a 'mom with courage'. I could be all these people too from the safety of my bed.

My scars were 'tiger stripes'. I was a big cat. I was fearless. No, I was pretty terrified.

I received another knitted boob or knocker in the post. It came wrapped in tissue and with a label saying it had been hand-knitted with love. It did feel it had been knitted for me. It was a myriad of colours and an exact fit. I ordered a similar aqua boob in acrylic too for the water. I had no idea these things existed. Only later did I find pages of designer boobettes and falsies on the internet.

My friends, family and colleagues had and have been very supportive. I made sure I updated them with how I was getting on and with my "Tackle the Tumour with Humour," mantra, I updated my Facebook status daily:

December 2nd 2017: Just Feeling a Right Tit Now

"I wonder if I could win both the first and the last prize if I entered a wet t-shirt competition."

"I'm fed up with all this talk of breast cancer and these mastectomy jokes; they're not funny.

Glad I've got that off my chest now!"

ENTERING NEW YEAR WITH STYLE

New Year's Eve I awoke shivering and my eyes hurt to open. My head also felt like it was exploding.

I knew I had to get to A&E and so I packed a mini bag for the long wait including a pillow for the hard plastic chairs in the waiting room. I couldn't change out of my pyjamas but changed shoes and pulled on a dressing gown. My best friend drove me, and I moaned quietly as my head was pounding.

Even though A & E was busy, I was seen quickly, and it soon became evident that I was fighting an infection. They treated me for viral meningitis, and I was given IV antibiotics and painkillers. The hospital was getting busier. I lay on a trolley still in A& E as there were no beds yet and the headache was getting worse. On a scale of one to ten, I would put the headache at 9.75. I had suffered from stress headaches and migraines and tension headaches, but this was like nothing else I had experienced.

The hospital was extremely busy, and it wasn't until very late that I got a room on the ward. I couldn't read my watch or phone but heard the night staff doing the countdown and wishing each other a happy new year. This was only the second New Year spent without family, and it was horrible, painful, lonely and sad.

"HAPPY 2018 TO ME!"

The next day my bloods had gone from 5 to 277, and I had also developed cellulitis. My skin was red and hot, but they couldn't give me the right antibiotics until the previous ones had finished. I was just glad to see the headache go away. My eyes grew less sensitive to light, and the Tramadol tablets seemed to ease the pain.

In the afternoon I watched how the two hand sanitizer machines, the paper towel dispenser and the poster in front of me in my side room, morphed into the Presidents of the USA like Mount

Rushmore. I called for the nurse, and she explained that Tramadol could cause me to hallucinate. Too right! She told me to think of something nice and to rest.

I thought of returning home to Phoebe. I imagined her running to greet me. We were both so happy, and her little tail was wagging. I calmly took a large box of matches out from my pocket and set her alight! Yes, I was now hallucinating setting fire to my dog.

I sat up bolt upright. I needed to stop taking these tablets. No wonder you can't take Tramadol into some foreign countries. They gave me shortness of breath too, and I had to go back on oxygen.

My temperature was high, blood pressure high and pain just about under control.

I was on an orthopaedic ward (no idea why), and as I sat on the seat in the shower with a dribble of lukewarm water on me surrounded by a stark white shower curtain, I remembered a previous shower curtain incident.

THE SHOWER CURTAIN INCIDENT
Staying in a Bed and Breakfast in Solihull on a University Swimming Competition weekend, I was horrified to see the amount of mould growing on the shower curtain. It was black and green, and it was impossible to shower with it there, so I wrapped the shower curtain over the top of the rail dislodging enough dust and grime to sink a battleship. It came down on to my head. As I shouted out a few expletives, the fire alarm went off. I grabbed a towel and followed other residents out as although the fire escape procedures were laminated and on the walls, I hadn't read them. I was a source of amusement and thankfully not the only one caught in the shower, but I was the only one whose hair was white with dust having been in the shower!

THE BEDPAN

After my mastectomy and node removal, I was connected to various drips and machines. I pressed the buzzer for the nurse and asked if I could get up to use the toilet. I wasn't allowed to, and so I was brought a bedpan. In all my years of life, I had never used a bedpan, and after a while, I realised it was going to be harder than using a 'She-wee' in the car in a traffic jam!

I slid the thick cardboard pan underneath and then stared at the ceiling. How on earth is it possible to go lying flat? This was almost impossible. I couldn't sit up, and I couldn't use my elbows to prop myself up. I got the giggles and then went. I had the distinct impression and feeling that I was sitting in it and I pressed the buzzer again. Yes, I was sitting in it, and the nurse in blue said that I had 'weed' for England. I leant over to get a baby wipe and wondered how was going to dry myself. To my horror, the nurse scooped up the plastic bed protector and used it in its crumpled form to wipe and dry me. I was sure that wasn't meant to happen, and it happened so quickly. I was still holding my baby wipe and was so shocked that I said nothing.

To be on the safe side, I didn't go on it again, and the next day I unplugged everything and used the en suite.

A TALE OF TWO NIGHTIES

The beds on the ward were fancy with controls to raise the legs and the head but were plastic underneath. With my regular hot flushes, I was regularly stuck to the bed.

I asked my daughter to bring in a nightie. She packed two, one extra, except they were both long sleeved satin pyjama tops. When I asked her why she hadn't packed a nightie, she said the tops were huge and like nighties on her!

However, the best and most excruciatingly embarrassing nightie story occurred in August 2016.

We have lovely neighbours where we live, always popping over with runner beans or jam or to collect a parcel. They are used to me taking the bins out in my pyjamas or screaming like a banshee barefooted chasing an escaped dog down the road. However, I am not sure my neighbours were prepared for the vision that presented them that August morning.

The fuel button on my car had flashed up empty a few days before. I was looking forward to a lie-in. I had told the girls I wasn't driving anywhere in the morning.

One daughter was late for school, and the other was late for work experience. It wasn't my fault; they were faffing about, on their phones and had wasted a lot of time. They each begged for a lift. You would have thought the world was ending with the amount of screeching and huffing when I said no, but reluctantly I agreed to take them both in separate journeys- just for an easier life. It's what mum's do!

I got out of bed wearing only a scruffy mixed wash nightie and put sandals not slippers on. I didn't even tame the hair. I drove one daughter to school and then collected the other from home to drop at the station. The girls were thankful merrily oblivious that I was going commando!

It was a hot sunny day, and about a quarter of a mile from home, the car spluttered and ran out of fuel. I knew exactly what was happening and managed to pull over to the side of the road. I'd just forgotten I had no fuel and their music was so loud in the car that I didn't hear the fuel button beep saying low.

I had no money, no phone and no knickers!

I had to walk home during the school run, to get my purse and phone. I remember pulling my nightie down for modesty reasons, and it made it look even more hideous at the front.

I swear it was the longest quarter of a mile ever and I spent the whole time cursing under my breath. I must have looked a real sight. I contemplated waving to the neighbours but thought better of it.

I got home, changed and phoned for assistance. That was yet another walk of shame that I had done.

MRSA?

I had spent one night on a ward after my mastectomy because of the risk of catching a virus. There was now a real risk of me picking something as there was a virus on the ward. I had to go home hurriedly, but it was fine. I had two nurses in the forms of my daughters and a pug at home.

I changed into my maternity jeans from 15 years previously. I was reasonably proud to still fit into them- even if they did have a large elasticated stretchy tummy bit! I was given a plastic bag full of tablets and my discharge papers. It was all a bit rushed but necessary. I was a bit apprehensive as I still didn't feel 100%

When I greeted Phoebe, I made sure I had no matches in my pocket! We were delighted to see each other. I may have been on boxes of medication- I took ten and a half tables daily to be exact, tablets but she was the best medicine I could ever have.

My medicine drawer was overflowing, and it was now that my daughters started compiling an A to Z of every ailment that I had ever had or suffered from! The finished list is Appendix II.

There's no place like home!

22

SHIRLEY VALENTINE

The summer of 2017 is when I penned most of these stories, before any mention of the C word. Using diaries and notebooks and my wonderful returned memory, I wrote down these stories under the Kentish and Spanish sun.

TENERIFE AUGUST 2017

I had gone on holiday on my own for two weeks. I had the desire, the confidence and the determination to start doing things my way. The girls were on holiday with N., so I went quite happily somewhere on my own.

While I was staying in the hotel in Tenerife more funny things were happening to me which only confirmed my belief that although this book would no doubt cause some embarrassment to my family, especially my children, it would also be an amusing read.

EASY PICKING

It seemed that it was alright for a man to holiday alone, he wasn't disturbed or talked about, but if you were a woman holidaying alone, then you had another agenda. I had hoped it was my suntan and glamorous attire that attracted attention, but I fear it wasn't. I heard some great chat up lines in various languages, but this one from a young man from England is perhaps the best of the bunch:

Him: Are you here alone?

Me: Yes

Him: Good, I gave up weed two weeks ago, and I need a woman!

I had a ball people-watching in the hotel. There was a mixture of nationalities. I felt a bit German as I laid my towel out on a sun-lounger before anyone else. I wanted first pick of the loungers not just for the all-day sun, but for the minimum amount of walking from lounger to the pool. The walk to the water's edge was when I was at my most self-conscious. I could feel eyes behind dark sunglasses all watching me. It was possibly worse than getting out of the pool and shivering back to the lounger- unless I had lost part of my bikini.

STUCK IN THE WATER

It was Sicily 1991, and I had dared to wear a red bikini into the sea. N. was waiting on the beach. I was doing the "jumping the waves thing" from about waist height as the waves were coming in strongly. They came so strong they whipped my bikini top from me and took it down to the water's edge. I was stuck. Modesty prevented me from coming out of the sea onto the packed water's edge where teenagers played paddle ball, and older men stood in their Speedos scanning the beach for easy prey.

N. was nowhere to be seen. He had taken himself up into the shade of the promenade. Despite coming from Morocco, he didn't enjoy the sun.

I'm convinced the beach became busier just as I wanted to come out. I tried to come out on all fours to distract attention. It wasn't at all like the Bond Girl moment when she emerged from the ocean. One last powerful wave and I had a face full of sand. That helped, at least I was partially covered, and I went on to do the "hot sand hop" quickly back to my towel. I dived on it headfirst and stayed there without daring to look up for a very long time. Well, at least until the beach had emptied a bit, the sun had gone in, and N. had come back to see how I was getting on sunbathing.

BEACH DAYS

In Tenerife meanwhile, I had no children, no partner, a lot of textbooks to read and some serious sunbathing to do. Lying on the sun lounger, I thought back to my childhood beach days.

Beach days in the 1970s/80s were full on major days out but secretly I enjoyed them. We were the family that brought the windbreak, sun loungers, air bed (no pump), chairs, soda-stream, Calor gas stove, cool box, buckets and spades, fishing nets, football, beach ball, cricket set, towels, beach mats, and two swimming costumes. Two costumes? Why?

I remember the hassle of changing into a dry costume and then wanting to go back in the sea and having no dry costume later, let alone waiting that hour after lunch to go back into the sea. That hour has to be the longest ever hour- even longer than the last hour of the school day on a Friday. All the stuff was brought down to the beach in shifts and then taken back more slowly at the end of the day.

No sand was allowed in the car.

You had to walk miles to the water's edge - the tide was always out -and gather water in a bucket for your feet. Wobbling, one footed washing your foot, drying it and then trying to put socks on and then fatally putting a wet foot on to the sand by mistake.

Sand was everywhere.

All in contrast with that one beautiful tanned woman in sunglasses that sat a few feet away from you, with one towel and a book.

Sand was in the car.

EUROPEAN HOLIDAYS

I still didn't understand why Europeans wore bikini bottoms with no backs, whatever size they were. There was possibly less fabric involved than on a thong. Maybe I was just jealous that I couldn't get the all over tan. Or perhaps I was saving the guests from a scary sight if I wore a pair.

I also felt a little left out in Tenerife that I didn't have a tattoo anywhere, so I drew a Kermit the Frog in biro on my arm just to fit in. It didn't matter what age or what nationality. It seemed everyone staying in my hotel was adorned with some paint, whether it was a massive tribute to their mum on their back or some squiggly motif on the ankle.

THE SUN LOUNGER

How is that I can never get comfy on a hotel sun-lounger? If they're plastic with slats, then I debate whether to pay the extra fee and get the foam padding that's been sweated on by hundreds of previous sleepers or stick with the plastic chair which then gets hotter and hotter throughout the day. Or do I get the toughened plastic one with the mesh-like cover? This sun-lounger can collapse at any moment spilling your drink everywhere or collapses flat so abruptly that you have to lay there pretending that you meant to do that.

It's also impossible to get comfortable on this type of lounger. If I lie on my back, everything lays like jelly, so you need one knee up to flatten the stomach, and then if I lay on my front, then my ankles and the top part of my feet hurt hanging over the end.

Then if I sleep on my side, I can't relax because I think I'm just going to tan on one side only so have to keep changing sides, and without a watch, it's just a guessing game. But looking around, everyone is lying perfectly still.

THE PRINCESS AND THE PEA

I have no idea why beds are so hard in hotels but possibly dependent on how cheap the holiday was. Anyway the first night I slept on my slab, I felt black and blue in the morning.

I love a soft mattress. I had two single beds in my room, so I piled them on top of each other finishing with two duvets.

It was far more comfortable. I left a note for the cleaner, or rather

I left a cartoon. The first matchstick person was drawn sleeping on the two single beds and was exclaiming "Ow!" with a miserable face. The second picture was of a matchstick me sleeping on the pile of beds and exclaiming "Ahhhhh!" with a happy face. It worked.

The cleaner made up my pile of mattresses and didn't inform the manager!

The funniest thing was when I was piling the beds up, apart from some euros; I found something that very much looked like a pea!

THE PEN

I was doing a lot of writing and had gone through four pens already. I was going on a trip up to a volcano crater and asked at the hotel's Reception to borrow a pen.

The two receptionists —an old and a young one looked at me. The old one said "No".

I laughed.

He didn't. He wasn't joking.

When I realised he wasn't joking I felt a bit awkward and tried again asking for a pen to do some writing.

The young one gave me the posh pen from his top pocket, his only fancy pen. I said thank you but could I have an old one if possible.

The old one said, "For how long?"

I said all day.

There was a standoff. I added that if I found a pen shop up the volcano, then I would buy another one to replace anyone they may give me.

They discussed this proposal in Spanish together, and the old one disappeared behind the back.

He emerged with an old plastic biro. Finally.

I said thank you and began to walk away. The old one then called after me, "Room number?"

It was unbelievable. I was to return the pen. It must have been a rare one or diamond encrusted or perhaps borrowed by Harrison Ford when he stayed in the hotel. I was trying not to laugh and spent the afternoon taking pictures of the pen in various locations, including on the edge of the volcano crater.

When I returned at almost midnight, I swear they were waiting for me. I handed back the biro in the hope they may say, keep it. But no, they took it away and crossed my name on the "pen borrowing list".

I told this story to some Belgian friends in the pool the next day. They were staying in a neighbouring hotel which had pens in the rooms. They grabbed a handful of pens and brought them to me as a present!

THE LADY IN THE CORRIDOR

I had begun to think I was staying in the Fawlty Towers hotel; there were so many things happening that were a little bizarre. This next story was no exception.

I couldn't sleep and went for a walk down to the buffet in the middle of the night. As I walked along the corridor on the third door, I could hear a lady moaning and groaning. She was doubled up near the lifts and talking in another language. I thought she was ill.

As I approached her, the moaning and groaning was getting more frequent. I tapped her on the shoulder to see if she was alright. She was on the phone. She stopped, angrily looked up and in no uncertain terms told me not very politely to "go away". The talking and moaning carried on.

I suddenly realised that she was one of those women that you can phone for a specific type of "conversation".

I was so embarrassed and quite relieved that I hadn't called Reception about a sick lady in the corridor!

AWKWARD

While in the pool I noticed a boy swimming out of his depth. He started going under, and I brought him back to the shallow end. Ten minutes later, the same thing happened again. There was a lifeguard, but I was nearest, and I pulled him back to safety.

The boy was African and spoke very little English.

I told the lifeguard in my mixture of Italian and French that this boy was swimming in deep water and to keep a beady eye on him. I then got out and went for a nap.

My sun lounger was at the back and well away from the cafe where the boy's mother was sitting on her phone.

I remember being awoken by something touching my legs. I opened my eyes to see a African boy sitting at the end of my lounger entirely covered in suntan cream. The cream had run in the sun. The boy- and his name I never knew, from the pool, was rubbing cream into my legs.

It took a while to register what was going on and then I looked around. This was awkward. I couldn't be angry, but that wasn't right. He wasn't speaking. I sort of said thank you and shooed him off the lounger in the direction of his mum.

I was very embarrassed. He couldn't have been more than 10 or 11. It was weird. I put my sarong on and went to find his mum. Her English wasn't brilliant, but the gist was that he thought I was burning in the sun. There was some more awkwardness. Should I be grateful- was this way of saying thank you?

It seemed that his mum had allowed him!

MESSY ROOM

I lost count of the number of times I lost things in my hotel room, especially the room key. There was only me and I had extra bed space with the two singles piled on top of each other. But my room was a tip. My recollections of all hotel rooms are of a mess and worse if sharing with the kids or sharing with the husband. There is a great need to empty everything from the suitcase into all the drawers, and then the 'floordrobe' takes shape and grows in quantity of items. Wet towels are drying on the balcony and the bathroom – once sparkly and white and a drop of every cosmetic in the sink.

When all my treatment is over, I'd like to go somewhere where the sea is turquoise, and you can see the sand at the bottom of the sea. I'd like to be served with orangey-red fruit cocktails with umbrellas in on a comfortable, non-collapsible sun-bed and do nothing.

23
KEEPING ABREAST OF THINGS

The wait from December 1st to the appointment with my consultant seemed to drag, despite all the Christmas activities and the surprise return visit to the hospital over New Year. It meant, however, that I could write more stories for this book and decide on what shape it was to take. Using my cancer 'journey' as they say on all reality TV shows, as a structure for writing this book seemed the best approach. It was like writing a novel that had no known ending. Some ladies suggest the journey is a train ride stopping at unknown stations along the way. You don't know how long you were to ride on the train and where you were going, let alone your final destination and you weren't even sure if the train was going to stop.

I don't know now what is coming next, how it is all going to turn out, or whether or not it has a happy ending. All I know is that I haven't felt sorry for myself. I haven't cried proper tears. Something seems to stop me from crying, and I have found strength from somewhere to go on. I was also still making jokes. The cartoon that made me laugh the most was one I saw of a man having a check-up at the doctors. The sign on the door read 'Dermatology'. The doctor was looking at a small tattoo of a crab on the man's back, and the caption was, "Yes, I'm afraid it's a sign of cancer!"

I'm not making a joke of cancer as it's not funny. I'm just trying to make light of the illness to keep going. As I said before, my mantra was and is "Tackle the tumour with humour" and definitely, "Do not take up running!"

THE RESULTS ARE IN

January 8, 2018, the tumour was confirmed as 90mm. Any tumour over 20mm is deemed large. Two out of the eleven lymph nodes taken out were affected and were cancerous, and the tumour was Oestrogen ER+ and Progesterone positive PR+.

In effect I was declared cancer-free, they had got it all. I didn't know how to feel. On the one hand, I was ecstatic; they had removed all cancer, and the decision to do a mastectomy had been the right one as the mass was so large. On the other, I was thinking of the girls' dance teacher of 12 years who had lost her battle with cancer on New Year's Day. I couldn't shout it from the rooftops. It was again one of the times when good news and bad news cancel each other, and you're left feeling nothing. Like when N. announced he had a visa and Cheryl died.

In 1987 my 'bestest' American friend along with her eleven brothers and sisters left Edinburgh after a year's visit to return to Utah. We had become incredibly close, and I had learnt so much about American traditions and the Mormon religion. I was so upset. That very same day, my German pen pal phoned to ask if he could come and stay for three weeks with my family in a few weeks which was unbelievably brilliant news. The two emotions cancelled each other out, and I felt flat. It's a horrible feeling to have.

THE NEXT STEP

The next step was a series of scans. A bone density scan would set the bar and give a starting point while I was on the Letrozole tablets. There was some evidence that the pill caused a decrease in bone density.

A bone, chest, pelvis and abdomen CT would also determine definitively whether the cancer had spread elsewhere as they were more detailed. All this data would give my oncologist the best picture to draw up a plan of treatment. So I couldn't relax- I needed the results of these scans to know that I was cancer free. I still couldn't relax.

The scar had healed well, but my chest felt very tight. I likened it to wearing a bra two sizes too small. It felt as if someone was hugging me too tightly. The skin also looked puckered, as if someone had pulled a cord at one end and it had all gathered up. The Breast Care nurses assured me everything was normal and I relaxed a bit.

The Pregabalin had stopped all the aches and pains and tingling and numbness attributed to my B12 deficiency and I only had my insomnia to deal with.

INSOMNIA

Waking up in the middle of the night and then not being able to go back to sleep is bad enough, but going to bed and not being able to fall asleep is worse. It's a horrible feeling.

You're tired, and you want to sleep, but your mind is going ten to the dozen. I try and think about nice things or play word association but nothing works. I've tried most of the old wives' remedies and even avoided cheese. The sheep had no intention of jumping over any fences, let alone letting themselves be counted.

Sometimes I read rubbish on my phone or trawled through the news. Sometimes I tried to see if I could beat my score at some addictive game- that normally passed a few hours. I've even bought things from EBay that I never really needed. Mainly they were an impulse buy from Hong Kong because they were cheap;

- LED light up earrings,
- White tile grout refresher pen,
- Bridget Jones-style big pants that hold everything in,
- Dog pyjamas with ducks on,
- Multicoloured boots- (actually they were a good buy)
- A 12ft pillow

HIDE AND SEEK

I was sucked into the advertising of the 12 ft pillow and chose a brown cover to go with my bedroom decor. However when I slid it on it just looked like a giant turd! Once I got the image of the turd out of my mind, I was able to snuggle up to it, and it was excellent support for my arm and side. Once snuggled under the duvet, wedged between a 12ft pillow, it was tough to get up. However, I couldn't lie in for long, Phoebe needed her breakfast and let out, and I needed the first cup of tea of the day. In the long days to come when I was always exhausted, it was somewhere nice to retreat to and hibernate.

While comfortably snuggled, it reminded me of the time almost 35 years previously when I ended up hibernating in a friend's bed under the pillows.

I was playing a massive game of hide and seek. My friend had a large family and an enormous house in the country. It was ideal for playing games in. It had started horribly when I had hid behind the shower curtain. The father of the house had then come into the bathroom to use the toilet. I thought it was someone coming to look for me, so I stayed quiet until it was too late to make myself known. It was a very awkward few minutes.

I wasn't discovered, but I don't know who would have been more embarrassed if we had seen each other.

I hid again across a double bed with pillows on top of me. It was a great hiding place and incredibly comfortable. However, I fell asleep.

When I woke up, the party was almost finished, the food had been eaten, and everyone was watching a video in the dark.

I don't know whether I was more upset at not being missed or that I had missed the food. That bed shouldn't have been so comfortable!

A NEW FOOBIE

The fitting for my prosthetic breast was quick and easy. I was supposed to bring a tight-fitting plain t-shirt, but as I told them, I never wear tight fitting plain t-shirts so brought a busy patterned frumpy top that was my signature look. I felt I was in Ollivanders-the wand shop in the Harry Potter books. The room had cupboards full of different artificial breasts- boxes of different sizes, colours and brands.

I had a small knitted foobie and the large soft NHS foobie, but I was now being presented with a prosthetic- 'silicone heavy duty soft squashy moulded heavy breast' that slid like jelly into a bra pocket. I tried a few on, and the lady pondered and wondered and then produced an even heavier one in a large box. It looked huge and was indeed huge, like some mini molehill with realistic creases and nipple bit.

However, it was surprisingly cool and on my sweaty, hot, flushed body, felt good. It did look realistic, and for once I turned and twisted in the mirror admiring my new silhouette. It then fell out on to the floor with a splat! I needed to get fitted for a proper mastectomy bra with a pouch. I couldn't have it falling out at work!

At night the prosthetic gets washed with soap and water and placed in a special box to keep its shape. Some people have a glass of water by their beds to keep their teeth in; I have a box to keep my boob in.

PROTECTING THE ARM

My appointment with the lymphoedema nurse wasn't so quick and easy. I was told off for carrying my bag with my left arm. I knew how serious having lymph nodes out was and the need for protecting the arm but I felt other people didn't know enough or were aware. I wasn't aware in fact a month earlier.

Lymphoedema is the swelling of the arm or chest or hand caused by the build-up of lymph fluid in the surface tissues of the body. It's not very nice, and the risk is real. There were compression sleeves I could have in the future – some patterned like tattoos or loads of flowers, but for now, the arm was alright.

It was hard listening to the nurse tell me that I could never have a sauna or steam room again and never to carry anything with a straight arm. I was told to wear oven gloves and washing up gloves and to protect the arm from all trauma, which included not letting it get sunburn. I queried that one mentioning my vitamin D deficiency and love of the sun and she said 15 minutes of exposure was ample. It was sinking in but not entirely, and when relaying everything the nurse had told me later to my mum on the phone, I did feel I was exaggerating.

Unfortunately, lymphoedema is serious and protecting my arm is no laughing matter; things would just have to change. The nurse even said take care not to rub hard with a towel while drying after a shower and to observe all insect bites, dabbing on antiseptic cream and watching for any changes in the skin.

CHEST CT

It was a struggle to get up and ready for this 8 am CT (computerised tomography) appointment and more of an effort to drink the jug of water they gave me as a prerequisite. I was told I could empty my bladder a little bit and then carry on drinking. Well, doing that is like just having one peanut from a bowl!

Sitting a little cross-legged, I was impatiently awaiting my name to be called. It reminded me of the pregnancy ultrasound days when you arrived having drunk a bath full of water and had to sit with a whole lot of other ladies all feeling uncomfortable on hard plastic chairs, desperate for a wee. On one occasion I sneaked to the loo and went 'just a little bit', but I got caught and was brought some more water by a very diligent nurse and my appointment time was pushed back later.

I didn't have many veins left in my arm and after a few attempts; they called a specialist down to find a vein for the cannula to be inserted into.

The CT machine was like a giant doughnut. Feet first you lie on a slab, and the doughnut encircles you to take a picture. When the dye is added, you experience a hot flush and the urge to wee which is somewhat bizarre, but it is over in a few minutes.

Before every scan and I've had a few, my height and weight are measured. Unfortunately, my weight has stayed the same, but I lost an inch in height in one week! I kept quiet, but no-one seemed to pick it up or was worried. Perhaps a side effect of the Letrozole is also bone shrinkage not just decreased bone density?

The next scan to have was the bone density one. The Radiographer was very friendly and asked me to take my boots off and hop up onto the bed.

"Nice socks", she said.

I had my Miss Piggy and Fozzy Bear mismatch combo on.

I never wear matching socks- there is something too conformist about it. At age three, my youngest daughter did not share the same love of wearing stripes with spots or floral with zigzags.

THE MISMATCH SHOP 2006

On being pushed in a buggy into the shop by my brother, my daughter took one look at the display of stripes with spots and plain with patterned and uttered the most blood-curdling scream imaginable. She could not bear the odd socks and mismatched clothes. She screamed to be taken out of the "horrible shop".

"Take me out," she was hollering. So much so, that my brother was shamed into buying a pair of the said socks to appease the bewildered sales assistant.

As she has aged her clothes are neatly organised in colour and size order, and she knows exactly where everything is and has a good fashion sense.

As time has gone on, I have got worse, and I know it. I rock the frumpy schoolteacher look, with comfortable shoes, duffle coat and sensible length skirts; although I have stopped wearing so many knitted cardigans.

THE BONE DEXA SCAN

I lay on the slab again, and this time a modern machine took pictures as a starting point. A bone DEXA scan was about taking measurements in three different areas and keeping a beady eye on those measurements as my treatment progressed. The risk of osteoporosis is real now that I've started taking the tablets and will also become greater with radiotherapy or chemotherapy. My feet were put into odd positions, and I had to breathe slowly but it was over quickly, and this time thankfully no needles were involved.

WHAT DID THE ONCOLOGIST SAY?

Strangely I was looking forward to meeting the consultant oncologist and hearing what my treatment plan was to be. However, I was disappointed.

I saw the Registrar and no treatment plan had been drawn up as the results of all the scans weren't in. Also, I hadn't had the full body bone scan as the appointment had only just come through. The Registrar had all my notes in front of her and said that I had to have radiotherapy definitely, but that chemotherapy was an option. I was a borderline case. In my favour for not having chemo was the fact that only 2/11 nodes were affected, the cancer was Her2- (which if there were any good cancers to have, this was the best one) and definitely hormone receptor-positive, so the Letrozole was the right tablet to be on if I was post-menopausal.

Against me was the size of the tumour- It was 9.5cm, not 9cm and the fact that it was metatastic- had spread elsewhere. I was to go away and have a think about what I wanted to do. I was also sent for more blood tests, to make sure I was post-menopausal.

I felt like a human pincushion. I was still bruised from where the cannula had been fitted and from all the failed attempts to get a good vein. Fortunately, it took only two attempts to get blood, and the back of my hand was spared. The skin was so thin there that it hurt. I cheered myself up with a hospital canteen dinner. I had watched Celebrity Master Chef, set in a hospital canteen on TV and had great expectations of the choice of food. I was a bit disappointed but had a pleasant meal, and the highlight was sitting at a long school dinner type trestle table with some rather good-looking doctors. I was in the minority as it was obviously 'doctor and nurse dinner time' and I felt left out that I wasn't wearing a hospital lanyard.

I didn't stop thinking about my possible treatment. To chemo or not to chemo, that was the question. Naturally, why submit my body to such a toxic regime if it wasn't necessary but what if in a few years I lived to regret my decision? It was, and if I'm honest, I didn't want any treatment at all. I just wanted to go back to teaching. It's funny how you only miss something when you can't have it, and in my case- couldn't do it. I had always wanted to be a teacher.

24

THOSE WHO TEACH, CAN

My teaching placement schools were lovely with only a bit of running on the stairs and overcrowded cloakrooms as their problems. I wanted more of a challenge and so came nearer to London.

I'd always wanted to teach, but I soon found out there was never a dull day in a classroom. You're always your pupils' 'bestest' teacher until their next teacher, but why is it at the end of each year do the kids remember the school trips the most and not the teaching?

SCHOOL TRIPS

Dropped off in the beautiful city of Rochester in March 1994 there was a freak snowstorm, and all the clipboards and sheets were destroyed. We spent a half hour slot in the cathedral and 2.5 hours in a cafe trying to shelter from the cold and make one drink and a packed lunch last.

We played games-a lot of charades and quizzes, and although thirty soggy children hogging all the seats all afternoon wasn't what the cafe owners were expecting, it was a memorable day. We made and sent thank you letters to the cafe.

THE PET SHOP

Walking thirty kindergarten children age 2-4 to the pet shop from school was itself an ordeal. They dawdled. They stopped. They ran on. They caused your heart to stop at each road crossing, but we finally made it to the large pet shop and began looking at the small animals and birds. The staff spoke to the children about caring for rabbits and chinchillas and gerbils. The children were allowed to stroke the animals, and the highlight was the squeaking guinea pigs. Unfortunately, this story does not have a happy ending, and if you're an animal lover or squeamish, you may want to miss this bit.

The children wanted to see the guinea pigs close up, so a member of staff went to gather a guinea pig up. As she came out of the enclosure, the lady tripped on the step and slam-dunked the guinea pig on the floor. It had broken her fall.

The children were oblivious and crowded round to stroke the guinea pig. The lady looked at me in horror, and I said "Shh everyone, the guinea pig is sleeping. Let's go and see the birds." The lady took the guinea pig behind the scenes, and the children, fortunately, did not find out. They were given a balloon to carry, and we set off to walk home. I'm not sure who made the loudest cry; the child who lost their balloon or the child that did not want to walk any further. I do know I ended up carrying home a sleeping two-year-old on my shoulder and several balloons home.

THE LONDON AQUARIUM 1997

In one school I taught in, it was school policy not to take parents on school trips because it was so hard to choose one parent over another and difficult for the kids too. So it happened that my husband, my dad and I took a class to the London Aquarium. I still remember the look on my dad's face explaining to a mum how a rubber stress ball they had bought in the gift shop had exploded in sticky gloop all over her daughter's blazer and was now all over his monogrammed cotton handkerchief. However, it brought a new meaning to "A family day out".

BIG BEN

Although it is a fantastic experience for the children to climb the clock tower of Big Ben, I have been three times now, and each time the rest station couldn't come soon enough. There are a lot of narrow stairs, and the rest station comes where the mechanism of the clock is housed. It is balanced by the original handful of Victorian penny coins and the works have not needed to be altered for years. It is possible to walk behind all four clock faces, but the most remarkable sight is the bell 'Big Ben' itself. It is indeed loud, but it is, and the views are amazing from the top.

The Big Ben trip was normally accompanied by a visit to Churchill's War Rooms or the London Eye. On one such trip, we were allowed to enter Downing Street. The children looked smart in their caps, blazers and straw hats and I had my selfie outside number 10 Downing Street. The children's uniform attracted a lot of attention, and I could see the children wearing it with pride and walking tall as tourists took their pictures. There is something very British about school uniform.

PADDINGTON

There's nothing more British than Paddington Bear either. I had an excellent snivel at both films, but in the second film, Paddington has a mixed wash accident in a prison laundry.

I had a mixed wash accident at home last year. It is amazing what damage a dark purple towel can do to anything with the slightest amount of white on- lace-trimmed underwear and lettering down leggings and grey stripes on tops. Nothing got the purple out and a lot of washing still now has a lilac hue to it in some types of light!

FLYING VISIT

However, any story involving royalty has to be important. Prince Charles was due to land in his helicopter just behind our school. We had brought the children down to wave their flags, look cute and greet the Prince. We had arrived early, and we were asked by the security to help them look in the grass for anything suspicious – knives, devices, anything dodgy before the helicopter landed. We couldn't say no as they needed to sweep the area but it was a health and safety nightmare, and we the teachers were running around behind the children urging them not to touch or pick up anything suspicious but to call or wave their Union Jack that they were holding. Fortunately, nothing was found and as the school, looked very smart in their uniforms with their hand coloured flags, Prince Charles came over, and I managed to shake the hand of the future monarch, in a field, in Kent.

SOMETHING SUSPICIOUS

My daughter and her friend aged ten found something suspicious. They found a discarded gun. It had been thrown away near some wasteland where they were playing on some wasteland. Fortunately, it was only a replica, but it could have easily been mistaken for a real one. The police were called but only after it emerged that the children had already picked it up 'to see if it was real.' Children do have to touch things.

DON'T TOUCH

I remember when I was at primary school in year three, we were allowed to go and visit the classrooms of the other classes. In a year six classroom there was a massive model of Tower Bridge made with junk- cereal boxes and the like. The class teacher said to everyone, "If you touch any part of the model, you will die!"

At playtime that afternoon I found one of my good friends crying in the corner. It was hard to console her, but it emerged that she had touched part of the model and now thought that she was going to die.

THE GIFT SHOP

The highlight of any school trip is the visit to the shop, but it can be a traumatic 15 minutes especially if the children haven't any concept of money. They clutch a pound coin in their palm, and the price says 50p so they think they can't buy the item. The shop owner would get increasingly impatient at the long queue of dithering children, and the teachers too were losing it trying to stop the children from picking things up to look at them.

£1 couldn't buy anything as the gift shops were always ridiculously overpriced. They couldn't even afford a pencil and the children more often than not went home disappointed with nothing or a couple of postcards.

HOMEWORK EXCUSES

The following are correct answers to my all so familiar question, "Why haven't you got your homework?"

- "I'm sorry my mum went out last night." (Obviously, their mum did their homework)
- "I'm sorry a volcano erupted in Iceland" – I remember a couple of my teacher friends used this one for not even turning up to school!
- "I'm sorry, my was dad lying on it and I didn't want to wake him."
- "I burnt it on an iron." This homework set was the popular 'make a letter look old' task. No one ever admitted to setting fire to the whole paper when burning the edges, or tea staining the sheet and all the writing smudging, but the iron was a new one!
- "I have half of it here; the other half is gone somewhere." "Gone somewhere? Let's see if it comes back for tomorrow then."
- "You know Miss; women are never satisfied." (This was a dialogue between a 9- year old and me, and yes his parents were informed!)
- "I'm sorry a fox ate it."

THE FOX

"I'm sorry a fox ate it", was once my daughter's excuse and I sent an accompanying letter into school for it was true. She had made a papier maché model of Saturn complete with rings. Painted, it was drying by the open backdoor. A fox (we were without a dog at this time) then had taken great chunks out of the planet, later on, leaving teeth marks while we were all watching television in the other room.

THE DOG

I had to write on a student's work "Sorry my dog ate your homework". Embarrassingly my dog had taken a shine to a leaflet on the English Civil War and had chewed most of it!

THE SAUNA

"I'm sorry; the ceiling fell on it."

Yes, this is another one of my daughter's excuses too. We had returned from an all-day dance competition to find an old corroded bathroom pipe had burst in our house. The hot water had continued to run all day from upstairs, and the steam had nowhere to escape. The house had had a sauna.

Every bit of metal was sparkling, the kitchen looked like a show home kitchen, yet all wallpaper had come off, there was plaster dust everywhere, a horrid damp smell, three ceilings were down and everything was wet and beginning to go mouldy.

The Viking project left out on the table downstairs didn't make it through the sauna.

OUT OF THE MOUTHS OF BABES

Every day children say precious things. Some I wrote down in my notebook as they showed the innocence of youth. No names are mentioned here.

Teachers either loathe 'show and tell' and 'news', or love it. It's like marmite to teachers. I challenge myself not to smile or be sarcastic. It's difficult not to, and I have been known to sound very much like Joyce Grenfell. I kept a book of memorable quotes. No names obviously and apologies if you read what you said!

Best ones over the years at both primary and secondary level have been:

- "My dad wear's a nappy. My mum makes him wear one when he comes home from the pub. She's fed up with him wetting the bed!"

- "We had four gerbils, but then they all ate each other, so we ended up with one".

- Me: What have you brought in for show and tell?
  Pupil: It's a stone, it's grey.

- Me: Can you count back from 20 to 1?
  Pupil: Yes

- Me: Name four animals that live in a polar region
  Pupil: 2 polar bears and two penguins

- What is the main difference between an invertebrate and a vertebrate?
  Pupil: Invertebrates are very, very shy. (Introverts maybe?)
  Pupil: Can I go and wash my hands in the toilet?

- Me: Please don't. Use the sink.

- Me: When you have finished the test, read a book or sleep on your desk. Just be quiet until everyone has completed.
  Pupil: Climbed up onto a double desk and was about to lie down and go to sleep before I showed him how just to put his head on his arms.

- Me: Would you like to spell "friend"?
  Pupil: No

- How do you change litres to millilitres?
  Pupil: Add the milli bit.

- Pupils were asked to list things not to do in a science lab, some
  of the best:
  Don't poke the chemicals.
  Don't light your tie.
  Don't lick any spoons.
  Don't put your friend's hand in the flame.
  Don't wear hair gel near a Bunsen Burner.

- Me: Name two classes of the medieval period (discussing The
  Feudal System)
  Pupil: Maths and geography

- Explain why it is that you weigh less on the moon than on the
  earth.
  Pupil: There's more food on earth.

- "Miss, what time are we doing the F Word? (They meant
  phonics)

- Me: Describe two reactions when you place a 1cm strip of
  magnesium ribbon in water.
  Pupil: Surprise and shock

- Me: Describe two effects of global warming
  Pupil: It kills snails and destroys satellites.

LETTERS IN CLASS

When I was at secondary school, we didn't have mobiles. We messaged each other with notes, sometimes scrunched into tiny balls and thrown or sometimes folded neatly and passed under the desks.

I'd buy a lollipop at break time which had a strong paper stick. I'd develop the art of bending the stick and leaning on my hand, so it was not apparent that I was eating. When the lollipop had gone, and the paper was a bit soggy, it was possible to unravel the stick into a small piece of paper. Then it was time to write a message.

As a teacher, I would work up a collection of such messages. One day I watched as a message was being passed around the class and managed to intercept it. I thought myself rather smug as I opened the folded piece of paper only to find the message; "This is an amazing lesson, smile if you think Miss is the best."

Referendums in the class were always done by small bits of paper. My favourites were the votes for the class captain or sports leader when you were told explicitly not to vote for yourself and not to vote for your friend. By habit, most children wrote their name on the top of the piece of paper regardless of how big it was!

REPORTS

Every child dreads what has been written in their report, every parent dreads the arrival of the report, and every teacher dreads writing the reports. So why don't we save all the dread and not bother?

To make life a little more straightforward in one school I worked in; we used a SIMS report system which meant that we could choose from hundreds of set comments and mark them on a form with a couple of linking words and 'he' or 'she' for variety. It did save a lot of time and was useful if you were saying the same thing about several children, but not particularly personal.

The name used as an example on the comment banks was Charlotte. I devised my own (joke) set of comments for some colleagues.

They followed a very similar format:

ENGLISH

A01 Charlotte has no problem talking in front of others

A02 Charlotte has no problem talking behind the backs of others

A03 Charlotte is beginning to spell

A04 Charlotte is beginning to smell

A05 Charlotte has begun to read

A06 Charlotte is beginning to read

A07 Charlotte is beginning to begin to read

A08 Charlotte has begun to begin to read

A09 Charlotte has used a full stop

A10 Charlotte has a vivid imagination

A11 Charlotte lies

A12 Charlotte can, has, and is often

MATHEMATICS

B01 Charlotte cannot do mathematics

B02 Charlotte could not care less about mathematics

B03 Charlotte can write the number 1

B04 Charlotte has difficulty counting with only nine fingers

B05 Charlotte can count from 1 to 3 without stopping

R.E.

C01 Charlotte has no opinion

C02 Charlotte has no soul

C03 Charlotte has no PE Kit

C04 Charlotte has created her demi-god status

C05   Charlotte believes

C06   Charlotte believes she is a fish

GENERAL

D01   Charlotte is a time waster

D02   Charlotte wastes time

D03   Charlotte has a tendency to waste time

D04   Charlotte eats pencils

D05   Charlotte has a tendency to eat pencils

D06   Charlotte is satisfactory

D07   is

D08   and

D09   Invaders and Settlers

D10   growth mindset

FUNNY MOMENTS IN THE CLASSROOM

- We were making rhyming dominoes, and a pupil had drawn a heart on one side and what looked like a little girl on the other.
  Me: What have you drawn?
  Pupil: A tart.

- • It was my birthday, and I was wearing an "I'm 21" birthday badge. (I was well into my 40s)
  Pupil: You wore that last year Miss. You're 22 now.

- Me: Are you eating in class?
  Pupil: No answer (obviously something in the mouth)
  Me: What are you eating?
  Pupil: (No answer)
  Me: If you are eating food in class then you are breaking one of our class rules.
  Pupil: (Spits out a whole chunk of glue stick) Phew Miss, it's not food -it's glue!

- Me: What colour is made by mixing blue and yellow together?
  Pupil: Green. When I pee in the loo when my mum has put that blue stuff down, it goes green.

- On a school trip to a zoo, we were all looking into an enclosure and trying to work out what animals were in there.
  Pupil: Dangeroos are in there.
  Me: Dangeroos?
  Pupil: Pointed to the sign. It read "These animals are dangerous."

PARENTS

I became a better teacher once I had children of school age. I realised it was almost impossible to hear your child read every single day even for just ten minutes and the weekly palaver of writing a sentence and drawing a picture to go with a book that had been read was often saved for Sunday afternoons was a nightmare and was dreaded by all involved.

However, the respect seems to have gone between parent and teacher and the child appears innocent until the teacher proves them guilty in an altercation, which is a real shame. Of course, there are lots of lovely supportive parents out there. I've met so many in the three decades I've been teaching. However, it just needs one or two negative comments, and they are the comments that stick.

Some memorable conversations:

- "My daughter has come home without her poppy. She says she has worn it all day and now it's gone. She paid 50p. I want the 50p back please."

- "My daughter says she is an alien in the school nativity."
  Me: "Yes, that's right."

- Me: "Your son has been caught walking to school along the train tracks."
  "He's not stupid; it's not as if he's going to walk on them!"

- "I've come to get back the pencil you stole from my son."
  Me: "I confiscated it, as he was poking it in another boy's ear."
  "You stole it and never gave it back. Teachers shouldn't steal."

- "My son said you said he could bring his pig in for show and tell."
  Me: "Yes please if that's ok. It's a micro −pig?"
  "No, it's a fighting pig!"

MRS CHIPS

I often wonder what I would be remembered for as a teacher. My 'Paddington hard stares' or my P.E. warm-ups to ABBA? Could it even be my very hard to earn smelly stickers- particularly the bubblegum scented ones?

GREAT WHALE

Teaching a group swimming one afternoon, I stretched out too far demonstrating and fell in fully clothed. I remember the look of horror as I came tumbling down towards a child, only just missing them. A teacher paid £1 for me to stand in the body drier, but the coach driver still made me sit on some newspapers on the way home. My hair exploded, my watch was almost broken, and I had to laugh the incident off with the children both on the coach and back at school.

TIN-CAN COOKING

What could go wrong with 30 children cooking fried eggs in pairs on tin cans with tea-lights as the source of heat? Quite a lot. The oil spilt over the sides of the can and little fingers, despite being told not to, touched the oil, the candle, the egg and the hot tin. One group even managed to set fire to a nearby dictionary- accidentally on purpose? Never again.

It was a day that my teaching assistant and parent helpers might never forget!

THE WASP 1999

One thing that is hard to do is reading a whole story in a classroom without any distractions. Whether it is a knock on the door, children nipping to the loo, funny sounds or wasps, there are always disturbances.

You would have thought that there was a scary dragon in the classroom this day for the amount of screaming and shouting and fuss that was being made over one wasp. I opened the windows and said, "If you ignore it, it won't sting you."

There was still an undercurrent of noise, but the screaming had stopped. I continued reading. There were constant knocks at the door, visitors to the classroom, messages sent, questions asked, hands waving in the air and a few trips to the loo.

I wasn't getting anywhere with the story and so a little exasperated I said: "no more interruptions, please".

The class settled and went surprisingly quiet, and I got on well with the story. It's quite an art to sit sideways and hold a book up so the pictures can be seen and yet the words can still be read. The class were still quiet.

I felt a sharp pain on my leg.

"Did it sting you miss?" asked one child.

The wasp had stung me. I looked at the class who had been trailing the wasp.

"Did no one think to tell me it was on my leg?" I asked.

"You said no more interruptions, miss."

LOTTERY WINNINGS 1995

When the National Lottery was first launched in 1994, there was a buzz of excitement. Life changing amounts of money could be won. The staff created a syndicate, and we would watch for our numbers each week.

One Saturday night I watched in shock as five numbers were drawn out. The phone was hot with us all phoning each other. We had to wait until Camelot had verified the numbers and see how many other tickets shared the same numbers. Only £10 for three numbers could be guaranteed. The week before five numbers had paid out £400K. It was ever so exciting.

I had mentally spent my money on:
- Flights home to Edinburgh
- A new school bag
- A kitchen extension
- A holiday/honeymoon to Egypt.

The winning numbers were popular numbers. There were unusually a lot of tickets with those numbers. Our winnings were shared between the twenty of us in the syndicate. I took home £43.17. I tried not to be disappointed. I bought the school bag nevertheless and put plans for a trip to Egypt on hold.

TGI FRIDAY

Friday afternoons in schools can sometimes be a challenge, especially after a long school week, which is why some schools close early on a Friday. In one school I worked in we had class assemblies on a Friday and for fun, some of the teachers would have 10p sweepstakes. It changed each week. Once it was bets on how many times a teacher would say the word "fantastic". Another time it was how many times we would hear shoe Velcro straps being pulled. But one favourite challenge- just for fun- was whether you could get a random word into your assembly or celebrity name.

I was given the name Richard Clayderman- the French pianist and my assembly was on the Aztecs. There was no link, so I started the assembly with all of the classes filing in to "Ballade Pour Adeleine" by Richard Clayderman. I then told the school who the music was by before introducing our class assembly.

Another teacher had the botanist David Bellamy to get into her assembly about Bonfire Night. But she got him in as he was a guest at the organised firework display that she went on to talk about.

David Bellamy was a charismatic, bearded celebrity and his son went to the same university as me. A touring choir I was part of was staying at his house one summer, and at dinner one evening we were all tired, and no one was talking. It was one of those silences that went on a little too long, so one American girl piped up:

"So, who can talk about the mating habits of a wombat?"

Primarily a botanist, Mr Bellamy was possibly one of the only people in at least a 50-mile radius that could answer that question.

The silence became even more awkward until there came a raucous laugh from Mr Bellamy.

There was no laughing at the end of this next story.

THE PUPPET SHOW 2003

When an Australian duo came to a local theatre with their "origami of their genitalia" show, a group of teacher's and assistants thought it would be a giggle to go an attend. It was the end of term and someone's birthday, and although not the kind of show we would have liked to have been seen at, it was a fun night out. It was indeed a giggle.

Two men dressed only in capes and boots, had their "bits" projected on to a big screen for the audience to marvel at how they made various animal shapes and famous landmarks. It was tastefully done and more an art show than anything dodgy, but it was incredible, and we all laughed until it hurt.

One friend bought the book and a few days later brought a few sheets for us. I knew there would be trouble if these pictures were found so kept them safe all day. But they were so safe when I got home I couldn't find them. I had lost them. I was panicking and sweating and didn't sleep at all. I phoned the caretaker and arranged to go into school early.

I looked everywhere. It was a lack of professional judgement to accept the pictures, and now I had mislaid them. I retraced my steps and looked through everything.

I was marking maths when I got given them. I looked through all the children's maths folders. I found them. Out of 30 children in the class, the sheets were in the vicar's daughter's folder! It was the same colour as my work folder.

I shredded those pictures into so many pieces and certainly learnt my lesson.

25

ALL BECOMING REAL

I popped into school on a Cake Friday, predominantly for a cake but also to see my colleagues. I hadn't been in since the end of November, and it was now the end of January 2018. It was like I had never been away and I felt a bit emotional. When everyone disappeared to their classrooms, I was left sitting in the staffroom. I did have a nice chat with the secretary and the head who were both of the opinions that it was far too soon to return to work and also if I returned too soon then like a sports injury, it may set me back further. The head mentioned something about me going home sitting in my pants and watching Jeremy Kyle!

I did go home. I was, but it made me more determined to fight and get better and to return to work. I missed the children and the staff so much.

DECISIONS, DECISIONS

It was worrying having to decide on my treatment. I tried the PREDICT predict.nhs.uk online tool. It suggested that chemotherapy would make a small difference as the hormone therapy and radiotherapy was deemed to be sufficient but fairly unreliable too as I didn't have to say what tablets I was on or whether I had had surgery.

However, when I tried the Nottingham Prognostic Index (NPI) scoring system that uses the grade and size of the cancer to determine a prognosis, it gave me a poor result: Poor 17% chance of surviving for five years.

These two online sites were featured in the Breast Cancer Care booklet amongst others, and it was going to be a starting point for a conversation with the oncologist when I next got to see her. I didn't sleep well that night.

FULL BODY BONE SCAN

Another early start and a visit this time to the Nuclear Medicine department at the hospital. I had blue dye inserted into the vein through injection and then had to wait three hours for the dye to circulate.

The machine again was large and modern, and I lay once more on the slab with a pillow under my knees. I then had a fabric belt put around my arms which felt a bit like a straight jacket so that my arms would rest by my side and not fall into the machine. A plate then came down on top of me to within a couple of inches. I felt I was the filling in a panini press! It took about 40 minutes for the scanner to travel slowly from my head down to my toes and then swivelled and did some side shots. It's incredible how far technology has come in only 100 years.

The sign on the wall said to avoid ports, airports and some train stations as I may set off the sensors. If travel was necessary, I was to carry a hospital letter with me. With my track record of luck at airports, I probably would have every sniffer dog on the premises barking at me. I decided it was possibly best to stay at home and not visit any airports or ports.

Now for some more waiting. Easy, I knew how to do that by now.

The insomnia was at an all-time high and not sleeping at night meant I was a bit ratty during the day, and after walking my dog and doing a few chores, I was worn out.

I didn't have to wait long. Within 24 hours I was face to face with my consultant oncologist. An appointment had come up.

OUT OF MY HANDS

I didn't get the choice about the chemotherapy. Due to the nature and size of the tumour (it was now 95mm apparently) the best option was adjuvant chemotherapy to start as soon as possible. The aim was to destroy any rogue cancer cells that may have spread from the breast to other parts of the body. I was to have four cycles of Epirubicin and Cyclophosphamide delivered by IV. Each cycle would last three weeks and then four cycles of Paclitaxel, every two weeks. I would also need Bisphosphonates (Zoledronic Acid - ZA) by means of injection. It was a bone-hardening /bone-strengthening treatment to reduce the risk of breast cancer spreading to the bones. Clinical studies have shown that breast cancers can sometimes recur in and spread to the bones even years after surgery.

I felt relieved, and I think I smiled. It was because things were moving forward. The full body bone scan from the day before was not back yet, but the other ones were, and the blood test showed definitely that I was post-menopausal. I was likely to be on them for the next seven years.

I signed some consent forms and was given a lot of reading. I was scared and apprehensive but still kept thinking that it was for the best. The first boxes ticked on my forms said that the chemotherapy was being undertaken to:

- Prevent cancer from returning
- Prolong life expectancy

I went to bed early and stroked my hair. I had found out that one of my chemo drugs- the red one- Epirubicin- was the one that caused hair loss. It was now highly likely/definite that I would be a 'baldie oldie', and lose my eyelashes and eyebrows too. On a positive note, it meant I wouldn't have to shave my legs for a while!

I didn't want to lose my hair. There was a cold cap I could wear, but most reviews said it didn't stop all hair loss. My best friend tried to cheer me up and said I might look like the singer Sinead

O'Connor. I replied I'd look more like the comedian Matt Lucas! I was sort of secretly intrigued to see what my scalp looked like. Did I have freckles or moles or any birthmarks there?

This would be the plaster cast I had wanted but not in this way. I didn't want strangers knowing my business, and now it was likely that everyone I passed would be mentally thinking, "That lady has cancer". Well, I haven't. I'm cancer free. All scans but the full bone scan were back and had shown up nothing unusual.

I wasn't eligible for any trials because I had been on HRT (Hormone Replacement Therapy) and Letrozole. The next step would be a phone call from a support nurse at the chemotherapy unit and an appointment to go and talk through any questions or worries. There were five pages of side effects that I could have, ranging from mild to life-threatening. It didn't make happy reading, and I knew I wouldn't get all of them, but the thing was no-one could tell me which ones I was going to get. That in itself was worrying. Also, my daughter was 14. That was far too young to have to shoulder the responsibility of making sure I was OK and didn't have a fever or a high temperature every day. I would be doing the checking, but she would still have to be very mature about things. The next few months were not going to be easy. Chemotherapy can affect the number of healthy blood cells in the body, and because of this the following can happen:

- Anaemia- not enough red blood cells
- Bleeding and bruising more easily
- Susceptible to infection- not enough white blood cells

The last one was the most important and why I had to keep a beady eye on what my body was doing. I began writing down a whole list of questions to ask at the next visit to the hospital.

DENTAL CHECKUP

The last thing necessary before treatment was a full dental assessment. My teeth were in a state anyway. The Zoledronic Acid injections that I was to have may cause osteonecrosis of the jaw bone. That's all I needed. I could visit the dentist for checkups during treatment but not have any invasive work done until at least six weeks after the end of treatment.

A WORRYING THOUGHT

Lying awake at night again it suddenly occurred to me that I had been celebrating being cancer free. I had told a few people, and a lot of messages had come through to me saying 'congratulations' etc. I had scans to see if any cancer cells had broken free. I was to have chemotherapy to destroy any cells that had broken free, and I was probably to have Radiotherapy to destroy finally any cells that had broken free. I was so confused. I was either cancer free, or I wasn't. Just as I thought I had got my head around everything and understood what was going on, I slipped down the slide again and was at the bottom!

26
FOOD FOR THOUGHT

I had a lot of information to read about my impending treatment in a few booklets. The pages I was drawn to first were what I wasn't allowed to eat! I had heard about the side effects of loss of appetite and taste changes, but I hoped I could still eat my favourites (chocolate, Chinese food and strawberry milk!) Fortunately, it appeared that it was only a few foods that I had to avoid, mainly foods that could harbour bacteria; yoghurt, shellfish, soft cheese, lightly cooked eggs, buffet food. I tried to ignore 'takeaway food' on the list. Surely it was a misprint? It wasn't. Any food that I hadn't seen cooked and could have been reheated was a danger.

It could have been a lot worse; the list could have said chocolate and all cheeses. For Lent this year I was going to give up giving up anything. It also depended on how I felt as to what food I ate, so that was OK too. I liked my food, and it was a little worrying to think that my taste would fail me. I needed to lose a bit of weight, but I also needed to have some comfort in life!

DIM SUM

I like eating. I like food. I especially love Chinese food, so when some Chinese students that I taught English too, wanted to take me out for a thank you meal, I was delighted. We went to China Town, and we're going to have Dim Sum – lots of little plates of delicacies.

The only food I thought I didn't eat was seafood apart from white fish – that you get in fish fingers, small peeled prawns - like you get in the 1970s starter prawn cocktail, and tuna. It didn't occur to me that proper Chinese food wasn't like ordering nos.45, 78, and 116 from the local takeaway!

In the restaurant, the first plate came out, and I felt I was doing a Bush Tucker Trial on the ITV programme "I'm a Celebrity Get Me Out Of Here."

It was chicken feet. I couldn't eat them. I could see the skin and claws and little hairs.

Then came a plate of squid. I couldn't eat it.

Then came some stuffed pig trotters, I couldn't eat them.

I was so embarrassed. But every dish that came out except the beef wrapped in leaves, I couldn't eat. Even the seaweed was salty, and I had to leave it.

Fortunately, my friends weren't offended. They thought it incredibly funny. They loved watching me trying to be polite and also it meant more food for them!

I was so hungry yet couldn't eat the dim sum, so we ordered some fried chicken-no claw in sight, egg fried rice and some prawn crackers. I finished off the rest of the beef in leaf thingies too.

THE GOLF COURSE 2000

It was winter in Edinburgh, and my mum, N. and I were going for a swim with our baby at the local golf club. My dad was due to play golf later depending on the condition of the fairway. My mum phoned my dad and said: "Yes golf is on, I saw a man go on the golf course".

My husband was puzzled. He was looking for mango on the golf course!

BARCELONA 2007

I went with my daughter on a dance trip and to save a bit of money we stayed in a basic hotel in Lloret de Mar. The food was difficult to describe, and most people went out favouring the fast food along the promenade. I was determined that my seven-year-old sample Spanish food, so we helped ourselves to a large plate of something. We looked at each other and then at the lumps in the sauce.

What could it be?

I had to find out, so I went up to the chef and tried to ask. They spoke no English, and I spoke no Spanish. It then turned into a fun game of charades with noises. I made a pig sound and squashed my nose- no it wasn't pork. I moved and made horns- no it wasn't a horse. I clucked like a chicken, neighed like a horse.

My daughter was in a state of embarrassment/ astonishment/ merriment. We were running out of animals until the chef did the under the sea movement, but it wasn't a fish.

We finally narrowed it down to squid – calamari in a tomato sauce with pasta ribbons. We smiled politely, left the table and I gave my daughter the go ahead and run. We found an excellent pizzeria with a sea view and a great range of ice cream flavours for dessert. Viva Espana!

FOAMING AT THE MOUTH 2014

Who leaves bubble-bath next to the sink? Well apparently not me, for after cleaning my teeth I took a large swig of what I thought was mouthwash. It was a bubble bath. I then made the mistake of trying to rinse my mouth out with water instead of maybe a dry flannel. I was foaming at the mouth. Bubbles emerged from my nose too. It was horrendous. The more water I drank, the more bubbles that were produced. My family just stood and laughed. I can laugh now, but if I had laughed then, I would've created a stream of small bubbles.

THE SUN LOUNGER

I bought a fabulous retro striped sun lounger in 2010 and carried it in the car in case I had the opportunity when I was out anywhere to sit in the sun- especially when the girls were dancing. At home, my garden was overlooked, but it was also a sun-trap.

I prepared one day for some serious sunbathing. I had a lovely iced Danish pastry I remember, and I put it under the lounger to keep cool.

The lounger collapsed,

I had quite hurt myself, but I was upset more about the Danish pastry which now squashed was coming through the mesh of the lounger. I lay there smarting a bit, mourning the loss of my Danish pastry. As I did so, the builder who had seen everything from next door said,

"Are you alright Luv?"

THE FLY 2012

If you've seen the Karate Kid film with Ralph Macchio, he has to practise his reflexes by catching a fly with chopsticks.

One night a friend and I were having a Chinese meal, and there were chopsticks on the table. I can never get the hang of them. This fly was bothering us as we ate. My friend tried to get it using the chopsticks. I cheated and tried to get it with the dessert menu. I splatted it, and it fell into my dinner. Dead.

If only I had had the soup!

I told the waiter there was a fly in the dinner. I only told her to get a reaction as it was hilarious.

The waitress was apologetic and called the manager over who gave us a drink and a dessert to say sorry, and the rest of the meal was on the house. I did feel a tad guilty.

But not as guilty as I felt about the chocolate mousse...

THE CHOCOLATE MOUSSE 1991

At University we took turns to cook food as cooking was stressful and no-one cooked properly? It was far too easy to make toast, noodles or get a takeaway. Cooking for flatmates or friends meant that we ate properly.

I was going to a party with some Italian friends, and I was bringing the dessert. I had forgotten until the last minute so made a gallon of chocolate mousse using a packet mix and milk.

Everyone loved the chocolate mousse. I had grated a chocolate bar on the top for effect too. My Italian friend wanted the recipe. She was very, and I couldn't just say it was an ancient family recipe. I kept making excuses until I felt so guilty I told her a couple of years later. I sent her some packets for Christmas too!

ONE WAFER THIN MINT

In Italy 1992 I had had a late huge afternoon Italian meal consisting of soup, pasta, meat, dessert with some student friends of mine. I had had breakfast and a snack for lunch much earlier, and it was a fun meal.

Feeling full I returned home to the family I was staying with, having forgotten I had said I would be back for dinner. I had to have a second substantial Italian dinner with all the trimmings.

Later that evening I had plans to meet friends at an ice-cream parlour, and although I tried to be polite and order something simple, I ended sharing one of the enormous desserts you eat with spoons. I was nagged continuously to eat my fair share. I'm not sure how I got home later, but I staggered in to find my family still entertaining their friends. They invited me to sit down with them for a coffee and liqueur, and when they brought the cake out, I wasn't sure what to say. It was rude to say no.

As I put the fork on the plate, I could see myself as the Monty Python character, Mr Creosote. I brought the fork to my mouth and could hear my stomach vibrating. After I had chewed on a small morsel, I let out the loudest belch. I was so embarrassed. It made the one Bruce Bogtrotter did in Matilda the musical seem like a squeak.

I felt all eyes on me and slightly shaking, absolutely mortified. I made my excuse to leave the table with a headache. I politely tucked my chair in and rolled into my room.

BLUE SOUP

Bridget Jones famously made blue soup once and had the dashing Mark Darcy come to the rescue. I made purple soup at University and in the days before allergy sufferers carried Epi-pens, almost triggered a full-blown nut allergy in a friend. I had learned a great soup recipe that involved celery, curry powder ketchup and peanut butter. There were other ingredients including rice, and the finished result can get rather thick because of the rice and look unappetisingly greeny-brown.

I added food colouring which turned the soup a purple colour, and I also forgot to mention to my friends that it contained nuts in my sheer desperation of getting them all to taste it. No alcohol was needed to get them to try it, and I'm sure some friends were polite when they said they liked it, but one friend who hadn't tried it yet wasn't feeling well, and her lips were starting to swell. She was allergic to the peanut butter fumes in the air from reheating the soup. Fortunately, she got medical attention quickly, but in the 1980s nut allergies weren't common. I soon learned about the severity of nut and other food allergies as a teacher when children in the class even reacted with coconut shampoo from another child or the trace of strawberries left on a table. All very scary.

THE FINES BOOK

I may have eaten some rubbish over the years, but at least I've had the freedom to eat it. My brother had been socialising with some Grenadier Guards who had told him about their fines book. You had a fine if you stooped so low as to:

- Bring Marmite to the breakfast table. Marmalade was OK. And the best one, not food related:
- Be caught writing to a girl who lived at a house with a number! Imagine! The shame!

27

SCOTLAND THE BRAVE

I took the plunge and had my hair cut short in February 2018, not shaved but very short. It was a relief and literally "a weight off my shoulders!" It was still incredibly curly and resembled a Brillo scouring pad. One friend did ask for a bit to scour her oven with!

I saved all the hedge trimmings in a plastic bag. I'm tempted to stuff a pillow with it, but I'm yet undecided.

Glancing in shop windows, I reminded myself of my brother. It made me look a bit butch. My friend agreed and said I looked like the manly one in a lesbian relationship! The hair that was left hadn't seen the light for years, and so was dark grey and wiry. If turned upside down I could be used to clean the oven! Fortunately, I knew it wasn't going to last, but now I started worrying that when my hair eventually did grow back, it would come back in the same manner.

I didn't sleep well during the night with hot flushes, restless legs and worry. I had been worrying about my mum. She was having her surgery for endometrial cancer while I was having my hair cut. Fortunately, all went well, and she had had a hysterectomy and the whole caboodle taken out including a node to be tested. She recovered from the anaesthetic well, and when I phoned to see how she was, she was sitting up with dad watching 'The Six Nations Rugby'. They had debentures at Murrayfield Stadium in Edinburgh and loved the game.

I put the rugby on too and snuggled on the settee with my dog to watch. Scotland was playing Wales. Although I lived in England and was English, there was part of me that wanted Scotland to do well.

UP NORTH SOMEWHERE

My family moved to Edinburgh in October 1981. I had just passed the 12+ grammar school tests and had had my bedroom decorated in a beautiful brown floral print. I didn't want to go. I thought Scotland was far away and they spoke funny. I didn't know many Scots and apart from Edinburgh, Skye and Glasgow, I hadn't heard of any other places.

The Scottish accent was tricky to get used to. The first programme I watched on television was late at night in the hotel we were staying in while house-hunting, and it was The Beechgrove Garden. I hadn't a clue what they were saying. We found it easier to wait until the speaker had finished and then nod or smile.

MISHEARD

At dinner shortly after arriving in Scotland, my mum listened to my dad's Scots boss talk about the Coney Fur he had just bought his wife for Christmas. Hearing "conifer," my mum asked his wife where she was thinking of planting it!

There were lots of alien words- girls were lassies and women were hens or dolls.

Yes was aye and no was nae.

Dirty was clarty and disgusting was minging.

But possibly the best new word was "seek" which meant serves you right/ tough luck/ haha/ hard cheese all rolled into one.

While waiting for a meeting my class and I were sitting on a stage, and they were told to move up. I moved up, off the stage and onto my coccyx. I'd never felt pain like it, but also I hadn't heard the word "Seek" either, which was roared by so many people.

Hogmanay (New Year's Eve) is enormous in Scotland. My family soon learnt that it was OK to knock on your neighbour's front door after midnight on New Year's Day and invite yourself in "first-footing". If you brought a bit of black bun, then it was okay to wander in and have a drink as a teenager first-footing was an excuse to go and have a street buffet- different food from different houses. At midnight in the city centre, it was also an excuse to kiss as many police officers as possible, a ceilidh (Scottish dancing)the morning away, listen to a band that everyone had thought had broken up years ago yet knew all the words and walk all the way home as there were no taxis. And all without a mobile phone either.

STARTING SCHOOL OCT 1981

The Scots have a Primary 7 class, so my brother instead of starting secondary school was in the last year again of the primary. He had an excellent first day and was complimented on the elastic, orange, floral tie which he wore proudly to school with his grey shorts and grey shirt. Unfortunately, on the telephone my dad had heard "yer oon tie" (your own tie) instead of maroon tie!

It wasn't easy starting a Scottish secondary Comprehensive School two months into the first year. I was known as "Wire heed" or "Bog brush" or "Enema" or "Sassenach". The Scots can be very cruel to the English.

MUM'S CAR

My mum was selling her car, and it was bought on by a Scottish television company. They were going to try an experiment. They painted a red cross of St George on the white car and put flags and other England stickers on the car. It was then filmed being driven through the streets of Glasgow. Abuse was hurled at the driver of the car, and eventually when it was parked at night, it was kicked and then set alight. It was sad watching the car on TV but even worse seeing it destroyed because of what it represented. You can still see the clip on YouTube.

WORLD CUP 1986

England was to play Argentina. You could wear blue to school or blue to work.

England played Nigeria, and at the airport, there was a billboard saying "Och Aye Kanu" in reference to the Nigerian player. With the fuzzy hair, scaly skin and an English accent, I was easy pickings for the school bullies.

My first-hand experience of being bullied however does have one positive. It has made me deal with bullying differently as a teacher. I had realised from a young age that racism wasn't just about the colour of your skin, but also about where you were born. Neither did I have any say in it.

28

CHEMO BRAIN

"You may develop what is known as 'Chemo brain'," said the chemo-nurse, "It may make you prone to memory loss and confusion".

Oh, joy. On top of my B12 deficient brain fog, I was going to get Chemo brain. Good luck to all my friends with that one I thought.

EARLIER BRAIN FOG

Forgetting where I parked the car seemed to be happening more and more frequently, and now I could use the excuse of having chemo-brain. In 2015 another incident occurred which was partly due to having B12 fog and also due to the real atmospheric fog.

My daughter and I went to Italy for a few days to have a break and I made sure I parked in the corner of the short stay car park in an easy place to remember. It was Zone B. Returning to the car park with suitcases in tow; neither of us could remember which zone I had parked in. I knew it rhymed with 'ee'. We looked in car park zones B C D and E, and there was no car parked in the corner. It was Halloween, 11 pm and incredibly foggy. The car parks were deserted and to be honest; it was a little scary. We tried the intercom help buttons at the bus stops, but they all weren't working. We finally decided to follow the main route back up to the entrance and to ask at the barriers for help. It was a long walk, pulling suitcases in the dark and in the fog along deserted roads.

I pressed the help button, and a muffled voice answered via the intercom. I felt a bit silly saying I had lost my car, but shortly a man appeared and ushered us to the office where he checked the CCTV. It was a simple process. On that day at that time of arrival, only one car park zone was open. Car park F! The attendant very kindly offered to drive us back to car park F rather than wait for the shuttle bus. It was one time that we were relieved to get into the car of a stranger, and we found ourselves crying with relief. If we had been searching in broad daylight and without dragging heavy suitcases full of authentic Italian food and pints of apricot juice, we might have laughed about losing our car and looking for it, but the fog and the shadows of the trees and the silence had spooked us both a bit, let alone it being Halloween.

We got a result too as the attendant gave us a pass to exit the barrier and saved us £100 of parking fees!

THE DAY OF POISONING

I had been fitted with a PICC line and had one last ECG (heart monitoring scan) to just double check I was fit and healthy before starting chemotherapy. The PICC line was a way of joining a vein in my arm with a thin, flexible tube to one in my chest and would mean no more attempts to find a vein in my arm and sore cannulae hanging out at jaunty angles from the tiniest of veins. One cannula would stay in for the whole duration of treatment.

PICC stands for Peripherally Inserted Central Catheter. Mine didn't go in that easily and took a wrong turn around my shoulder and went up a vein near my ear. Two x-rays later it travelled down the right vein and stopped just near the heart. It didn't hurt; I couldn't feel it.

The night before my chemo was due to start; I slept poorly. I was worried about not knowing how it would affect me. When I finally did wake up, I felt like death warmed up before even starting! My

Vitamin B12 injection was due soon too and was causing fatigue and muscle ache. I was also very short tempered and getting cross over the slightest of things.

I drank lots of water, and the first drug- the red one- Epirubicin was administered via four syringes and the second- Cyclophosphamide was administered similarly, flushed through with saline. The room was warm, and the chair was comfy with a reclining footstool. I had watched too many TV programmes and had envisaged a light and an airy dayroom with flowers on the windowsill and people in headscarves chatting away with each other while bags of liquid dripped down long tubes.

It wasn't quite like that, and for a start, the unit was down in the basement and very quiet apart from a radio playing. The patients were either reading quietly or asleep and of a mixed age range and sex. Some had brought a relative too. There was no Wi-Fi.

I had waitress service; however, with a cup of tea refills and biscuits and even a choice of sandwiches at lunchtime. We were spoilt. The second drug made my sinuses hot, and I had a nose bleed. It was an odd side effect, and I was quickly given hydrocortisone and antihistamine. They knocked me out and after an embarrassing hour's snooze; I was ready to go home.

I had a doggy bag of injections for my stomach, anti-sickness drugs and steroid tablets to take home. The district nurse would also be popping in to flush through the PICC line. That was me for the next three weeks. Fingers crossed everything would be all right.

The first three days were hard. I had to take steroid tablets and anti-sickness tablets, but I felt intense tiredness that I couldn't shake. It was nothing like the B12 tiredness. This was like jetlag. I was light-headed and dizzy and couldn't sit still watch the TV or read. Everything ached, and I couldn't get comfortable anywhere. At one point I was sitting with my arms dangling over the back of the settee trying to get some rest.

My B12 injection was due, and on the way back from the doctors I was sick in the street, just as the local school were walking to their PE lesson — nothing I could do. I hoped the new short haircut meant I wasn't recognised.

The steroid tablets make sleep difficult. The leaflet says "an agitated feeling". I second that. Even my memory foam bed had begun to lose its memory and kept waking me up. This tiredness was more irritating than wearing camel hair pants! The best word I found that could sum up my mood was "exhaustipated"- too tired actually to give a s***!

To make my house infection free took a bit of work. The inside of the washing machine and tumble dryer had never seen such a deep clean! Phoebe's toys were washed and sprayed, and an anti-bacterial gel was put in every room. I didn't want to pick up an infection that I could stop.

My immune system was gradually decreasing and to counteract this I had to self inject for five days. The first day, my hand was shaking. The needle was thin and the flesh on my stomach thick and vast to stab, but still, the thought of actually inflicting pain on myself was worrying. As it turned out, I didn't feel a thing and was quite proud of myself.

I had noticed a dip in my mood. I watched the opening ceremony of the Winter Olympics in Korea fighting back the tears. I think it was something to do with the hope of peace and countries uniting in one goal- to triumph through a struggle. That was how I felt. I wanted to triumph through struggle. I grew even closer to my dog. She didn't understand what was going on but knew if she played her cards right she would get lots of cuddles and snuggles and strokes if she came and sat next to me. I swear somehow she sensed something was not quite right and she followed me everywhere in the house.

The extreme tiredness lasted a week and then I managed to get some rest. I then had something else to moan about – I now had a metallic taste in my mouth and was prone to sicky burps- nice! The weather was freezing so it was an excellent excuse to batten down the hatches and hibernate.

As I got dressed into fresh pyjamas, I looked down on my mastectomy scar and wished myself a Happy Pancake Day! I had pancakes for breakfast by habit for Shrove Tuesday, not for love, but by now all foods tasted very similar and horror of horrors, I was going off tea and coffee. I also decided that I was giving up giving up anything for Lent. Simple.

Valentine's Day brought lots of messages of support and love from a UK breast cancer support group on Facebook, and as I woke finally with some energy, I enjoyed a day pottering around the house and changing the furniture around. I also bought a posh leather chair and footstool that could be "my chair". It was a present to me from me. I was worth it.

NOW, WHAT?

Another day, another side effect. This time my lower back started aching. I had been warned that the Filastrim injections that I had been taking to encourage the growth of new white blood cells might cause back pain. It wasn't too bad but enough to take painkillers. The district nurse came to "flush my PICC line". I had bought a fancy floral covering for my arm- another impulse buys in the middle of the night, although I must have been bored to have searched for 'PICC line cover'.

My energy levels increased around day 10, and the weather seemed to improve too. I spent a fabulous two hours sunbathing in February in the garden. My hot flushes were keeping me even warmer, and although it was only 12 degrees, I was warm and imagined I was somewhere exotic. I took a photo of my foot against the blue sky- I was one of those who did that and posted on Facebook rather than the customary 'hot dog knees photo."My leg was silky smooth. The hairs had dropped or rubbed off during the last few days, and now there was no need for a razor, any foul smelling hair removal cream or waxing. Surely this was a bonus?!

OFFERS OF HELP

The offers of help were now coming flooding in. Maybe it was the short hair or glimpse of my PICC line, but suddenly friends seemed even more concerned about me and offered to cook food, walk the dog, take my daughter to dance class, bring dinners around, drive me places. It was lovely. I didn't say no. My eyesight was still pretty blurry, and I didn't want to drive any long distances. I took people up on their offers, and they didn't seem to mind. My pen-pals abroad began face-timing me and emailing, and I even got some care parcels in the post and my favourite sweets sent from the USA. Everyone kept saying I was an inspiration.

AN INSPIRATION

I didn't feel I was an inspiration. I didn't have any choice. It was either go through the treatment or face a higher risk of recurrence. There were still no guarantees that it wouldn't come back, but at least I was trying something. Someone who was an inspiration to me was the girls' dance teacher. She had had bile duct cancer and went through chemotherapy and radiotherapy. The cancer returned with a vengeance, and she died on New Year's Day. She never stopped fighting and carried on choreographing and teaching when she could and arranging trips abroad and shows. She was taken far too soon.

I went to the memorial service, and it was then that I cried for the first time. It was too close to home. There was I, and another lady near me who were responding to treatment. I was surrounded by 15 years of friends and their children from the dance centre, and my daughter was singing and dancing. In that church, I sobbed. I sobbed for their teacher and their family and then for me. I felt utterly helpless.

It was then I thought truly about what makes someone an inspiration, and I wondered if it was a belief that I was not as brave or smart or good as that person, and so they became some role model and if they could do it, then so could I.

A few years ago, the writing in the year 6 SATS (end of the year) government insisted exam was to write about "Someone Who Inspires You". I would have loved to have answered that question, although I would not have known who to choose over my mum or my dad. Most of the 11-year-olds wrote about their sports' heroes or their grandad but we as a teaching staff were an amalgamation of shocked saddened and mortified to find out that one pupil's inspiration was 'Jeremy Kyle'!

MUM'S THE WORD

On 15 February 2018, my mum got the all-clear after her surgery. It was such brilliant news. I felt happy for my mum and my dad too. The nodes investigated weren't cancerous, and the consultant was pleased. My mum had now to decide whether she wanted to undergo brachytherapy. This was an internal radiation treatment taken over a couple of days that would blast anything ominous left over from surgery. There were pros and cons, but it was a simple treatment. I wished I had a simple treatment. As I sent into school my doctor's certificate for absence, I longed for treatment to be over and to feel healthy enough to return to the classroom. I missed my colleagues.

29
FRIENDS

Having both a mental illness and physical illness showed me who my friends were. Very few people stuck by me when I had the mental illness. It was partly fear and ignorance of what to say or how to help and also somewhat because I had been rude to some people and told them to stay away. Reading me during that time was hard.

My family didn't have the choice, and they were stuck with me regardless. Some friends were supportive by text and inspirational quotes and phone calls. I also had a couple of guardian angels who had been through something similar so knew what to do and say and sometimes would turn up with a takeaway coffee or food for the children. In my life, I needed people that would "elevate not constipate". I was able by now to know the difference.

One person who never left my side was my best friend D. As a teenager we had been boyfriend and girlfriend, but we were more like brother and sister. We had too many things in common for things to work and also because we valued our friendship we didn't want to break up and not speak to each other ever again as sometimes happened with young relationships. We accompanied each other as friends to concerts, to swimming galas, to game shows. D. Taught me to ski and ice-skate and we shared piano music. We were both studying for grade 8. D. Visited me in St Andrews and we met up every Christmas to visit the Edinburgh street entertainment.

D. was a best friend, and because he had a serious girlfriend, it wasn't awkward at all. He was worried about my relationship with N. but from a neutral friend's point of view. He had never met N. and just thought we had all the odds stacked against us for a successful marriage.

As we grew older, we both became teachers. D. Started as a music teacher in a secondary school and then became involved in pastoral care and eventually a Deputy Headteacher. I was never interested in management, and we used to joke about our different roles. I suffered from depression, and D. was on medication for severe anxiety and stress. We both understood each other and could text at any time of the day and night and know someone was there. I had never met his wife or his son, and similarly, D. never met my family, it was about us. There was no sexual chemistry at all between us, which is why it worked. D. was protective of me and I of him. He would send me silly postcards or toys from the 1980s, and I would find fun things to send to brighten his day at school.

There was no secrecy, yet I didn't talk to anyone about our relationship. Outsiders may find it strange or insist that we were having an affair, but it was not true. We were both loyal to our partners. D. Was just D. I couldn't bear the thought of losing him or things being awkward, so we were just rude to each other and took the mickey out of each others' film and music tastes, only agreeing on the wonder of the musical theatre star Kerry Ellis. My phone had nothing to hide, yet it was private. I didn't want the kids reading our conversations. D. was my friend. I didn't even sign our texts with an "x" D. understood why I didn't leave the house during my illness as he had had similar days. He would then feel better by going off walking on his own into the Munros- large hills near Edinburgh. That was his 'D. Time' and I understood that. I had to have "me time" too.

I introduced him to musical theatre, forcing him to watch Billy Elliot and Wicked and also to eat pickled onion Monster Munch crisps. He made me listen to Scottish pop music and made me use Shea hand cream- silly things but so important now. He also wrote a daily diary without fail for his son to give to him on his 18th birthday of things his son did that day, and things in the news, to keep forever. It was such a sweet thing to do.

At the end of April 2017, he texted how much he was looking forward to going walking into the hills. A week or so passed and I hadn't heard from him. It was the end of the term, and he would never pick up his phone. I assumed he was busy. Days then weeks passed. I still heard nothing.

I looked back at my text messages; he hadn't said anything about going away. I texted a long emotional message from Tenerife and again got no reply. At first, I was upset, then I got cross and hurt, and then I didn't care. He was throwing a perfect friendship away and over what? I was no threat to his wife. We were just really good friends.

When the schools went back in September, I wrote him a letter to his school. That way he had to read it and I asked him to keep in touch if only to let me know how he was from time to time. In October I still hadn't heard anything. I plucked up the courage to phone his school and speak to him directly. I hadn't anything to lose. I wanted to tell him that I had cancer. I hadn't told many people yet, and I wanted him to be one of the first to know.

I spoke to the secretary, and she said that D. didn't work at the school anymore. I said I was a good friend and could she let me know a contact number for him as I had some important news to tell him or if not, could she pass on a message please to him.

"I'm sorry; I can't do that," she said, "D. died last May".

I was in shock. My heart was racing. I couldn't say anything, and I was fighting back the tears. I couldn't believe it.

I got online and searched his name. It was true. There was an article in May regarding a 47-year-old hill walker that had had a heart attack and was found by other walkers. He had died alone walking in the hills he loved. He was so looking forward to going away that weekend.

We were the same age.

I don't know where I got the strength to keep my head up and high during those days. The very next day was when I was diagnosed with cancer. I had lost my best friend. How was I going to get through my cancer journey without him? How was I going to cope knowing I would never see him again?

I had missed the funeral; it had been six months ago. I messaged his wife, and I got a lovely reply from her. She was going to continue the daily diary for their son. I wasn't able to grieve properly until a few weeks later.

"SEE YA BILLY"

One of the older men that I had met at Billy Elliot had suddenly died. He was such a kind-hearted man that had taken the time to chat with me, and he loved the show as much as I did. We had often sat next to each other in the cheap seats, and I thought he was lovely. His funeral wasn't too far away, so I went along. I held it together until "Electricity" from the musical Billy Elliot was played, and I grieved for both him and D.

Knowing I had cancer, I wondered how many people would come to my funeral and it was as I was filing out to a Millwall football song with a slight smile on my face, that I thought I just had to have a cheerful or funny song at my funeral for family and friends to remember me by.

30

LITERALLY TEARING
MY HAIR OUT

VEGGING FEBRUARY 2018

I spent many hours slumped in my new posh chair. I didn't have any energy. I was being good and drinking litres of water to flush out the toxins, but it meant numerous exhausting trips to the toilet. I liked the contrast between my vegetative state and the super fit snow-boarders and speed skaters that I was watching compete in the Olympics. It didn't inspire me or make me feel guilty if anything it exhausted me and made me feel cold. The thought wearing one of those specially designed NASA clingy catsuits also scared me. I had put on quite a bit of weight since diagnosis, and those suits were unforgiving.

I had got a waterproof PICC line cover for the shower and bath and took great fascination as it sucked like a giant leech onto my arm expelling all air. It was only during one of my hot flushes at night around 3 am did I realise I was still wearing it after my bath. Almost, but not quite in the same league as my mum who caught a bus and realised she was still wearing an oven glove!

WIG REFERRAL

I had become used to my short hair. Despite looking like my brother, it was so easy to manage. I took a more significant interest in the wigs on sale in the hair shop, although not daring to try them on alone. I went to my official wig referral at the hospital. I was quite excited thinking I'd be able to try a few on. It wasn't quite like that. I was shown a glossy catalogue of models wearing wigs- not cancer patients and told to choose one. I had an NHS voucher that could be put towards one, but my goodness I had no idea how expensive it would be.

I could choose a colour according to hair samples, but I wanted to try one on to see if I looked like a clown or looked quite cool. It would take a week to arrive, and I didn't have to commit to, so that was a relief. I had chosen one with a slight fringe and much straighter so I could "swish". The lady looked a little confused when I asked what it did in the wind. I didn't mean did it fly off your head. I meant did it flare out like a lion's mane, all unruly like my own- or rather like my own used to do.

COMPUTER TIMES

Writing and editing these stories was good therapy for me. It meant I could look back on the past and then see how far I had come, but it also highlighted how terrible I was with I.T. I was forever cutting and pasting into the wrong places, losing work and confusing fonts. At times I felt like throwing the laptop out of the window. However, if I had had a laptop during my university years, I would have saved so much paper that lay in scrunched up balls around my room during essay days!

The hours I wasted playing games on our ZX Spectrum in the 1980s. It took absolute ages to type in the program code, only for the game not to load. The games were simple but ever so addictive. My favourite game was Manic Miner which was an adventure over different levels, but it was ever so frustrating as every time you lost a life you had to start from level one again. The day that someone gave me a code for 'unlimited lives' was one of the best days ever. My diary entry read, "Can't believe it; I can play Manic Miner forever now!" It wasn't quite forever, but I'm sure I have been secretly programmed to do something while listening to the repetitive electronic soundtrack that went with the game. I haven't yet worked out what it is, but if I ever hear the tune again, I fear I may do something stupid!

I dislike computers mainly because I don't understand them and how they work (like cars) and when they don't do what I want, I cry. Just as I get to grips with the software, it changes. The girls both grew up with a computer in the house, and we all have laptops to allegedly 'study on the go'. I seem to have so many passwords for so many electronic devices and accounts and websites. One time I phoned home to get a password for a laptop and my daughter, she replied, "Start with a capital S then star, star, star, star." I was getting so frustrated as it still wasn't logging in. I was typing, "Start ****". Just as I was about to throw the thing across the room, I realised what she meant. I should have been entering "S****".

Still, without computers, I wouldn't even have a box of scrap paper at home with perforated holes either side!

WINTER OLYMPICS

The winter Olympics were continuing, and Great Britain had triumphs and disappointments. I felt myself wanting to hug or the athletes that fell over or were beaten at the last minute. Maybe this was my medication too, but I was fairly tearful watching, especially when the athletes fell over or were disqualified or beaten by 0.01 seconds. Four years of training for a disaster, one minute or competition or performance and it was all over. Where did they get that kind of strength?

I also wondered why it was that every female snowboarder or skier took their helmets off to reveal long flowing, mainly blonde hair and was also beautiful. Maybe it was because I was fixated by hair at that time, but also the men had flowing locks. It seemed you could only ski or snowboard if you were young, gorgeous and had long hair. Whereas the criteria to do the biathlon of cross-country skiing and shooting was to have a beard and to be completely bonkers! Who thought of that as a sport? I mean to ski cross country up and down hills and then while you were out of breath and frozen, to lie down and hold a rifle still enough to shoot a tiny target five times. What fun. Early ice-age hunters!

The figure skating was nervous watching from behind the sofa; I didn't want anyone to fall. This was my favourite event in the Olympics, possibly because I kept thinking of my own relatively recent attempts to ice skate. I hadn't mastered how to stop and crashed into the sides between beginners hanging on for dear life to stop, and it had taken nearly 50 years to go a few metres backwards.

These 15 and 16-year-olds in South Korea were performing triple jumps and spinning and dancing on the ice. I was chuffed to keep upright for more than one lap of the rink. The only thing I did find funny was the girl's costume malfunctions. Leotards were getting munched up behind, and straps and poppers were pinging undone as they span, Luckily there was no "fall-out" but if that had have been me on the ice it would have happened and in front of millions of viewers!

HAIR TODAY, GONE TOMORROW

I pulled my PICC line out around 10cm just taking off my coat. The district nurse came round and wasn't able to save it. This was a blow as I needed it in because of my dodgy veins. It meant another visit to the hospital.

I was also literally tearing my hair out with tearing my hair out. It was moulting everywhere and also hurting. My hair felt sensitive to touch, and my scalp felt like it had static electricity running through it. Typical, it had started to come out just as I was getting used to the short cut. I had even perfected the boys' "Meet me at McDonald's cut"!

I tried to shock my family pulling large clumps out without wincing. It was a great party trick to perform over Facetime on the phone, although I don't think my mum thought it as funny. I was reminded of this joke:

"What is the first sign of madness?"

Ans: "Finding hair on the palm of your hand."

"What is the second sign of madness?"

Ans: Looking for it.

Both of my palms were covered with hair, and like white school glue, it was a nightmare to wipe off!

The PICC line had come out of my arm too far, so it was removed entirely and blood tests now had to be taken directly from a vein. More and more hair was falling out, and despite people saying that I looked good, I felt like the stuffing had been knocked out of me. The only smile I could muster was when stationary in my car at traffic lights, I had pulled clumps of hair out from my head to the horror of the watching driver next to me and then casually thrown the fuzz out of the window. The birds would soon find it.

I had ordered some soft beanie hats, and they had arrived in the post. The first one made me look like a World War 2 land girl, the second like a housewife and the last one had a flower on the side and I felt I had to burst into the Charleston dance as I wore it. However, they were comfortable to wear at night.

I took my daughter to the wig shop and tried a few on. We had a code for "Mum, that is hideous," so that we wouldn't hurt the sales assistant's feelings. As I tried some on I realised that this was just for me. My friends would know I was wearing a wig so it would only be to face strangers. I went for a longish blonde 'Agnetha from Abba' one that I could tie back and alter and then a short black bob with pink ends. Well, why not? It was never the style I could grow myself, and it was fun. Next, I needed to work out how to draw in eyebrows and do my makeup to go with my new hairdos.

I did my bit for the community, well- for the birds, and pegged all my fallen hair on the washing line. It would make excellent nesting material, especially with the snow on its way. I can still remember the double take my friend did over coffee as she looked at my washing line. I could see her trying to work out what it was and then politely not say anything, so I put her out of her misery and told her.

Fortunately, my garden is not overlooked.

EC AND T

Epirubicin is a bright red chemo drug that makes your wee red. I was at the hospital when I first noticed and to say I was a wee bit surprised was an understatement. I thought I was losing my internal workings and I hadn't even touched any beetroot. Once reassured, it made a fun experiment. Would it turn purple with a loo blue?!

I also couldn't quite get into the habit of flushing twice for 48 hours after chemo. This was to protect other healthy people from the toxins. It was ok at home, but when I was out, it was awkward flushing then waiting for the cistern to fill up again just reading the healthy living poster or the graffiti on the back of the door. I once waited outside in a restaurant toilet but then as soon as someone came in, I had to rush into the cubicle to flush as if I had forgotten- even more awkward.

31

IN SCREENSAVER MODE

Once again the extreme fatigue dragged me down. I just sat in my chair. I couldn't read or text or watch TV; I could only listen to it. I called it being 'in screensaver mode' as I was there in spirit but not necessarily in body. My arms were covered in bruises from collapsed veins. The nurse had tried unsuccessfully to re-insert the PICC line, and so I had to wait for an appointment to have a Hickman Line put in. This was a heavy duty line going in at the jugular vein. Chemo no.2 went in the back of the hand.

I slumped waiting for the "Beast from the East" to come sweeping in.

CHEMO AND SNOW

I had no reason to venture out, and as the UK froze, I stayed in bed and tried to work through the chemo symptoms. I still had hot flushes and my beanie hat would make my head hot and then I would take it off and feel cold. The stubborn spiky hairs left acted like receivers, and I could feel the wind even from opening a kitchen cupboard- they were that sensitive. I also got my scalp infected as I would scratch during the night. It took a while to get used to the Uncle Fester look but I wasn't upset, I was impatient. I had almost had enough and wanted it all to be over. Insomnia had returned, and the online cancer forums were a great support at this time, and I've made a lot of virtual friends. It was also a space to vent and rant and generally moan because everyone would understand. Bone pain and mouth ulcers were manageable with painkillers but there was nothing I could do about the wooziness, and I had resorted to going downstairs on my bottom.

The winter storm was aptly named Storm Emma. Schools were shut, and supplies ran low locally, but I had squirrelled supplies, and fortunately, we were ok. I also had help from friends and a volunteer dog walker.

Phoebe turned two years old, and the snow melted. Daffodils tried to pop their heads out, and my eldest daughter visited for 24 hours to spend Mother's Day with me. My mum had had positive oncology appointments and needed only three radiotherapy sessions. She had an end in sight. I focused on the school summer holiday; hopefully, that would be my end. I was on half pay now and soon no payment. Things were getting tighter. My clothes were getting tighter. There was nothing wrong with my appetite and despite fuzzy mouth and a constant metallic taste; I was still eating for England.

I attended a neurology appointment, and blood tests revealed that my B12 levels did drop around week 7-8 and I was prescribed injections at eight weekly intervals. I had too many symptoms going on as to accurately evaluate any improvement in mood and fatigue, but this was a step in the right direction, mainly as these injections were for life. I was so pleased, mostly as I knew what a difference the injections made to me in normal health circumstances.

SWEATY HEAD

On my good days, I tried to go out and socialise. I alternated between beanie hats, bandanas, bobble hats and my wigs, depending on the weather. I went out for a curry with my work colleagues wearing my two-tone black and pink wig. There was a lot of new staff, and I got chatting with some ladies. One friend was particularly puzzled as she thought the school's policy was not to have bright hair and I took great delight in telling her it was a wig. My head was so hot- a hot flush and the curry and sitting near a radiator had made me want to fling off my wig. I was also not used to having hair that fell around my face and with every mouthful I was eating my hair and the fringe I couldn't get right at all. After a bit of a struggle, I did indeed fling it off, and apart from a few stares, I was quite happy to reveal my bald head.

On leaving the restaurant, it was raining, and I enjoyed the sensation of cold rain on my shiny head. I can't describe the feeling, but I must have appeared a little eccentric to passersby as I looked up at the sky squealing in delight!

Wearing my bandana in a vintage 1940s tearoom with my parents, I looked at the waitresses in land girl costume. I turned my bandana round, so the knot was at the front and was so tempted to ask if any jobs were going! This was the real me. I had to make jokes and see the funny sides in everyday situations.

I then faced a big dilemma; to soap, to shampoo or to polish my head?!

If I am sincere, I enjoyed having no hair. I saved so much time in the mornings, I didn't smell of wet dog in the rain, and it was a talking point. I wore a bandana mostly, and I didn't get the stares I thought I would. One friend did exclaim "Wow you look like you have cancer now"! She immediately regretted it, but I knew what she meant. This was the first time my friends had indeed seen a visible sign of my illness, except I was hopefully cancer free as I told her. The cancer had been removed back in December with the mastectomy.

There were some other positives too to looking the way I did, even disguised under a headscarf; I got some sympathy avocados! They were meant to cost two for a pound, but the vendor looked at me and slipped in another two. I didn't complain.

I was joking a lot about my bald head. I think it was my way of coming to terms with it. I thought it would shock rather than get sympathy. However, I was in control. I was laughing and joking at myself. I found the first time someone said a joke about my head strange. In a supermarket, the cashier dropped all my change while handing it to me. All flustered she told me she was having a bad hair day. Then it got a bit awkward as she looked at my head. I was desperately thinking of a witty reply, but nothing sprang to mind, so I just smiled. It wasn't funny. Some youths shouted "Hey Baldy!" once in a car park to get my attention. I tried to smile but again it wasn't funny, and then a close friend made a Kojak joke. I realised if the timing or situation wasn't right then it could be quite hurtful.

It is interesting though, the stares you get when you are bald. It is only hair. I feel more self-conscious when my tooth crown falls out than with a bald head, but the stares and comments still come. In a shop, the lady serving said to me "'ere why did ya go and shave your hair off eh?". I paused, and resisted the urge to swear obscenities at her and then politely replied," I had to; I am undergoing chemo for cancer". Afterwards, I tried to think of some witty remarks, but the moment had gone. I think it is a woman thing; her hair is meant to be her crowning glory. I'm sure bald men not going through chemo don't get all this attention.

Looking at pink cancer t-shirts too online saying "Killer Boobs" on them was just too close to home. "Tragedy plus time equals comedy," I think the old saying goes. Laughter is a good medicine though, and that is precisely what I am hoping to achieve by penning this book. It should bring a smile to the reader's face. It does to mine, particularly reliving some of the situations. I read that apparently 'the actual physical act of laughing produces endorphins that help to alleviate pain and lessen anxiety and discomfort' and in some cases 'to boost the immune system of cancer patients'. Well, that sounds to me all very positive for everyone. But there is a line not to cross. Having cancer is no laughing matter and particularly for those diagnosed at a late stage with no positive outcome, but if laughter is therapy and can alleviate pain if just for a few minutes, then laugh away.

The next couple of weeks for me, however, were a bit grim. There was little laughing going on. The chemo had weakened my immune system, so I ended up with a few sores that didn't heal, some bruises and my scalp wasn't healing. Two different lots of antibiotics made me very tired, and I didn't really accomplish much around the house and instead watched a lot of films and rested.

I also planned my next fun venture. I wanted to make a fundraising calendar for breast cancer using pictures of me with my bald head, dressed up as various celebrities who had bald heads- Harry Hill, Kojak, Duncan Goodhew, Yul Brynner and Matt Lucas. I began looking in the loft for suitable accessories and ordering a few online. This was going to be a fun thing to do on a good week!

ALL I WANT FOR CHRISTMAS IS MY TWO FRONT TEETH

I ended up in fact with two consecutive good weeks.

I woke up one morning with an excruciating toothache. It travelled around my jaw and by the time I visited the emergency out of hour's dentist, I was holding my lower jaw, and the infection on x-ray was in fact in the root of my front tooth. I was given antibiotics and told to take strong painkillers. The knock on effect was that chemo cycle 3 had to be delayed by a week. I could cope with pain; I was pleased. I was also very, very used to toothache. My dentist and I were terrific friends. She had also banked most of my savings over the last ten years.

I like teeth to children. You can't live without them, yet they cause you a lot of grief and cost you a lot of money!

I always had problems with my teeth. Like the recurring dream of crumbling teeth, my teeth were crumbling. The Vitamin D deficiency meant that bits just fell off and having a severe Vitamin B12 deficiency also meant that my teeth were weaker. I was regularly seeing the dentist, getting antibiotics, having root canal treatment, having fillings, getting fillings replaced, having teeth out and it was getting me down. Even the gums were shocking and the bone too which was receding.

My oncologist and my dentist had had a long chat about the state of my gums and teeth and decided to delay the Zoladex injections.

It had also cost me a small fortune.

I had a night guard which is unsexier (made up word) than the wet eczema wraps. I would spit it out in the morning and then try and retrieve it covered in fluff from the carpet in the morning! Even though I regularly cleaned it, it still went yellow and then mouldy, so I binned it. It was a complete waste of money. I mean who wants to go to bed feeling and looking like a boxer?

My front tooth then fell out in Cairo.

I'm sure that's a title of a Monty Python song!

It's strange how just one tooth can alter the appearance of someone. I had six days of speaking only when spoken to. I needed a crown. I didn't fancy going to a dentist in Egypt. I had seen a table of teeth laid out in the souk; I didn't fancy wearing someone else's tooth.

Losing a tooth at aged 45 does not evoke the same feeling of excitement as it does at aged five.

APPEASING THE TOOTH FAIRY

My daughter had a wobbly tooth, and while I was in a staff meeting, it came out. Out and down the sink.

She was inconsolable. Fortunately, a lovely teaching assistant helped her to compose a letter to the tooth fairy explaining what had happened and giving her address, so the fairy knew where to visit.

Thankfully the tooth fairy did visit that night.

In a few years to come that fairy too was to forget one or two or perhaps more times to visit, until much later on into the next day!

I still now in 2018 would like two new front teeth for Christmas, four if the fairy is feeling generous.

Fortunately, the antibiotics and painkiller mix did the trick, and the tooth infection soon settled down, my bloods were ok and chemo no. Three went ahead. Despite a freak weekend of snow, the daffodils were out, the clocks went back, and spring sprung!

FABULOUS POST

I began being more brave and adventurous on Facebook, and more friends came round to offer help and to visit. They changed their mind at the hospital and decided to have another go using x-ray to insert a PICC line. I was relieved. The thought of a Hickman line attached to my jugular vein was a bit daunting. The frustrating thing was that I had sent my floral fabric PICC line cover and the waterproof cover to a lady in need from a Facebook group.

I too received some fabulous post. Anyone who knew me at St. Andrews may know about my addiction to fudge doughnuts and coffee towers. I would treat myself on a Tuesday after a long Ancient History seminar, and they were bought from a unique Scottish bakery. A few years ago, a small bakery near to my parents, became another outlet for the cakes and pastries. My parents had sent me two doughnuts in a Chinese takeaway box in the first class post, and it made my day. I even sent my mum a photo of me with cream all around my mouth.

However, this parcel I received was of a similar size and wrapped in unicorn wrapping paper and tied with a pink bow. I had been sent another two fudge doughnuts in a plastic takeaway box in the first class post. The accompanying card from the bakery owner in Scotland said they had seen my photo and if fudge doughnuts could bring me so much joy, then they would continue to send me a weekly delivery until I was better or until I said stop. I was a better charity case than donating anonymously. I was both touched and happy and also on that day, stuffed!

NAILED IT

One of the nurses suggested wearing dark nail varnish on my fingers and toes to save my nails from falling off as a side effect of chemo. They hadn't begun to go yet, but it wasn't me to wear any colour of nail varnish and just as I was admiring my handy work, Phoebe my pug knocked the bottle over. I'm glad she didn't run off with the brush, but I was so, so tempted to paint her nails. I didn't, and the varnish was easily mopped up. I then spent the day looking at my nails and I even though they were cut short, felt all girly all of a sudden.

PICC LINE BACK

I attended my appointment to have the PICC line put back, but it was a different set up to the casual nurse's room before. This time I had to change into a gown and hat (incredibly fetching). I'm sure the hat was just one of those blue outdoor shoe covers you get at the swimming pool. As my immune system was low, everything had to be sterile. I was covered in more sheets, and as I lay in the x-ray room, I was relieved that I had had this procedure before. It was just all very formal and serious; well it was until my arm was swabbed with orange antiseptic and the doctor said I may now look like Donald Trump's love child!

The x-ray machine came down, and it was easier to guide the line into the correct place using the wonders of science. It went quiet and serious again until the doctor said:" Can I just move your boob out of the way, as it is in danger of invading the sterile area". With a bit of an undignified shove, he moved me over a bit on the bed, all very embarrassing, but necessary. I didn't want an infection at this stage of treatment.

"Going through chemo is like the world's worst advent calendar- what surprise will it be behind the door today? Constipation, nausea, bone pain, an ulcer or even a cold sore"?

I love this quote. It is so true. This week its heartburn, and memories of pregnancy reoccur. I also suffer from horrible acid reflux and wind. One attack had me lying face down on the lounge carpet with my daughters rubbing and standing on my back. We were all laughing which was making it worse, and then I exploded; air came out from every orifice. It was incredibly funny but hurt so much. I lay on the carpet, feeling too like I had eaten a whole chunk of it – my mouth was so dry and fuzzy, and felt relieved. "Better out than in," Shrek said. My heart was beating fast, and my baldy head was sweating profusely.

Trapped wind hurts but with chemo can come out at any time: the unexpected loud fart in a lift or belch in a queue. Sufferers call it 'chemo-mist'! I've learnt to be polite and say "I'm terribly sorry", but the girls can't cope. The look on their faces says "ground swallow me up now please," especially in public, but it can't be helped. It happened when I was pregnant, and now it was ten times worse and more during chemo!

MISSING THE SUN

The weather fortunately changed. I was able to potter about in the garden and sit and read in my garden chair. Suffering from Vitamin D deficiency, just a few minutes outside made all the difference. It wasn't hot enough to be coated in sunblock yet, and I longed to be lying on a sunbed somewhere far away. I am determined to visit a beach with white sand and turquoise water once treatment is over. It is first on my bucket list!

I had read somewhere that during radiotherapy I was to avoid sunlight. Rads were planned for the summer, and the summer in England was forecasted to be the hottest on record. I tried to put that thought to the back of my head. After all, it was only Easter.

The girls were planning their holidays- I seemed to be the last one consulted. My eldest wanted a girls' holiday with her new university friends, and my youngest wanted to go to the Highlands where all the family were going.

CHILDHOOD HOLIDAYS

Family holidays for me as a child were mostly spent caravanning. I did enjoy it when I was very young, but it wasn't cool the older I got. Which teenager truly wants to sleep next to their brother, or use a port-a-loo, or go to the bed and wake up at the same time as everyone else or to the sound of sheep chewing the awning strings, or wash in a dribble of boiled water, or hear everyone's bodily sounds, or go without TV, or drink milk that has been standing in a bowl of water all night, or fend off insects, or keep saying excuse me please as you pass someone, or wear clothes that haven't been ironed, or eat tinned meatballs and fruit, or scrape your skin on the zip of a sleeping bag?

Or maybe that is just me?

Some people love caravanning, especially in the middle of nowhere.

THE HIGHLANDS JULY 1985

After fishing off the rocks, my brothers and I used to go round other caravans trying to flog our mackerel. One evening an awning was opened by my current history teacher. Why is it a weird phenomenon to see your teachers out of school? I felt it as a child and see it now as a teacher. Children go mute when they see you in the street or mutter a couple of words or stare.

To go kayaking, you had to wear a wetsuit. The Irish Sea even in the summer is freezing. I quite fancied going kayaking but didn't fancy wearing a wetsuit. Two children and a lot of food had left me bigger than average. I looked out of the caravan and checked there were no tourists on the beach. There weren't. I squeezed myself into the wetsuit. Every lump and bump was on show, and I squeezed my feet into wet shoes.

I took a deep breath and walked down to the dunes, really happy the beach was deserted. As I came over the hill the beach was full- the people were sheltering from the wind under the dunes. There was no return, and I did the walk of shame down to the waterfront.

Kayaking isn't a relaxing sport you imagine. There's cold water sloshing around in the kayak, and your paddles pick up random strips of seaweed. Where my family kayak is safe, a bay in the north -west of Scotland and on some days it's like a mill pond. My mum has phoned me from her kayak. She had paddled out with her friends with a mini -picnic and her knitting!

Getting out of the wetsuit is not as easy. Even with talc, it's a nightmare. It's a two person job to escape.

TRAPPED

In M & S in the summer of 2016, I tried on some of their shapewear. It's meant to hide excess body fat and pull your figure into an hourglass shape. I had a party to go to and was going to be wearing a dress.

I needed some strong Bridget Jones type underwear and thought maybe the 'one piece nude lycra contraption' I was holding in my hands was just the thing. I struggled to roll it in the right place. It was like getting a bag of jelly into a sock. My flesh was compressed rightly, but it had to go somewhere. I had excess tummy flesh under my arms, and the Lycra was digging into my thighs. I couldn't breathe in it, let alone walk or dance or sit. Then I tried to take it off. It wouldn't move.

Just as I thought I'd freed one leg, it clung to the other. I banged elbows, hips, knees on the mirror of the ever-decreasing changing room. I contemplated asking for help and then had another go, resting for a moment on the tiny seat. It was no used I was trapped in the Lycra and perish the thought if I had actually bought it and needed the toilet quickly. I suddenly felt myself falling, and inelegantly I appeared through the curtain and onto the floor where a somewhat bemused old lady asked if she should get help.

I declined and somehow managed to struggle out of the shapewear, pulling every muscle in my body as I did so. It was all so embarrassing.

32

BACK TO WORK

I went back to teaching on a phased return to work, just for a couple of hours a week. I was tired, but I enjoyed it. It gave me a purpose to get up and something to look forward to. I wondered whether to wear a wig or a bandana and settled for the latter. I got boiling in the wig, and the boys would all know it was one. I taught a lesson on the Black Death and managed to incorporate facts about my chemotherapy when I talked about immune systems being weak in the 14th century.

WORDPLAY

On stressful days during chemotherapy, I found it difficult to concentrate. I couldn't read or watch TV, so I just lay in a vegetative state on the sofa with my dog. I could think and dream and began making up a new dictionary of words. I'm quite proud of them too.

CHEMOAN- verb

To chemoan is to rat about side effects of chemotherapy. I found myself chemoaning regularly, but it was a good thing. Once I had chemoaned, I felt better.

CHEMOPE- verb

This was precisely what I was doing as I couldn't concentrate, just ended up moping around the house, flitting from one thing to another. I chemoped mainly on days 4-7 after treatment.

CHEMOJO –noun

To beat this cancer, I needed to get my chemojo working. This was precisely what would make me successful and how people were going to react to me.

CHEMOTIVATION –noun

I didn't need cheesy inspirational quotes to get me through each day. I needed honesty and help with some simple things. I needed lifts when I couldn't drive and a dog walker when I couldn't walk. I needed a friend to listen when I wanted to chemoan, and I needed to be busy. When my eyes were good, I could cross stitch in front of the TV. I was recommended some Netflix Box Sets to watch but secretly quite enjoyed watching old Fresh Prince of Bel-air episodes. I started watching "Suits" too, and although I know nothing about the legal world, it was strangely addictive. I had seven seasons to catch up on so would treat myself with a binge of episodes.

THE ZOMBIE LOOK

One of the rather inconvenient side effects of chemo is frequent nosebleeds-, especially during the night. Having no nose hair means that I often awake looking like a zombie film extra! They also come by surprise and without even having knocked the nose. It's a great one when you're on public transport or out without a change of top. My nose drips too without warning because I have no nose hair, which is a nightmare if you're teaching and worse if you're leaning over a pupil's work!

CLOTHES CHANGE

I needed a whole change of clothes after a day out in Florence, Italy in 1992. I know the Italian for wet paint, but when sitting on a metal bench, I didn't expect the sign to be placed a few metres away. My jeans were blue with dark green marks. What was more was that it didn't seem to dry off me, and I was leaving a trail of green wherever I sat. However, soon I was to recreate the entire Italian flag when sitting at one of those al fresco cafes, I managed to tip half my plate of spaghetti in red sauce down most of my white top. Nice.

HOTTEST APRIL FOR 70 YEARS

Having coped with the snow and the wind, we finally got some nice weather, but I had to keep my hat on. I could feel heat leaving from my baldy head in the cold weather, and it certainly sweated or rather perspired for England in the hot weather. I had an array of bandanas on hand to mop not just my brow.

Sunlight can react badly with some chemotherapy drugs, so I needed to slap on factor 50 rather than my usual no.6 and watch for sunburn. Most recommendations say stay in the shade and out of the sun while on current chemo treatment, but I needed this dose of Vitamin D. There was no way I could sit in the shade.

Three days in a row we had good weather. For all I knew, that could have been summer over; I had no idea when it was going to be sunny again, and possibly if I was having radiotherapy when we next saw the sun, I couldn't go out in it at all.

With the hot weather came a new sound; what could only be described as a cross between a tearing and a giant lick. It was the sound of my baldy bonce sticking to my leather armchair and my leather bed headboard. It wasn't uncomfortable, but it was not a sound that a year ago I ever thought I would hear, let alone so regularly.

PARENTAL VISIT

My mum finished her last radiotherapy treatment and was able to travel with dad from Scotland to visit. I knew I had a couple of good days before treatment and we made the most of the beautiful weather. It must have been difficult for them to see me with no hair, but they had come to help. My dad did all the DIY jobs needing, and the garden and mum bulk cooked and filled the freezer with food. She didn't notice that I had put a few of the worst things to iron on the airer as if they had just come out of the dryer. My mum is one of the minorities that enjoy ironing, and to this day she hadn't mentioned the coincidence of the same tablecloth, blouse and pleated skirt that seem to be always on the airer ready to be ironed when she arrived!

My mum did notice, however, that I was undoing the cellophane on the dishwater tablet before putting it in the machine. Well, how was I supposed to know you weren't meant to? I hadn't read the back of the box. I had enjoyed digging my nails into the tablet to try and get the wrapper off and stopping the red power ball thing from pinging onto the floor!

I tried to put on a brave face when the side effects of chemo kicked in, but it was a relief just to let my parents take over. I secretly enjoyed the breakfast in bed routine, and my daughter got a lift to school every day. Scones were on baking trays, and bread was freshly made every few days. What wasn't there to like? There was one evening that was particularly difficult for me, and I regressed into a child and let them put me to bed.

Just as I was entering my 'good week' with fewer side effects, they had to go home. The house was eerily quiet, and I had to find the strength to be jolly and keep looking forward.

As I put the bins out for the first time in a couple of weeks (dad had done that job), I thought of the analogy I had read about the cancer journey being like a ride on a bin wagon;

Every part of it is rubbish, it stinks, but you have to stay on regardless. Well, I was now four cycles of EC in and four cycles of Paclitaxel away from the end. A slight wobble, but I was still "tackling the tumour with humour."

33
GLORY, GLORY MAN UTD

ROYAL WEDDING

Saturday 19 May I was up early and out of the house. The local vintage cafe was selling slices of lemon and elderflower cake, a replica of the royal wedding cake. Prince Harry was going to marry Meghan Markle, and I needed to be back and in front of the TV to see the guests arrive, more importantly, what they were wearing.

The service was lovely with an inspirational American preacher – Bishop Michael Curry giving a speech. He came out with some great lines which reminded me of the inspirational quotes on the cancer web pages. However, when my daughter asked about the relevance of the "bombs of Giliad", it was me that was doing some smirking, not just the wedding guests. "Balms of Giliad," I told her, "balms!"

THE CUP FINAL

It was an unusually sunny day, and Windsor looked great on the TV. I felt very patriotic, but later that day was the cup final between Chelsea and Manchester Utd, and I felt a tinge of sadness. It was because I remembered how I used to feel on cup final day in my replica kit, one of the only Man Utd supporters in Scotland. Apart from the manager, I can't name a single current Man Utd player- not even the captain, yet from 1977- 1987 I was one of their biggest fans and could reel off statistics of each player. People remember where they were when man landed on the moon and JFK was assassinated. I remember where I was each time Man Utd reached the final.

In 1986 I was a typical teenager who spent a lot of time in their room, but it wasn't decorated in cute kittens or Depeche Mode posters. My brown floral wallpaper was covered in Manchester United football pictures, in particular, the Danish striker Jesper Olsen!

He was one of the two foreign players allowed to play for a premier league club (How times have changed!) and my favourite of all the Man Utd players. I collected the Panini stickers, and my school pencil case was covered in MUFC graffiti.

I had the league table on my wall, and I squabbled over Shoot! Magazine with my brother- a lifelong Spurs fan, as it arrived through the letterbox. I knew the offside rule, and I watched Match of the Day. The only problem was I lived in Scotland, and the Scots fiercely promoted their football on TV. I rarely got to see a United match.

OLD TRAFFORD 1985

When my dad had to go for a meeting in Manchester, I jumped for the chance to go with him. I was on school exam leave and studied in the car on the way down. While my dad was at his meeting, I was going to go to Old Trafford, Manchester United's stadium.

I caught a bus going to Old Trafford from the centre of the city and couldn't contain my excitement. My excitement, however, was short lived as I had arrived at Old Trafford, the Cricket Stadium!

Fortunately, I was soon pointed in the right direction, and I swear I had felt myself well up as I arrived at the ground. There was no one around, and no training going on.

I stared up at the clock which was permanently set to mark the time 3.04pm that an air disaster in Munich robbed Manchester of some of its finest players- The Busby Babes, in 1958. The tears were flowing now. A groundsman came over and asked if I was alright. I told him I had come down from Edinburgh to visit the stadium and to my joy of joys, he asked if I wanted to see inside. There was no stranger danger here, he most obviously worked for the stadium and

I toured everywhere- the museum, the changing rooms, the baths, and he left me to sit for a few moments at the Stretford End in the stadium, admiring the new roof. I was so happy.

I spent most of my pocket money in the merchandise shop- the most memorable purchase was a single duvet set, and a pair of shiny knickers with the badge transferred on!

I collected the football Panini stickers with my brothers and particularly in 1986 had a whole bundle of World Cup stickers to trade. I wanted the Danish ones. I had even learnt the Danish "We are red, we are white" World Cup song. I was fan-girling Jesper!

TYNECASTLE 1986

As winners of their leagues, Hearts were playing Man United at Tynecastle in a friendly.

A friend's dad offered to take me, and I had been counting the days.

Having not been able to buy any scarves or souvenirs with Man Utd on ever in Edinburgh, I couldn't believe all the pop-up stands that had "popped up" along the route on match night. I spent a lot of pocket money and bought a whole ten pin badge collection of Jesper Olsen. I couldn't decide which one to buy, so I purchased the lot.

Ok so I had seats in the family enclosure, and I was one of the only fans in red and not in maroon, but it didn't matter as I was going to see my heroes. I leant over the tunnel and slapped gold stickers with my name and address on the backs of Jesper and Frank Stapleton and some others as they came out.

Jesper scored a penalty. It went silent where I was sitting, and then I went for it, screaming my support at the top of my voice. I could still see the sticker, and I'm sure he could hear my screaming. I know most of the Hearts fans around me did. Not sure how I wasn't lynched.

When the Man Utd players came out after half time, the stickers were gone. I imagined they had been saved nicely in their wallets and that signed photos would soon be arriving in the post.

Man Utd lost to Chelsea May 19 2018

34

NEW CHEMO DRUG

THE T PART OF E.C.T.

Paclitaxel was another chemo drug that was given to me by infusion. I had read up on side effects, but I didn't realise it would take three hours to administer. I had anti-sickness meds, steroids, saline and Piriton first and then a half an hour wait before the Paclitaxel. The chemo room was relatively empty, and immediately the antihistamine made me sleepy. It is almost an instant reaction if injected into the vein. I used the remote and lay back in the chair. Two and half hours later I awoke to find the room packed, and it dawned on me that I may have been snoring. The chair was uncomfortable, my head was stuck to the leather, the sun was shining outside, and I didn't want to be there anymore.

For the first couple of days following treatment, I thought my luck was in, and I would escape side effects, but then the leg pain came. I can only liken it to labour pains that started from the hips and shot down into the ankles. I had never felt anything like it. Over the counter, painkillers didn't touch the pain, and after 20 hours of suffering I phoned the chemo unit, and they said to come in.

I was prescribed Oromorph and some stomach settlers and spent a morphine-fuelled evening watching the Eurovision song contest. It didn't make the songs sound any better, but I felt the pain had lessened a bit and now was a dull ache. Combined with the five days of injections I had to take, the week was a tricky one. I had thought that I would prefer pain to nausea, but it wasn't the case. I also felt that the painkillers I was taking weren't working.

I tried to keep busy, and I had my calendar photo shoot to look forward to.

DRESSING UP FOR CHARITY

I had sourced twelve different outfits for my charity calendar, trawling around charity shops and ordering off EBay. The day had arrived, and I went round to my good friend's studio. I am so glad her studio is soundproof as we laughed so much.

We had roughly chosen which character was to go on which month, but they were all so different, and I wasn't a natural model.

January- Phil Mitchell from EastEnders:

Holding a bottle, I sneered at the camera while trying not to look too drunk. I came out with these aggressive grunts which in turn made me laugh. I don't know how my friend kept her camera still. I was supposed to be wishing Sharon "An 'appy New Year."

February -Telly Savalas as Kojak:

Sucking on a lollipop and wearing a retro 70s shirt, shades and trilby hat, I was also holding a red rose. "Who loves ya baby?" was his catchphrase and I tried to entice the camera with a suggestive yet knowing look. No chance, I held the rose firmly against me as my shirt which was one of those that had a plunging neckline to reveal a hairy chest and medallion. I didn't want any chest exposed.

March -Gregg Wallace from MasterChef

Sucking a spoon and holding beetroot I tried to look as if I was enjoying my food (my normal face would show enjoyment of food). I wore a black jacket and pulled on my stomach thinking no one who enjoyed life had a flat stomach. I couldn't help it, but as the camera clicked I was making odd 'Mmmmm' sounds!

April –Yul Bryner as King Mongkut of Siam

The King and I musical had just opened at the Palladium, and my best friend had bought me tickets to watch for my birthday. I had ordered an embroidered tunic online and had stuck a plastic gem on my ear to look more like the character. I then practised my snooty look, folded my arms and became the King of Siam.

May –Blofeld (Donald Pleasance) from the James Bond films

I was quite excited to play a Bond villain and debated whether to put on eye make- up or not to represent the scar. I settled for an eye patch and then sat "evilly" in a chair. I had sourced an ugly tan shirt with long collars and a soft toy cat that had quite a mutant expression. "We've been expecting you, Mr Bond" I kept saying, although Blofeld never said that line and it was all a rumour. I said it anyway to stay in character. This was going to be a close-up photo, and to my horror the way the shirt fell over my bloated stomach made Blofeld look pregnant! We cropped the picture higher up to terminate the pregnancy, and I think Donald Pleasance would have been pleased with the result.

June -Richard O'Brien

I chose to portray Richard O'Brien as the flamboyant presenter of The Crystal Maze rather than as his Rocky Horror character and enjoyed mismatching spots with leopard print.

July -Patrick Stewart as Captain Picard from Star Trek

I had to order the correct tunic and thought maybe f I went to a Star Trek convention I could get the wear out of it again. With no space ship to fly or control panel to sit at. I decided to stand a look thoughtful instead, well to try to anyway.

August- Sigourney Weaver as Ellen Ripley

It was challenging and expensive to source a replica alien- there must have been a high demand for them at this time of year, but finally got one sent from Japan. This picture would be made up of a close up of me looking sweaty and terrified and a side-view of the alien and then cropping them and putting them together. I had no problem looking sweaty but emphasised the look with baby oil. My head felt good with the oil, but I had to concentrate on looking terrified....of a plastic alien.

September - Harry Hill

With a large oversized white shirt on, my black jacket was a bit snug, so my photographer friend borrowed a large jacket from next door. I have no idea what she said she wanted before, but I'm sure her neighbour wouldn't have believed her. I then created silly poses in the glasses, and although I kept doing the "jazz hands" thing, all I wanted to keep saying was "One way to find out.....fight!"

October - Uncle Fester from The Addams Family

I was incredibly hot in a big black overcoat, but this photo was my favourite. We had chosen October as he was pretty scary and set to work on creating the face. Talcum powder stuck to my sweaty face in patches so we used makeup instead and black eye shadow around the eyes. We shot Uncle last as it was the messiest and even when I arrived home with black circles around my eyes, my youngest never stared or asked where I had been. Perhaps I looked like this normally with the lack of sleep I was having?

November Matt Lucas as George Dawes from "Shooting Stars"

I had on a pale blue babygro with diaper flap and had a toy drum-kit and sticks. I padded into the studio and started pulling cheesy faces. "What are the scores, George Dawes?" I kept saying, and I would pull a cheesy grin and bang the plastic drums! I adore Matt Lucas; he is so funny. I was now 100% him!

December -Duncan Goodhew 100m Breaststroke Olympic champion

Growing up with swimming as my sport, I remember watching and cheering on Duncan Goodhew in the Olympics. A 15-year-old girl from the local swimming club, Suki Brownsdon had also qualified, and my year 6 class at school did a big display on the classroom wall. We learnt about Duncan lost his hair after a fall from a tree, and he became our class hero after he won gold. I wasn't taking the mickey, I was honouring a childhood hero with this picture, even if I was clutching a plastic gold medal from a party bag from a few years ago.

This calendar I hoped would be a good way to fundraise I thought and give back something to a breast care charity. I was yet to choose one.

EVERYTHING ACHING

I thought that I had a high pain threshold- especially with the amount of teeth problems I had had over the years, but there is nothing like the constant pain from Paclitaxel. It was almost as painful as labour pains, and there was no let-up. Watching the TV or resting was worse as you felt the pain more. I couldn't get comfortable, and I was ratty. Fortunately, I had an oncologist appointment, and I collapsed into her room and looked up at her with the "please help me eyes". She wasn't surprised that I was in pain and said that painkillers don't work for induced pain. She changed my prescription to weekly Paclitaxel chemo doses and assured me that although I would be having the same amount of the drug; it would be spread across the weeks and would possibly not cause as much pain. I still had a week or so to go, but at least there was some comfort in sight. I had to endure four days of jaw and cheekbone ache before that day, however.

THE LETTER

A copy of the letter sent to the radiographer by my oncologist arrived in the post. It was just a copy and had all the terminology, nature of the tumour and history of my treatment. At the bottom, there was a plan including restarting the Letrozole tablets and having a CT scan. I was just about to file it away when I read the two reasons given for the scan;

1. To check for "? Postoperative changes."
2. To check "? Small colonic node".

My heart was pounding. What small colonic node? Was this a mistake? Why did I not know anything about it? What were the queries?

I didn't dare to pick up the phone, choosing to wait a couple of days until the next chemo cycle. It ruined my day. I was tearful and panicky, yet couldn't tell anyone except my mum. I tried to find something to cheer myself up, but with the jaw and cheek pain at its worst, it was easier to go to bed. I didn't sleep and made the wrong decision to check with Dr Google.

In the morning I felt like death warmed up, and I found it hard to forget what I had read.

At my next meeting with my oncologist, I plucked up the courage and asked about the colonic node. She said that several enlarged colonic nodes had shown up in the CT scan before chemo started. I stopped her there and asked why I didn't know that. At first, she said that she had discussed it with me and then she suggested that there was a lot to take in back in January and that I hadn't listened. We agreed to differ. I wouldn't have forgotten something like that, and I was recording every meeting in note form for this book. Another scan after chemo would recheck them. Fortunately, there was a simple explanation, and a gut infection could have lead to this result. Unfortunately, I couldn't remember having any gut infection. I would have to wait now and not worry.

A FAT WEEBLE

I didn't overeat during chemo, and in fact, my mouth was so sore, it was difficult to enjoy the food. I longed to taste chocolate properly or crisps. Possibly as a result of the steroids or lack of real exercise, I had ballooned and put on a lot of weight. I was supposed to eat little an often and when I was hungry. Apart from the craving for banana milk and garden peas I wasn't eating unhealthily. The tea tasted like sludge, and fizzy drinks stung my mouth. Most foods tasted like cardboard or as if someone else had eaten them before me. I longed to be able to taste a meal fully. Cheese and green vegetables seemed an exception to the rule, and I could taste them no problem. My stomach was always bloated, and now I struggled to paint my toenails without holding my breath-my tummy was in the way. My suntan was coming along nicely – still with the neck-rings from last summer, but as I stared at myself in the mirror I thought I looked like a "Fat Weeble!"

SUMMIT NOT RIGHT

The bone pain from the Paclitaxel got worse. I wasn't sure where I preferred the pain to be but not in my jaw or cheekbones. There was no point holding my face as it made no difference and hot and cold flannels didn't seem to work either. Even the weight of my face on a pillow hurt. I spent a few nights wide awake and even found myself writing this book and wrapping Christmas presents. Yep, I did say Christmas presents, but although it was June, there was some reasoning behind it as my eldest daughter was going to be visiting my brother and nieces soon abroad and would be taking their presents with her.

I bought Epsom salts and having a hot bath seemed to ease the pain a bit, except that it was hot outside and I would have preferred a cold bath. I would have liked to have a proper bath without one arm being covered in a giant sleeve called a Limbo or as some on the Facebook group called it – an elephant condom! The PICC line needed to be protected but holding one arm up and out in the cold and away from bubbles wasn't particularly relaxing. I'd previously tried cling film but couldn't for the life of me find the end to unwrap it, and it nearly pulled the line out. In the end, my arm had to be brutally freed with scissors!

EYE PAIN

After days of jaw pain, my luck turned again, and I awoke one night with excruciating eye pain. At Urgent Care, they weren't sure what it was, and I was referred to the eye hospital. A paragraph ago I was citing jaw pain as the worst pain, but this new eye pain waltzed in and took over the number one slot. Even with my eye closed, the eyeball wandered around and wouldn't keep still. I was too early for the hospital and wandered the dark corridors finding a quiet waiting room. It was a bit eerie and reminded me of a horror film set in a hospital where there is no staff. Fortunately, after only a couple of hours or so, I was seen and quickly diagnosed. My eye had dried out during the night and had pulled off some of the cornea. Like sticky back plastic it had settled down in the wrong position- hence the pain. The doctor numbed my eye and put the cornea back in the right position, smoothing down the blisters that had occurred- definitely like sticky back plastic.

It didn't hurt, but I felt dizzy. I fainted.

When I came round, I remember telling the nurse trying to do my blood pressure to use the other arm, and I felt a bit silly lying on the floor with my head on my hoodie. I was OK just a reaction to the numbing agent in my eye. As I slowly got up off the floor, I thought of the time I fake fainted once at Uni.

THE FAINT

Have you ever wished to faint at a man's feet? At University I had a friend that would pretend to faint especially when there were good looking boys around, and then come round and be all girly. I had a flatmate too that suffered badly from epilepsy and fainted after stressful situations, and that wasn't a laughing matter, hours were spent on cold pavements or church hall floors waiting for her to come round. However my "fake fainting friend" would check to see who was coming down the street first, after all, once her eyes were shut, they were shut. Then another friend or I would guard her and ask a passerby for help. This was all pre-mobile phones, and if anyone were about to phone 999, my friend would miraculously come round and be OK. It wasn't about wasting the emergency services' time; it was about flirting with boys. Sometimes when she came round, she struck up a conversation and then a friendship with whoever was attending to her and even exchanged details. It was mainly about attention!

One evening we were together, I thought I would have a go at doing the fainting. The lads from the Leuchars barracks were in town. My descent to the ground was quite dramatic, and I hurt myself. I timed it just right, fake fainted and lay on the ground with my eyes shut. My friend was a fine actress calling to the lads for help. However, I wasn't swept into someone's arms. Instead, I found my legs were lifted above my head, and I was rather roughly slapped around the face. I was wearing a skirt, and I couldn't come round soon enough to adjust my decency.

A taxi was hailed, and my friend and I were bundled into it in the direction of our halls of residence. No sympathy or invitation out for a sugary cup of tea or something stronger. Not even a phone number. I suppose it was funny looking back- not at the time- and we both have never done it since.

My eye was still numb and dripping yellow stain. My blood pressure was fine, and I was allowed home. With a prescription for antibiotic cream and an eye gel to use for life, I felt a bit sorry for myself. What else was in store for me?

I didn't have long to wait for something next to happen. The phone rang to say chemo was to be put off for a week because my blood count had come back too low. I wouldn't now be finishing my journey in June now; it would be July. I scribbled out the circle around June 27 on the calendar and put my big girl's pants on. This was a tricky night. I didn't cry but watched footage of the historic summit meeting between the leaders of North Korea and the USA and downed three bottles of banana milk! I was fed up.

TOE-TALLY EXHAUSTING

The next few days were spent in bed, but it was a completely different feeling to the dark days of 2015. The sun was shining outside, and I had the TV on in the background and my gorgeous pug with me for the company. I had to rest. My eye was healing nicely but I was utterly exhausted and a bit run down. I suppose I had been trying to carry on as usual but not making any allowances for being poisoned at the same time.

I then came down with a toe infection. At first, I thought I had stubbed my toe in the dirt- it was filthy. However, on closer inspection, my toe was weeping a bubbly light brown liquid from behind the nail. I had had my toenails painted dark blue in the hope to save them from falling off, but the big toenail had begun to come away, and there was a lot of gunk hiding behind the nail. I felt a wee bit squeamish and covered the whole toe in a dressing. It didn't hurt, but it meant another trip to the doctors and more antibiotics. As a cruel turn of fate, I couldn't take any milk products two hours either side of taking the antibiotics, so no cup of tea in the morning and no banana milk at night! Someone somewhere was laughing at my expense. Surely I couldn't pick up another infection? Chemo was delayed another week. The nail fell off two weeks later, but I couldn't bear the thought of it gone, so I taped the neatly shellac polished nail in place and ignored it. The tops of my fingernails snapped off too, but they didn't look too unsightly. It just meant it was a nightmare finding the end of the Sellotape or itching that itch!

There was chickenpox in school, but I weighed up the risk of catching shingles and still went in. I was managing to work in the grammar school a couple of hours a week despite all the hospital appointments I was attending, which gave me some sense of normality, but unfortunately, there wasn't going to be a full-time position for me in September. September was still a long way off, but I needed to start thinking about what I would do. I had no energy to attend any interviews, but at least I could do some groundwork. I enjoyed secondary teaching so much now.

What other jobs could I do?

35

THE WORK YEARS

My first job was in a chemist. Walking home from school one day in 1984, an old man pulled up in his car alongside me and wound down his window. I didn't know him. "Come and work in my chemist," he said and pointed back to the parade of shops. "Come in and see me tomorrow." It was a peculiar and bizarre way of getting a job, but apparently, he had often seen me walking home and thought I looked "cheerful and good-natured". Of course, I was. If that had have happened nowadays, the police might have been called!

I accepted the job and began a Saturday job in a chemist shop. The customers knew me as 'The Bonnie One.'

I worked there in the days when prescriptions cost £1.75 an item and prescriptions were handwritten. There was a knack to reading the doctor's handwriting, and a bit of schoolgirl Latin helped me decipher them, and I was allowed to mix up the potions and lotions in the pharmacy. I loved working in the dispensary, and it also meant I was privy to a lot of confidential information about friends and family and friends' family!

It was great fun working in a shop, but I was not cut out to stand up all day and sometimes it was so dull I would resort to tidying the same shelf twice or spraying testers.

I used a printer to print out the labels for the brown medicine bottles. To relieve the boredom, I would make my funny personalised labels prescribing myself large doses of TV, no homework and the caution that attending science classes may cause drowsiness!

A colleague once sprayed Old Spice aftershave at me. My hair just absorbed the smell, and I smelt of an old man for days! I used to try out all the testers. Little old ladies, in turn, would try out testers of bright lipsticks on the back of my hand to see the colour. Nice to think that the back of my hand resembled an old ladies' mouth.

When the shop was busy, time flew but when quiet all the assistants would squabble over the jobs to do to ease the boredom. I remember once breaking a Hoover in the enthusiasm fighting over it because Hoovering the shop floor killed at least 30 minutes. I knew I would never be cut out for any career in retail.

I would also spend most of my wages on new products that came in just for the sake of it. I could never work in a cake shop! The chemist didn't sell food as such, but I would eat a jar of strawberry pudding baby food with a sugar-free lollipop for my break- far tastier than a biscuit!

DIABETIC JAM 1985

I worked in the chemist in the days when you had to ask the assistant if you wanted to buy condoms as they were kept behind the counter. As a 15-year-old it was embarrassing when customers asked, so I usually invited them round the back of the counter so they could choose what they wanted. However, one day when a gentleman came in and asked for "preservatives" I remember showing him the display of diabetic jam.

I wish I could remember the expression on his face, but the manager hurriedly came out from the pharmacy section and showed the customer to the back of the counter. I was blissfully naive. Preservatives were condoms.

THE GREAT ESCAPE

I have fond memories of serving customers but not on this particular Bank Holiday. I'd gone home for lunch, and The Great Escape was on. I'd been whistling the theme tune most of the day. While trying on sunglasses and spraying perfume testers and whistling the theme tune to the Great Escape, I was tapped on the shoulder by a customer. It was the boy in the sixth form that I had such a crush on. There was no way he would ever ask me out; a few months he came into the shop again. I thought he was the prescription delivery boy and as he came in I shouted,

"Err look what the cat dragged in!" (We had that sort of exchange).

He looked at me, and I looked at him, and again I wanted that hole to swallow me up. It wasn't him.

MISTAKEN IDENTITY

After a school music concert around 1985, we were all filing out to find our families. In a freak accident, my violin had been squashed to bits by a friend's trombone – the trombone had fallen off a table on to my violin which was lying in an open case. I was a bit upset, so in my defence, I did have a bit of blurred vision, but when I saw my dad with his back towards me, I went running up and hugged him from behind. I was so upset about my violin. Except it wasn't my dad. It was my English teacher!

THE LANGUAGE BARRIER

I worked as an English teacher for a while. I got my TEFL (Teaching English as a Foreign Language) qualification in 1991 and used it to get a job teaching Italian and Spanish teenagers in Edinburgh over the summer. I had always been in awe of anyone that could speak another language fluently.

I spoke schoolgirl French and German and a bit of Arabic. I had studied written Latin and Russian and was reasonably good at 'Gobbledegook'.

On a long train journey, one day in 1992, a friend and I were passing the time by speaking utter rubbish to each other. We changed the intonation and length of words, but it was absolute rubbish. Just before we got off, a lady who had been sitting behind us leant over and said "Where do you both come from? I have been desperately trying to work it out or a long time but can't seem to place it?!"

I swear my answer was, "Why England of course!"

Her face!

I arranged a fantastic treasure hunt around Edinburgh for the international students. It involved clipboards and questions for students to ask passers-by safely. Out of the 120 students that set off on the trail, only 4 did it. The rest used the time to go shopping or sit in McDonald's. This was my first experience of teaching or dealing with teenagers, and I vowed I would work in a primary school in the future, not a secondary.

At the end of the stay, the students gave me a thank you card from all of them and some flowers. Amongst the comments were these;" I learned some small things", "You is good teaching", "I will always forget you" "You are my fourth best teacher" and "I thank you from the heart of my bottom!"

HONG KONG STUDENTS 1997

It got easier in 1997 but only after I had got over the names issue. I taught a class of 20 Hong Kong teenagers. I couldn't read Chinese, and also their Chinese names were reasonably long, so each student had adopted a more English sounding name. It made taking the register easier.

The first day was an orientation one around the town of Bromley, looking at landmarks and using a map. They were to familiarise themselves with bus-stops and the location of the language school and then had some free time.

I had met the students for registration only and again on the bus. I went along to be a point of reference, and I sat on a bench outside the main shopping centre.

It was a long morning and after a couple of hours or so a Hong Kong student came and sat on the bench and started eating their packed lunch. I asked her if she liked the town and we got chatting about shops. Her name was Cherry, and yes the town was charming and had more flowers than her home town. Later at our designated meeting point, the students were milling around showing each other things they had bought. I couldn't see Cherry anywhere. We counted the students over again, and the numbers were right yet Cherry wasn't there. I didn't want to be responsible for losing a student.

We were late in returning home due to me being adamant we were missing someone. We got the registers out. There was no Cherry on our registers. She wasn't even with our language school! Luckily Cherry was merrily oblivious of the panic she had caused, and I hope she went on to enjoy her holiday.

36
RADIOTHERAPY

February and the start of chemo now seemed a lifetime away, and as I hung my knitted knockers on the line to dry, I felt the end of my chemo days were in sight.

RINGING THE BELL
I had followed friends in Facebook groups that had rung the bell to celebrate the end of chemo, and I was somewhat jealous. But it was my turn now. The date was 11 July 2018. My hospital didn't have a bell to ring as some patients never actually finish their chemo treatment, so I posted a picture on Facebook of me ringing my doorbell-well it was a bell at least!

My eldest daughter was now home from her first year at University (along with eight machine loads of washing), the sun was shining, and I only had radiotherapy to go. Yippee!

SURPRISE PARTY
My birthday came three days later and I went out for a morning coffee with friends. The sun was shining and both of my girls had presented me with breakfast in bed. Returning home at lunch time I was merrily oblivious that my garden was full of over fifty friends. I arrived home to quiet and went out searching for the girls. "Surprise!" came a multitude of voices and I stood lost for words as friends from all different friendship groups were eating and drinking some sort of

buffet in my own garden. My daughters had secretly arranged it all and had been in contact with my friends. They had even arranged for people to bring food too. I stood there speechless for a while and then had a wee snivel. It was all a bit overwhelming.

GUY'S

I had my preliminary appointment at Guy's Cancer Centre. I had never been there before and caught the commuter train early. Unfortunately, I had a bad nosebleed amongst the commuters and had to leave my precious seat and brave the train toilet. I squirted loads of the pink soap onto my hands only to find to my dismay that there was no water. I then tried using toilet paper to wipe the stuff off, which just left my hands hot and sticky and smelling of well not an exact scent, but just of pink train soap.

Guy's Cancer Care Centre was nestled between the Shard and the main hospital. It was modern and reminded me of a space station. My name flashed up on a big screen to tell me when my appointment was ready and where to go. It was quite cool. Lifts took me up to a floor with a beautiful panoramic view of London, and a nurse was excited to come and weigh me. I stood on a machine that weighed and measured my height remotely, the wonders of modern technology! I mentioned the "Fat Weeble" thing again as it honestly looked like in reality that I had put on no weight on in five months, yet my trousers didn't do up, my cheeks look like those of a chipmunk, and one side of my stomach was permanently bloated. The nurse blamed the steroids for blowing me up, so I felt content in also blaming the steroids too. Apparently, in time, it would all settle down. My hair was now falling out again with the Paclitaxel, and I began hearing the "shlumph" sound once again, of my head sticking to my leather chair. It was if I was giving my head a strip wax and Phoebe my pug gave me that look as if to say that it was "her job not mine" to leave little hairs on the furniture!

AT THE CHECKOUT

I was more confident in going out in public with my bald head, especially in the hot June weather, but at a supermarket checkout, one look at a toddler in their trolley seemed to scare him. He screamed the place down and wouldn't look at me. I tried to pretend it didn't bother me and I carried on loading my groceries onto the conveyor belt. His mum was very apologetic but as she was apologising she was oddly scanning her eyes over my food. She then pulled out her purse and emptied the contents into my hand saying "please buy something nice, I was looking to see if I could treat you to something, I'm so sorry". As she packed her bags and hurriedly pushed her whimpering child away, I wondered about what luxury I would spend the £1.83 in my hand.

A SKINHEAD WITH TATTOOS

Radiotherapy wasn't going to come without its fair share of side effects, but the positives and benefits of stopping any reoccurrence of cancer outweighed any negatives. It wasn't going to be as relaxing as the name implied and there was undoubtedly no radio in radiotherapy. I signed the consent form and listened as the doctor explained about targeting nearby lymph nodes too. There were some in my neck that needed blasting just in case and some in the chest but whether they could blast them depended on a CT scan as the heart needed to be protected. The risk of heart disease increased in later years if the heart was zapped. I was given a booklet to read and a leaflet about holding my breath for 30 seconds- a procedure that pushed the heart back into a safe place. It was okay; I was used to holding my breath:

- In order to fasten my trouser buttons
- While picking up Phoebe's waste in the park
- While retrieving cups and bowls from my teenager's bedroom.

- While passing that soap shop in the shopping centre.
- While trying to paint my toenails in one go!

In my booklet, it said "Radiotherapy uses radiation- high energy x-rays to treat cancer. The radiation damages the cells within the treatment area, killing the cancer cells but allowing normal healthy cells to recover." So it was slightly different from chemotherapy, and any side effects were isolated to the area being treated. My neighbourhood was large; the tumours being 95mm – considered very large and the area of lymph node involvement and the precautionary extra lymph nodes. I bought in the moisturising cream recommended to be stored in the fridge and was relieved to find out that out of a maximum of 6 weeks, my treatment was to last three weeks- 15 sessions. I was also to have cabbage leaves ready as apparently putting them on the affected area was meant to be soothing. I was yet to go to the market and examine cabbages for this purpose!

I also booked an appointment to have three small tattoos. They were to help line up the radiotherapy machine, apparently. Finally I was going to be a skinhead with tattoos. My mum would be so proud!

Looking at the calendar it did appear that I wasn't going to get a chance to go on holiday anywhere before the schools went back in September as I had just too many appointments, but I tried to see the positives and thought about who could come and visit and what I could do and see locally. I could even go somewhere hot in the October half term possibly if I could sort out dog care and childcare or take my youngest with me. I still had my heart set on a hot country with turquoise waters and white sand.

It wasn't all doom and gloom. My health was the number one priority. That thought had taken a backseat recently as I was busy with end of term and fundraising paperwork.

THE REAL FACES OF CANCER

Doing exactly what I had told my pupils not to do and talking to strangers in the middle of the night on social media had been a real comfort. My chemo unit didn't offer a social side, and I had only met a handful of people who had had breast cancer, and they were friends of mine already and not strangers. I wished there was a Maggie's Centre or drop-in centre to go and have a coffee and chat with other sufferers locally, but there wasn't. It occurred to me too that I had gone this alone, I didn't have a chemo-buddy or friend that was going through the same thing; instead, they were all strangers online.

One local photographer- Imelda Bell asked for models for a project she was doing. She was also a breast cancer sufferer and wanted to do an exhibition of portraits showing the real faces of cancers- gritty black and white images of the suffering and recovery process that weren't necessarily all cheesy and smiley. I met her and had some photos taken exposing my PICC line and clutching my head. As she took the pictures, I was suffering from bone pain in my skull, and the images were very real. She took a nice one of me as a reward, and on the same day, I was able to email the picture to my family. It was also really nice to talk to someone who really understood how uncomfortable bone pain was and we laughed as she explained how difficult it was to sit still in the cinema the previous night and I told her how I slid off the hard school chair at work as it was impossible to get comfortable and how Phoebe my dog thought I was playing as I lay flat on my lounge carpet in pain, and proceeded to put some soggy soft toys on top of me! I realised how beneficial it was to "chemoan" to someone who understood.

Imelda's cancer photographs were so successful she became a fellow of the Master Photographers Association and her photos were turned into a large coffee table book. It is the third book in the Monster Series by Donia Youssef called "Facing the Monster." It is odd to think that my tormented picture is on coffee tables around the country!

SPIRITUALLY SPEAKING

I don't mention my religion or beliefs (or politics) in this book on purpose, but apparently being diagnosed with a life-threatening illness does make you question things and although I took great comfort from reading inspirational and spiritual quotes on the internet, I did also wonder if someone was keeping a beady eye on me. I won't lie and say I don't think about having secondaries (cancer that has spread elsewhere); every ache or pain I think it's cancer coming back and I'm sure this feeling isn't just going to go away. A lot of my friends have prayed for me, for which I am truly grateful. I will need strength from somewhere.

BURNT TO A CRISP

The radiotherapy didn't hurt, but after a while my skin starting turning red and burning away. I tried the cabbage leaves but cream felt better. I was actually quite proud of the burns, they looked worse than they actually were and attracted a lot of attention. I milked the sympathy I received.

End of treatment was celebrated with a hot chocolate and then a photo shoot. I jumped about outside the Cancer Centre pausing as a car or two went by, feeling just a tad self-conscious while my daughter took the photos.

37
AUTUMN TERM 2018

BACK TO SCHOOL

My school was supportive during my active treatment, but there was no science post to return too. Luckily I was still offered one history class, but it wasn't enough to make ends meet. I had to fill out endless forms, visit the Job Centre and apply for some help. I felt embarrassed sitting on the plastic chairs awaiting my appointment, but strangely I wasn't worried; I knew something would turn up. It did. I was soon offered another history class and some more supply days with the potential for more hours. I was happy and immersed myself into making the most of each day and planning the holiday of a lifetime in the school half term.

NETFLIX AND A CHILL

October 2018 saw me put the central heating on and go to bed early. The Letrozole was making my joints ache and me getting very tired. I rarely went to bed after my teenager, and I caught my first cold. It wasn't flu but knocked me for six. I was burning the candle at both ends, and it was all a little too much. My earnings were going on new brake pads and new tyres, and I was making numerous trips to the Post Office posting everything that wasn't tied down in the house to EBay buyers. I either vegged on the sofa after work watching Netflix or lay in my very uncomfortable bed, coughing and sneezing and imagined myself swimming in turquoise waters.

After N. moved out, I invested in a new king-sized bed and memory foam mattress. I changed the colour of my bedroom and looked forward to a good night's sleep. After a week or so the wooden slats of my bed started giving way. I checked with the shop that I had put them in, and unfortunately, the problem worsened. It was an embarrassing problem, and I had to assure the shop that they gave way by themselves and had begun to warp.

I began to be afraid of rolling over in the night for fear of the slats going. I would wake up in a jolt. One and half years on and the same thing is still happening and generally around 3 in the morning. Sometimes the noise of just one slat falling wakes me, but I can go back to sleep. However, sometimes four or five wooden slats give way so that I am plunged into a dip and stay wedged there. I've tried sleeping sideways and across the dip but it's impossible to get comfortable on a slope.

A couple of times I've heard a laugh from my daughter as she recognises the sound of my bed giving way. I've taken photos, and the bed shop has promised to contact the manufacturer, but the bed is out of warranty, so all I can do is gaffer tape the warped slats, wait and hope for the best!

CARIBBEAN QUEEN

The half term could not come soon enough. H. and I had got a fantastic deal on a cruise around the Caribbean. We flew to Havana, Cuba and boarded a cruise ship that stopped at Belize, Roatan (Honduras), Costa Maya and Cozumel in Mexico before returning to Cuba. The holiday was exactly what I had wanted, and it was a thank you too to H. for looking after me during the last year and through my depression months also. L. was understanding; she was busy at University and wished us well.

It was hard the first time I saw the white sand and turquoise water of the Caribbean Sea. I cried, but they were happy tears. I waded into the warm water and enjoyed the feeling of the hot sun on me. We had been told to expect poor weather due to it being the end of the hurricane season, but it was in the 30s with just a light breeze. The skies were blue, and all around me were palm trees.

The water was indeed turquoise, yet you could see the sand below. You had to wade a while out to get any coverage, and I soon felt rather exposed so did a kneeling crawl thing in the water. I desperately tried to look as if I wasn't weeing or was a whale in distress. I ended up floating. I half hoped everyone on the beach would disappear, so I get out of the water in peace, but the water's edge just got busier.

I floated looking up at the sky; one hand was ready to grab my new ' aquaboob' in case it floated away; it had done It was warm, idyllic, picture perfect but there was one thing I struggled to get to grips with; sand got everywhere! It was impossible to sit at the water's edge without the stuff clogging up my costume. It was also impossible to swim without it clinging to me, and there were no standpipes anywhere to wash your feet at the end of the day to put your trainers on. It got in my phone, in my sun cream, in the little hair I had and also in my ears. I even brought some in my suitcase home!

IN THE PINK

Aboard the ship, no one knew my story or even anything about me. My aquaboob in my swimming costume disguised any obvious clues and my hair was going lighter and thicker in the sea air. However, I found myself volunteering information to strangers I met.

One example was while cave snorkelling in Cozumel. We had to lock all our belongings except for the swimming costume we were wearing in special lockers in a hut in the middle of nowhere. As I paid for a key, there was a display of jars of honey and salsa sauce on the counter with a pink collection tin for cancer. It was a surreal moment. I tried to tell the man collecting the man that I had had cancer but got nowhere in Spanish or hand gestures, and he must have thought I was a bit strange; almost as odd as walking through the jungle in just a swimming costume and water shoes while carrying a mask and snorkel. No, I hadn't had any insect injections and no I hadn't planned to see tarantula spiders or hundreds of bats that day. But I did exfoliate with mineral-fuelled grains of stalagmites and stalactites to get, in the words of our Mayan guide, "a smooth baby butt face"!

It seemed Mexico, apart from celebrating the upcoming day of the dead, also supported the "Wear pink for cancer" charity. Our guides wore pink caps, and there were posters and collection tins in lots of places. I played the "C" card once, while haggling for two hand- embroidered bags; I showed a picture of myself with a bald head on my phone, pointed to the poster and got a good deal on both bags.

WHAT LURKS BENEATH

I booked a snorkel tour of the Belize Barrier Reef. We were taken out to the middle of the ocean and deposited in the sea. I found it funny winding my daughter up with the jaws shark noise and a more tuneful rendition of the tune "Baby Shark". Our guide was Spanish and swam with a prodding rod. He very unceremoniously awoke big angelfish, eels and a stingray although was careful not to disturb the coral. I had snorkelled once before in Greece, but I hadn't realised how dark it would be. I had forgotten that all the brightly colourful fish I had seen in magazines had been photographed with flash photography. The water was clear but the scenery just not as vibrant as I had hoped. Suddenly some French girls swimming near me started screaming. At first, I thought they were laughing but then it was apparent that they were upset about something. The guide shouted out "Ignore the shark". I looked down and saw a two-metre black shark complete with dorsal fin and big mouth beneath me. It's strange how terror can affect people in different ways; my first reaction wasn't to protect H. or swim for it, it was to keep snorkelling and watch our guide use his prod to guide it away in a different direction, going beneath H. as it swam. The guide had shouted "It's a Nurse shark," and I was supposed to know it was harmless to humans. I didn't stay long in the water after that.

H. made a point of reminding me that my first thought was not of her, yet we were soon equal as a week later while walking in Cuba, a car backfired, and it sounded like gunfire. I stood still, and she ran and hid behind me leaving me exposed!

The rest of our cruise ran smoothly with no useable anecdotes and H., and I made memories to last.

49 SHADES OF GREY

The sun-bleached my hair, but to a lighter shade of grey. Only two weeks back in England and the roots had come in darker. It was soft like baby hair, and I suppose if it was an entirely new set of hair then that made sense. However, it was curling with a vengeance. L. thought it felt like a cushion whereas I thought I looked like a little old lady fresh from having her perm. More worryingly, I thought I resembled "Mrs Brown" from the TV programme "Mrs Brown's Boys!" I liked it short, but there was a fine line between looking smart and trendy and looking like an old lady or a toilet brush.

At one point of growth, I thought I looked like Paul O'Grady. I even contemplated another photo-shoot for calendar number two, impersonating the likes of Judi Dench and Julie Walters too.

As soon as the school term finished for Christmas, I dyed it bright purple. It was non-permanent but fun and festive. I was tempted by an electric blue dye but thought as it faded out I would look even more like an old lady with a blue rinse than ever before- particularly as I did indeed pull a trolley- for my school books though not shopping!

CHRISTMAS 2018

This time last year I was merrily going septic. This year I was able to celebrate relatively calmly with parents, daughters and pug. The highlight of the celebrations was perhaps the fact that the first time since being a young child, a paper hat from a Christmas cracker fitted me over my short hair. I kept my orange hat on for most of the 25th and refreshed with a purple one on Boxing Day: it's the little things!

On 27 December I went for my mammogram. I knew the appointment was coming and I was fine until I arrived at the hospital. There was no one waiting for an appointment, and I felt a sense of déjà-vu as I wriggled on the seat.

I was tempted the day before to practise running into a wall or slamming my remaining boob in a car door in preparation for the mammogram, but decided to grin and bear it. I smiled to myself as my boob slapped down on the slab and came to a standstill like a blancmange on a plate. The vice came down, and I was trapped. The technician only took two pictures. I suppose that's all they needed. I had thought that like last time if anything ominous had shown up, I would have been sent next door into the ultrasound room for further investigation, but I wasn't. On my calendar, 10 January had been circled for almost a year. This was when I would see my surgeon again. I would find out the results then, fortunately, earlier than the average 6-8 week wait but a nervous wait nonetheless.

"I don't want a lot for Christmas,

There is just one thing I N.E.A.D. (No sign of active disease)

38

HAPPY NEW YEAR

2019 This year surely has to be better than last year!

My resolutions are:

- To continue being positive and look at the glass half full.
- To exercise more and eat the right stuff so I can be and look "Fabulous at Fifty."
- To continue fundraising for Breast Cancer Charities.
- To make each day count.

10 JANUARY 2019

Today was the day.

Seems only yesterday that I was sitting in my surgeon's room and he broke the news to me- Unfortunately you have cancer. What is the saying? "Time flies when......"!

SOCKS

Today as I swung my legs nervously on the chair in the waiting room I wondered what he would say. I was glad I had taken a friend with me, and as I sat there I realised for the first time in a very long time, I wasn't wearing my fake boob(foob). I was going into school later, and there was no way I would get away with a lopsided look! It was then that I planned to use my socks to stuff into my bra, something I hadn't done since about the age of 14!

My name was called and still trying to think where I had left my foob or if indeed it had fallen out en route, I went into the room to find a strange lady reading my notes. She asked how I was and if I had received the results by post already. I looked a bit puzzled and replied "no," and she casually said that my mammogram was fine. It is odd how matter of fact she said it; the mammogram was fine! The treatment had worked; there was no sign of active disease.

She examined me, and it was after that I took the courage to ask who she was-fortunately she was a consultant surgeon, and she apologised for just assuming I would know. She reassured me that I now had a 1/8 chance of cancer appearing in the right breast; the same 1/8 chance as had every other woman.

As I walked out of the hospital I felt a little numb; it was almost like an anticlimax. That was it; it was all over. I should be happy, but I felt guilty. I thought of all those people I knew that hadn't been so lucky and all of those patients still fighting their battles in the building behind me. I phoned my family, and it was only when I heard their shrieks of delight did I finally break into a smile. I had done it. What was the expression? Oh yes:

"I had whipped cancer's butt!"

39

SO EMBARRASSING

Some of these stories have been all so embarrassing for me, but I wonder what makes a situation awkward? Is it the judgements and looks of others or the lack of confidence in oneself?

As these red-faced moments seem to be regular occurrences, I've developed a coping strategy. I mean, does it matter what you look like or if people are laughing at you? I hold my head up high and carry on. Well sometimes. Writing these stories has brought back such wonderful and genuinely excruciating memories.

The following are not long enough to have their paragraph, but all have happened:

- The time I lost a shoe on one of the rides at Chessington Amusement Park as we went upside down and then spent ages one socked looking for it.
- That time my daughter handed me a fabric rose, and I tried to put it in my hair except I forgot I was bald and ended up stabbing my head!
- The moment my ice-cream got knocked out of my hand by a football at the school fete and into my face.
- The time I was in a cinema and thought it was too loud. I started looking around for the controls to turn it down.
- The time I wound down the window, beeped and shouted like a madwoman to my friend when stationary at a zebra crossing and everyone looked my way except my friend.
- The time my brother and his mate won a holiday to Spain on

a Scottish TV game show wearing a Bert and Ernie t-shirt and a kilt, and got mistaken for being a "couple".

- The time my mastectomy drain leaked all over the floor of a cafe, and it looked like I had wet myself.
- The time my dad sneezed, and I jumped up suddenly off the sofa launching the dog sky high and jarring my knee out of place for five minutes.
- The first time I ever went to Starbucks I thought the barista was flirting when he asked me my name!
- The time I realised my underskirt had fallen right down in class and I calmly stepped out of it and picked it up as I was talking.
- The time on choir tour that the Vicar of Chipping Campden told me in detail about his noisy mating tortoises.
- The time my mum wore just a pair of coconuts and a grass skirt at a Hogmanay Party.
- The time in class I had to take my beanie off revealing my bald head for the first time and then mop it down with a flannel.
- The time your friend was laughing about pet owners that put pants on their dogs when they were in season. I listened and then admitted that I had bought special season pants with Velcro adjustment belt that had insertable panty liners! And yes my dog had gone out in public in them.
- The time I got terrible rope burn for not letting go of the ropes properly while bell-ringing.
- The time my mum was panicking thinking my brother's cat was in the washing machine, only to find out the supposed cat was, in fact, her black pants.
- The time I drove my family out for dinner in fluffy slippers (I hadn't realised). The slippers then broke in the restaurant, so I borrowed my mum's shoes which were two sizes too small. My mum then went up to the buffet in her socks, and as we both hobbled out later, we both looked as if we were drunk.

- The time I was crying my eyes out in the cinema at Disney's "Princess and the Frog" and got up to go and was greeted by a whole row of pupils in my class.
- The time I was hobbling home along the road as a student fairly late and the police pulled over thinking I was drunk. I had to explain to them that I had a badly ingrown toe-nail and it was difficult to walk. Fortunately, it was true, and they gave me a lift home!
- That time my brother chased me around the house with a dead fish, and I almost broke my toe running into a door. Spent three embarrassing weeks limping and trying not to tell anyone what happened.
- That time N. made me a glass of undiluted orange squash by mistake, and I took a large swig from it and spat it out on the floor in front of his family.
- That time I dislocated my knee in a portaloo tent. I went in, and there wasn't much room to manoeuvre and came out with a dislocated knee!
- The time I made Angel Delight with water instead of milk and then wondered why it didn't set. My dad brought this tale up in his speech at my wedding. Not in isolation, however, he told it as more of an example to justify his worry that he and my mum had sent me off to University without knowing how to cook.
- The time I nipped into a car park space before another car and my daughter pulled silly faces at the driver, and he got out and started ranting at us. (That was scary, and we locked the internal doors and tried to avoid eye contact.)
- The time I woke up on an overnight coach to find an unknown gentleman asleep on my shoulder. (Actually, he was more embarrassed than I was.)

- The time I had a dinner party, and when I returned to my two guests after clearing the table, they were fast asleep on my sofa!
- The time at parents evening when I didn't recognise the student, chatted away to the parent and then found out later I didn't even teach him!
- The time I began registering a year nine class and didn't recognise any of the students in the class until I realised I was in the wrong room and with the wrong class. (They didn't butt an eyelid.) I've seen a Mexican frying an egg! I was in Ensenada, 1988 with my cousin and grandmother looking for a fake Gucci purse to buy, and there he was, a Mexican in the street, just frying an egg. He was wearing a sombrero too. There was nothing nearby either that I could climb on to see what the bird's eye view of him looked like. So the moment passed, yet the memory has remained.
- The time I realised the reversing lorry that woke me up at the same time every morning for work, was my lodger's alarm clock.
- The time I texted my headmaster instead of my friend a whole rant about not being appreciated by my husband by mistake.
- The time I went for a bra-fitting and was assisted by a former pupil.
- The time my mum arrived at US Immigration and asked the Official if she was "on their special list".
- The time I was at a boot-sale with my dad and a stall holder thought we were a couple.
- The time I fell asleep in a staff meeting and woke myself up with a snort.
- The time I was looking into the orchestra pit from the front row and the trumpet player smiled and waved at me. I wave back only to realise he was waving at his family behind me.
- The time my three-year-old daughter told the cashier at Tesco with severe acne not to scratch their chickenpox.

- The time I had to sit through the whole of Physics next to a school inspector with no tissue with a severe cold, running nose and sneezes.
- The time I did pass wind in a lift.
- The time I had severe morning sickness and couldn't find a bin in the street quick enough that opened at the top so was sick all over the top of one.
- The time I wasted 1-2 hours, 40 weeks pregnant just outside the shop Mothercare in the hope, my waters would break and that I would receive baby vouchers.
- The time a child in my class tried to sharpen his finger in a pencil sharpener in the attempt to have Wolverine claws.
- The time my two-year-old daughter tried to use the display toilet in B & Q.
- The time I came in way too early singing the chorus of a song as a teacher in whole school assembly.
- The time you take your teenage daughters to watch The Rocky Horror Show and realise they are the youngest in the audience by about 30 years, and it isn't a suitable show for them.
- The time you watch the film Love Actually with your family forgetting it has some dodgy bits in.
- The times when you are between bus stops and the bus comes and you sort of wave, and then jump up and down in the hope the bus stops, then have to run to the next stop where the whole bus is waiting for you, or it drives off without you.
- The time the pantomime Snow White was on, and I saw five dwarves in the local supermarket. I then started looking for the other two- as if they would all be shopping together!
- That time I rushed Phoebe to the vet as she wasn't moving her back legs, only for her to jump up and start licking the vet as soon as we got there.

- The time my daughter aged six dressed up as Sandy from Grease in the very tight black trousers strikes the pose at the beginning of "You're the one that I want," and says, "Tell me about it, Doug!" (Instead of Stud)
- The time in church when N. turned to other members for the 'Peace Be with You' and handshakes and says 'Pleased to Meet You' instead.

40

<u>TO CONCLUDE</u>

These are my embarrassing tales to date, but all pale into insignificance when you are speaking too loudly to your children in a public place- a doctor's surgery or on a train. No more displays of public affection and hand holding when a teenager and if you have to pick them up for school you have to park a mile away. Perish the thought too of getting out the 'spitty tissue' to wipe dinner off their face. It's a phase; I was a teenager. I know it won't last, but I miss the recounts of the day in detail rather than the one word answers I get now.

Actually that isn't entirely true, we all talk every day at length. I have two very talented and loving daughters and I know they are proud of me. I hope my readers enjoy the book, be inspired, know that there is no stigma about mental health, be aware of what to look for when checking your breasts and be comforted in the knowledge that a cancer diagnosis is not all doom and gloom.

As a professional, I thought hard about each story and whether or not to include it. They happened, they are true and to be honest I saw no harm in sharing them. I also made sure no names were used. No offence is meant to anyone.

I'm sure there will be more tales to come; I will continue to record them. It is only a pause in my cancer journey. A time to rest, look back a little if only to realise how far I have come. So in this world of sadness, sorrow and difficulty, why not read about me and laugh?

As I wrote earlier, I do feel like Kent's own Bridget Jones. I've met Mr Bingley, and I have the big girl's pants. However, I'm yet to find my Mr Darcy. Although I am not actively looking yet, I know he's out there somewhere.

Please feel free to retell these stories to your family and friends, and in some way, I will feel like Ronnie Corbett. I hope I have helped you the reader, even in a small way understand what it is like to have both a mental and physical illness.

As for me, my recovery will depend on taking Letrozole for the next seven or eight years and coping with the awful side effects that drug inflicts. I will also have four more annual mammograms. Then there is "Survivor's Guilt" – the fact that I got so far, and "Onco-Anxiety"- the worry that comes with every twinge or pang that occurs; has cancer come back? Great, I can't wait.

My hours were increased in the grammar school and I helped cover for teachers on placement terms, trying my hand at Economics, Business Studies and Geography. I loved it. I was kept busy and it really did wonders for my confidence.

I continue to work in the fabulous school- as of printing- full time, back in the KS3 Science and History departments.

I accompanied 40 teenagers on a school trip to Italy in February and although it was a struggle moving my Letrozole-filled limbs, I climbed Mount Vesuvius. Now that I've climbed a volcano, every mountain or hill will seem like a molehill to me. Bring it on!

I will continue to record my journey, but for now, this chapter of my life has come to an end. I made it. I'm a warrior princess, a survivor, a pink sister, a fighter!

I will also be happy knowing that my collection of personal stories are being read and retold and in the process, I will be entertaining you and still raising funds for breast cancer research.

And don't forget when it comes to your boobs- men and women- you should be;

"MAMMOGRAMMING not INSTAGRAMMING them!"

APPENDIX I

THE MOUNTAIN LION

To conclude I have to include this story written by an unknown author. It is by far the best cancer treatment analogy I have ever read. The author is amazing.

'What's it like to go through cancer treatment? It's something like this: one day you mind your own business, you open the fridge to get some breakfast and OMG there's a mountain lion in your fridge. Wait; what? How? Why is there a mountain lion in your fridge?

No time to explain. Run! The mountain lion will kill you unless you find something even more ferocious to kill it first.

So you take off running, and the mountain lion is right behind you. You know the only thing that can kill a mountain lion is a bear, and the only bear is on top of the mountain. You had better find that bear. You start running up that mountain in the hope of finding the bear.

Your friends desperately want to help, but they are powerless against mountain lions, as mountain lions are merciless killing machines. But they want to help, so they're cheering you on and bringing you paper cups of water and orange slices as you run up the mountain. They are yelling "Get lost mountain lion, no one likes you", and you really appreciate the support, but the mountain lion is still coming. Also for some reason, there's someone in the crowd who is yelling, "That's not a mountain lion, it's a puma", and another person is yelling, "I read those mountain lions are allergic to kale, have you tried rubbing kale on it?"

As you're running up the mountain, you see other people fleeing their mountain lions. Some of the mountain lions seem comparatively wimpy- they're only half grown, and some even have three legs. You think to yourself, why couldn't I have gotten one of those mountain lions?

But then you look over at the people who are fleeing mountain lions the size of a monster truck with substantial prehistoric sabre fangs, and you feel guilty for even thinking that- and besides, who in their right mind would want to fight a mountain lion, even a three-legged one?

Finally, the person closest to you, whose job it is to take care of you- may be a parent or sibling or best friend, or in my case, my husband- comes barging out of the woods and jumps on the mountain lion, wailing and screaming "Get lost mountain lion, stop trying to eat my wife!".

The mountain lion punches your friend/husband right in the face. Now your husband is rolling around on the ground clutching their nose, and he's bought you some time. But you still need to get to the top of the mountain.

Eventually, you reach the top, and the bear is there waiting for both of you. You rush right up to the bear, and the bear rushes the mountain lion. The bear has to go through you to get to the mountain lion, and in doing so, the bear kicks you to blazes, but not before it also punches your husband in the face. Your husband is now staggering around with a black eye and a bloody nose and shouting "Can I get some help, I've been punched in the face by two apex predators, and I think my nose is broken". All you can say is "I'm kind of busy in case you hadn't noticed; I'm fighting a mountain lion".

Then, if you're lucky, the bear leaps on the mountain lion and they are locked in epic battle until finally the two of them roll off a cliff edge together. Maybe the mountain lion is dead, perhaps.

You're not sure- it fell off the cliff, but mountain lions are crafty. It could come back at any moment.

All your friends come running up to you and say, "That was amazing! You're so brave, and we're so proud of you! You didn't die! That must be a huge relief!"

Meanwhile, you blew out both your knees; you're having an asthma attack, you twisted your ankle, and also a bear has mauled you.

And everyone says "Boy, you must be excited to walk down the mountain!"

And all you can think as you stagger to your feet is, "I never even wanted to climb it in the first place."

APPENDIX II

<u>AN ALPHABET OF AILMENTS</u>

Just for fun and started by my girls, I've compiled an alphabet of every illness, operation or ailment as of printing that I have ever suffered from!

An anaemia, abscess, allergies, adenoids out, amnesia, anaesthetic allergy, atopic eczema, anxiety, acne, acid reflux, arthralgia, alopecia

B B12 deficiency, burst eardrum, butterflies, brain fog, bee-sting, breast cancer, bipolar disorder, burn, bump, blister, bruise, blackheads, blocked nose, brain freeze, burp, blood blister, bad breath, backache, bloating, blurred vision, boil

C cellulitis, cancer, chest cold, constipation, chub rub, carpal tunnel syndrome, cold sore, common cold, caesarean section, catarrh, contractions, chapped lips, cyst, chickenpox, cramp, cuts, cellulite, cough, coccyx inflammation, constipation, concussion, chafing, cavities, chest infection, cold sore, corneal abrasion, cystitis, conjunctivitis, cricked neck, chilblains, chemo-brain

D dandruff, depression, diarrhoea, dermatitis, dehydration, dyshidrotic eczema, dental abscess, dizziness, dead arm, dry skin

E earache, eye infection, eczema, endometriosis, ear infection, esophagitis

F flu, flatulence, fainting, folate deficiency, fever, fatigue, folliculitis

G gingivitis, grommets, glands swollen, goose bumps, graze, German measles, glue ear

H hiccups, headache, heatstroke, heat rash, heartburn, hives, haemorrhoids, hay fever, head lice, haemorrhage, high temperature, hunger, hot flush, hair loss

I impetigo, insect bites, insomnia, itching, intubation fail, indigestion, ingrown toenail

J jellyfish sting, jet lag

K?

L labyrinthitis, laryngitis, labour pains, leg cramp,

M migraine, mumps, menopause, mastitis, mastectomy

N neuralgia, nosebleed, nausea, neuropathy, nappy rash

O obesity, oral thrush

P plantar fasciitis, pregnancy, panic attacks, pernicious anaemia, postnatal depression, pins and needles, puberty, paper cut

Q queasiness

R ringworm (not a worm!), rash

S sunstroke, sepsis, stitches, scabies, shaving rash, sweating, snoring, sore throat, stress, stitch, scratch, stretch marks, sickness, splinters, stye, sinusitis, stretch marks, sunburn, spots, stomach cramp, stitch, sprained ankle, seroma

T tonsillitis, tonsilloliths, tooth decay, trapped nerve, tinnitus, toothache, baby teething

U ulcer,

V vitamin D deficiency, vitamin B12 deficiency, verruca, vomiting, viral meningitis,

W warts, wasp sting, water retention, Whitlow

X ?

Y ?

Z ?

Appendix III
<u>ACKNOWLEDGEMENTS</u>

This is the part where I can write my BAFTA thank you speech, thanking people that you won't necessarily know. It's all very polite, personal but necessary. So here goes.

There are so many people to thank for supporting me. The last four years have particularly been a rollercoaster of emotions and experiences.

Firstly I would like to thank my amazing family - my wonderful mum, dad, brothers and beautiful daughters.

Thank you to Katharine, Alice, Andy, Julie, Chrissy and Jeanie.

Thank you to the staff at MIND and the doctors at my local practice.

Thank you to the 'Strictly' table at work who have kept me going.

Thank you too to my oncology team, my consultants, my breast care nurses and surgeon, my chemotherapy nurses, and my radiology team.

Thank you to Matt Lucas and to Donia Youssef.

Thank you to Rosie www.rosiestillphotography.co.uk for my wonderful calendar photos.

Finally a massive thank you to my close circle of friends who never gave up on me despite me trying to push them away and to all my friends, relatives, colleagues and pupils at my current school that have offered support in a whole host of ways.

I love you all xxx